Macmillan Building and Surveying Series

Series Editor: IVOR H. SEELEY
Emeritus Professor, The Nottingham Trent University

continued overleaf

Information and Technology Applications in Commercial Property
Rosemary Feenan and Tim Dixon (Editors)

Introduction to Building Services, second edition Christopher A. Howard and
Eric F. Curd

Introduction to Valuation, third edition D. Richmond

Marketing and Property People Owen Bevan

Principles of Property Investment and Pricing, second edition W.D. Fraser

Project Management and Control David Day

Property Finance David Isaac

Property Valuation Techniques David Isaac and Terry Steley

Public Works Engineering Ivor H. Seeley

Resource Management for Construction M.R. Canter

Quality Assurance in Building Alan Griffith

Quantity Surveying Practice Ivor H. Seeley

Recreation Planning and Development Neil Ravenscroft

Resource and Cost Control in Building Mike Canter

Small Building Works Management Alan Griffith

Structural Detailing, second edition P. Newton

Sub-Contracting Under the JCT Standard Forms of Building Contract Jennie Price

Urban Land Economics and Public Policy, fifth edition P.N. Balchin, G.H. Bull and
J.L. Kieve

Urban Renewal – Theory and practice Chris Couch

1980 JCT Standard Form of Building Contract, second edition R.F. Fellows

Series Standing Order
If you would like to receive future titles in this series as they are published, you can make
use of our standing order facility. To place a standing order please contact your bookseller
or, in case of difficulty, write to us at the address below with your name and address and
the name of the series. Please state with which title you wish to begin your standing order.
(If you live outside the United Kingdom we may not have the rights for your area, in
which case we will forward your order to the publisher concerned.)

Customer Services Department, Macmillan Distribution Ltd, Houndmills, Basingstoke,
Hampshire, RG21 2XS, England.

Property Finance

David Isaac

Professor of Real Estate Management and Associate Head
School of Land and Construction Management
University of Greenwich

MACMILLAN

First published 1994 by
MACMILLAN PRESS LTD
Houndmills, Basingstoke, Hampshire RG21 2XS
and London
Companies and representatives
throughout the world

ISBN 0–333–57681–0

A catalogue record for this book is available
from the British Library

Typeset by
Richard Powell Editorial and Production Services
Basingstoke, Hants RG22 4TX

Printed in Great Britain by
Antony Rowe Ltd
Chippenham, Wilts

10 9 8 7 6 5 4 3 2 1
03 02 01 00 99 98 97 96 95 94

For Simon and Katie

Contents

Foreword

In a world of increasingly intense competition with bankers, accountants and lawyers, property professionals need to understand the dynamics of the finance world if they are not to be poor relations.

The skills of the property profession are unique, but are often seen as being narrow when compared with competitors'.

This book provides an opportunity to understand the financial world and how it relates to property. It will be invaluable to students and practitioners wishing to learn or better understand the mechanics of property finance.

Property Finance offers an overview of the theory of finance, explaining the technical jargon and removing the mystique which all industries jealously guard as the 'entry ticket'.

Corporate, debt and equity finance – the main engines of the property market – are dealt with in a practical way, using examples which will help put the theory into context.

The book also examines the property vehicles that drive the market, namely institutional investment, property companies and joint ventures, enabling the student to see in practice how finance is used to produce returns for investors.

The ability to 'add value' to any transaction is the hallmark of a true professional. In the property market, the provision of financial advice is part of the complex process of adding value. The true test will be the level of return provided by, for example, an acquisition or a development restructuring.

As a comprehensive guide to the world of property finance, this book will help those eager to learn, and will quickly become an invaluable reference point.

Michael E. Riley
Managing Director
Chesterton Financial

Preface

This book is an introduction to property finance, bringing together the professional disciplines related to finance and to property investment and development. The book intends to do three things: establish the basic concepts of finance; examine the applications of these concepts in practice; and, finally, give an overview of the market – its history and present position as of 1993. As the reader will appreciate, this is a wide field and I have tried to be as selective as possible in the text.

I believe the book will be useful for a number of different groups, including students in property-related areas, practitioners who are not specialist in the area or who have limited experience of it and those professionals involved in developing, investing in and administering property assets. For the student it provides a text at second- or third-year undergraduate level and is also useful as an introductory text at postgraduate level for those without previous knowledge in the area. Finance is an essential and arguably the paramount agreement in the process of land and construction management. Estate and land managers, surveyors, construction and project managers, architects and engineers need an understanding in this area and, at the same time, those involved in finance, commerce and business require an insight into finance as applied to the property asset. The book provides an overview for progressing to more advanced and specialised texts. For those concerned with property and construction I hope that the book will provide a view into the area of applied economics in the same way that, for those with a business background, the text will help to explain some of the peculiarities of dealing with land, property and construction.

I have endeavoured to structure the book by initially establishing the basic concepts and then looking in some detail at the main characteristics of finance, the instruments involved and the players. Where possible, I have introduced recent research and make no apologies for using and referencing this work to bring the reader up to date in a rapidly changing sector. Where possible, simple case studies have been added to assist in the understanding. I would have liked to have incorporated more extensive applications but this was beyond the scope and scale of this text.

I believe the book comes at an important time in the development of the property market; hopefully, we are now seeing the signals of partial recovery in both the residential and commercial sectors, and with recovery it is hoped that the practitioners and financiers involved in the market will be older and wiser, and that both the lessons of the slump of 1973–4 and the false hopes of the booming late 1980s will be understood and taken on board. In fact it will be expected of professionals in the market to be older and wiser. In a previous book entitled *Property Valuation Techniques* (written with Terry Steley, Macmillan Press, 1991), we wrote about the need to clarify valuation techniques to make them more accessible and applicable; the intention here is to provide an insight into property finance that will also seek to clarify this process.

Chapter 2 is about the theory of finance; and some readers may wish to bypass this in the first instance if they find it difficult or wish to move on. Hopefully, they will come back to it at a later time when the overall picture becomes clear and they feel more suited to the material. I have endeavoured to keep the chapters self-contained and apologise for any duplication of material; the intention is to reduce cross-referencing and provide easier reading.

Finally, I would like to thank those who have assisted me in writing this book, Professor Ivor Seeley, the series editor, who has stimulated me to write what will hopefully be a number of texts for the series, and Malcolm Stewart, my publisher. I would also like to thank Mike Riley and his staff at Chesterton Financial, who over the years have provided me with valuable insights into the practice of financial services. Many colleagues and external organisations have provided me with information and assistance and these are listed in the acknowledgements. I would also like to thank Terry Steley and Maxine Davies of the University of Greenwich and Neil Woodroffe of South Bank University for their help. Finally, I am reliant on the continued support of Professor David Wills, Lewis Anderson and the staff of the School of Land and Construction Management at the University of Greenwich to develop my research and studies and I am grateful for their help.

University of Greenwich, 1994   David Isaac

Acknowledgements

The author and publisher wish to thank the following for the use of material:

> Butterworth-Heinemann for the use of extracts from *Real Estate Finance*; *Estates Gazette*; the *Journals of Property Finance* and *Property Valuation and Investment*.
> S. G. Warburg Securities, UBS Philips and Drew, and Paribas Capital Markets.
> Chesterton Financial, Savills Research, DTZ Debenham Thorpe Research, and Richard Ellis.

Every effort has been made to trace all the copyright holders, but if any have been inadvertently overlooked, the publishers will be pleased to make the necessary arrangements at the first opportunity.

1 Introduction

1.1 INTRODUCTION

A property or building can be owner-occupied or rented, i.e. an investment property. In the present market (1993) it may of course be vacant, resulting from being surplus to the owner's requirements or a poor investment! From the beginning it should be noted that a large proportion of property is owner-occupied, but most of the texts and theories are applied to an investment market. The commercial property industry is a relatively young one in terms of the realisation that profit can be earned by producing and renting space.

Property finance is money raised on the back of existing properties or raised for the purpose of expenditure on properties. Whether the property is owner-occupied or an investment property may alter the criteria for the raising and application of the funds, but the fundamental concepts may well be the same. For instance, funds could be raised internally or externally by an organisation but the criteria for the internal loan or transfer of funds may well need to match those in the market. In this text, the presentation is mainly about the application of funds to property in the investment market and funds are considered to be private rather than public sector monies. This is to make the analysis simpler but, as has already been said, the principles and concepts could well be similar.

The investment market for property cannot be seen in isolation from other investment markets. The application of funds to property has to reflect competition from other forms of investment. The decision to invest in a particular area will be a comparison of return and security, for instance; thus, knowledge of alternative investments and, more interestingly from a property finance point of view, knowledge of the application of finance to other investments could be very important. This can clearly be seen in the securitisation and unitisation of property, which are discussed later. Another important point to be made is in respect of the nature of the lender and the property to which finance is applied. At its simplest it is an individual purchasing a single property with a single loan. This is rarely the case. Much finance is raised by corporate entities, such as property companies, lending on the back of existing property and other assets for the purchase of a portfolio of assets which may include property assets but not exclusively so.

1

Finally, it is important to realise the significance of property and its finance to the economy. The importance can be shown in three different ways: as a factor of production, as a corporate asset and as an investment. As a factor of production, property is the space in which economic activity will take place; the efficiency and costs of such space will affect the cost of goods and services produced. As a corporate asset, it forms the major asset value in the balance sheet and the majority of corporate debt is secured against it. As an investment, it is one of the major types of investment held by the financial institutions on which pensions and assurance benefits depend (Fraser 1993, p. 3).

1.2 THE STRUCTURE OF THE INVESTMENT MARKET

There are three major areas of traditional investment opportunity (ignoring gold, commodities and works of art): these are fixed interest securities, company stocks and shares, and real property. The Stock Exchange provides a market for listed shares and certain fixed interest securities such as those issued by the Government, local authorities and public bodies. The market in real property contrasts with that of company shares and other securities. The property market is fragmented and dispersed, while that of shares and other securities is highly centralised. The London Stock Market is an example of this centralisation. The centralisation of markets assists the transferability of investments, as does the fact that stock and shares can be traded in small units, thereby assisting transferability. Compared with other traditional investment opportunities, real property investment has the distinguishing features of being heterogeneous and indivisible, and having inherent problems of management. The problems of management may include collecting rents, and dealing with repairs and lease renewal, and thus, together with the other problems noted, may lead to real property being an unattractive proposition for the small investor. A decentralised market will tend to have high costs of transfer of investments and also there will be an imperfect knowledge of transactions.

Thus, the nature of the real property market makes property difficult to value. There is no centralised market price to rely on, as the price may be too difficult to ascertain unless a transaction has recently taken place. Many of the problems of valuation relate to difficulties of trying to relate comparable transactions to properties being valued or even trying to assess what transactions could be considered comparable. Because of the nature of the real property market, individual investors have tended to withdraw from the market. This is also due to the channelling of savings into collective organisations, such as pension funds and insurance companies, rather than individuals using their savings for direct investment.

Property company shares

Property company shares provide a medium for indirect investment in property which deals with some of the disadvantages of direct investment outlined above. Equities are available in smaller units and can be easily traded. Property shares, specifically, have been viewed as an effective protection against inflation because of the durability of property. Shares of a property investment company where most of the revenue to the company is derived from rental income also provides the investor with a high degree of income security. Thus, property shares traditionally were seen to provide both an element of protection against the effects of inflation and greater security to the investor.

Two types of property company are discernible. The investment company holds property for long periods normally and takes its revenue from rental income. The trading company will develop and sell property, earning revenues on disposal of the property rather than through income. Because of different tax positions the functions should be kept separate, but the most extensive developers will also often be investment companies which may or may not retain a completed development within the portfolio of the investment company.

1.3 FINANCIAL STRUCTURES

Property finance is important in the property investment market. The costs and availability of finance will affect the cost of the provision of new investment property and therefore its supply. It is through finance that the structure of the investment interest in property may be created, so finance has effect on the form of the interest. While the costs and availability of funding are obvious in the case of the funding of development property, it is important to realise that it is critical to the investment market also. The value of an investment may be driven by the opportunities or lack of opportunities to fund it and, of course, this was the main impetus of the move into the securitisation of property, a repacking of the property asset into appropriate financial packages which add value. Securitisation is covered in Chapter 12.

There are basic principles of the financial structure which have been identified by Fraser (1993) among others:

- A company must maintain a balance between equity and debt capital. Traditionally property companies are highly geared; this means that these companies carry a high level of debt capital relative to equity or total capital. The issues of gearing are covered in Chapter 2. The security of property and the growth in rental values and capital value have provided an appropriate environment for increasing debt capital. Apart from the balance of equity and debt, the nature and composition of equity and debt in themselves are important.

- There should be a balance of maturity dates of the debt, with the majority being long-term. Redemptions should be spread evenly to avoid the risk of a major refinancing operation occurring at a time of adverse financial conditions. The needs of a major refinancing could have an adverse effect on the market, making available monies scarce and putting up the costs. A proportion of the money should be flexible so that it can be repaid without cost or penalty at any time during the duration of the term.

- A company should match short-term assets with short-term liabilities and long-term assets with long-term liabilities; this is asset matching. If long-term property investment is funded through short-term borrowing, e.g. overdraft or short-term debt, then there could be major problems for refinancing, as an appropriate stock of new capital may not be available at the crucial time of refinancing; this may mean that the property asset would have to be disposed of at an inappropriate time, leading to a collapse in its value.

- Companies should maintain a balance between fixed interest money and variable interest money. Fixed interest rates protect the company in a period of rising interest rates but obviously are expensive if rates fall, so are a hedge against future risk. A hedge is a means of avoiding financial risks associated in this case with changes in interest rates, and this is covered in Chapter 4. Variable rate monies need to be available if interest rates fall so that the benefits of the reduced cost of money can be obtained. Excessive high fixed interest money could have a disastrous effect on a property company in a period of low inflation.

- Debt should be structured so that interest repayments are spread over the year so as to even out the cash flow for the company or, better, to coincide with income received.

- To avoid foreign currency risk, companies with operations overseas should reduce their exposure to this risk by matching overseas assets and debts in the same currency.

- The financial structure should aim to maximise the tax shield, i.e. the avoidance of tax payment to maximise the after-tax cash flow. Thus, where appropriate, the interest repayments should have tax relief and be available to offset against income.

- Apart from interest rates, the arranging costs should be minimised. The price of capital includes not just the interest rates, but commitment and arrangement fees, penalties for early repayment, and is based on the frequency of repayment and how interest is calculated on the outstanding amount.

The finance function

Management and finance theory tells us that in a well-organised business each section of the business should arrange its activities to contribute to the attainment of corporate goals. Central to this function in a corporate entity is the maximisation of shareholders' wealth. This is basically done by the generation and management of cash. This is the fundamental concern of finance. Pike and Neale (1993) suggest the simple cash flow diagram shown in Figure 1.1.

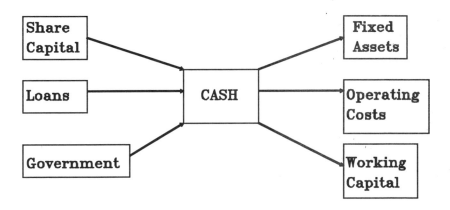

Figure 1.1 *The importance of cash (adapted from Pike and Neale 1993, p. 8).*

The sorts of questions which may be key in our understanding of what finance is all about in a generalised corporate context are:

* What long-term investment strategy should a company take on?
* How can cash be raised for the required investments?
* How much short-term cash flow does a company need to pay its bills?

These are basic decisions which will determine the strategy for generating cash and at the same time ensure that the company is liquid.

One way that companies raise cash to finance their investment activities is by selling or issuing securities. These securities are also called financial instruments or claims, as they are claims on the cash and assets of the company. These securities may be roughly classified as equity or debt and are called, respectively, stock or bonds in the US, and shares and loan stock in the UK. The differences in terminology do make this a problem when dealing with finance literature from the US. Sometimes the basic concepts behind a security or its operation may differ between the US and the UK, as in the operation of financial options, which are discussed later.

The difference between equity and debt is a basic distinction of the modern theory of finance, and this book uses the distinction to classify the instruments available. To summarise, all the securities issued by a firm are claims that depend on or are contingent on the value of the firm. Maximising shareholders' wealth is the primary goal of the company and thus financial decisions are made to increase value for shareholders. A company raises cash by issuing securities to the financial markets. There are two basic types of financial markets, the money markets and the capital markets. Money markets deal with debt securities that pay off in the short term, usually less than one year. Capital markets are the markets for long-term debt and equity shares.

The balance sheet model of the firm

The concept of the finance function as a corporate activity can be seen easily in the use of a balance sheet model of the firm (Figure 1.2) (Ross *et al.* 1993). The balance sheet is a yearly snapshot of the assets and liabilities of the firm.

The assets of the firm are shown on the left side of the balance sheet; these are current or fixed. Fixed assets are those which last a long time and are durable, such as buildings and plant. Some fixed assets are tangible, such as machinery and equipment; others are intangible, such as patents, goodwill and trademarks. The other category of assets is current assets, which have short lives and are intended to be turned to cash. For a property company the distinction may be between properties held for investment and those which it intends to trade in the short term.

In order to invest in these assets, the company must raise the cash to pay for the assets, and this is shown on the right side of the balance sheet. The firm will sell claims to its assets in the form of debt (loan agreements) or equity shares. Just as assets are classified as long- or short-term, so are liabilities. Short-term debt is a current liability and consists of loans and other obligations which must be repaid in one year. Long-term debt is thus that debt whose repayment date is more than one year from issue. Shareholders' equity is the difference in value between the assets and debt of the firm and is thus a residual claim.

The balance sheet model highlights the questions that have already been mentioned and provides an appropriate response:

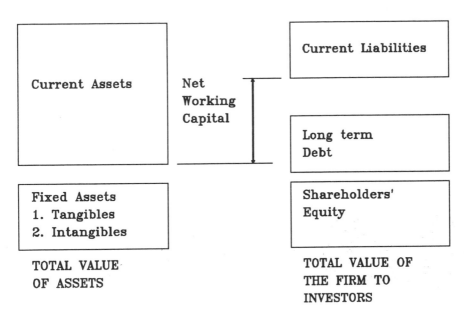

Figure 1.2 *Balance sheet model of the firm. Source: Ross* et al. *1993, p. 5.*

- In what long-term assets should the company invest? This is a question about the left side of the balance sheet. The type and proportions of the assets invested in will depend on the nature of the business. Making and managing expenditure on long-term assets is called *capital budgeting*.
- How can a firm raise cash for the required capital expenditures? This question concerns the right side of the balance sheet and the answer involves the firm's *capital structure*, which represents the proportions of the firm's financing from current and long-term debt and equity.
- How should the short-term operating cash flow be managed? There is a mismatch between the timing of cash inflows and outflows during operating activities; financial managers must manage these gaps in cash flow by managing the firm's net working capital (current assets less current liabilities). This is the subject of *short-term finance*.

From a property perspective we may see these activities as, respectively, the areas of property investment, finance and operational financial management. This book is essentially about finance but seen in the context of property investment and financial management.

1.4   THE FINANCING OF PROPERTY SINCE THE SECOND WORLD WAR

The post-war property market can be divided into a number of periods (Brett 1990, pp. 231–6). These are the post-war development boom, the financial boom of 1967–73, the investment boom of the late 1970s, and the finance-led development boom of the late 1980s with the subsequent collapse into the 1990s. Differences between the boom periods reflect the different finance sources and methods available during each period.

The post-war boom period

In the post-war boom period immediately after the war there was a shortage of space. This was especially so in the office sector, where the shortage of office accommodation was fuelled by the destruction of approximately 750 000 square metres of office space in the blitz. The economy was growing at a respectable rate against a background of low interest rates and low inflation. Property had been destroyed during the war and space was scarce, so this led to a growth in rentals. At the beginning of the 1950s the Conservative Government of the time recognised the need for a 'dash for growth' and encouraged a period of rapid economic expansion. Interest rates were low at this time and thus the yields on property investments were higher than long-term borrowing rates. Fixed interest institutional money was available and readily used by the property companies. Financial partnerships between institutions and property companies were frequently established. Financing of property investments could be carried out using long-term mortgage funds at low rates which were fixed. Typically these funds would be provided by an insurance company. Short-term finance for the construction period usually came from bank sources or else from the building contractor. There was an overall attempt by the developer to raise the total funds necessary for the development from lending sources, thus not committing any of its own money. Property developments were thus intended to be 100% debt financed with no equity involvement. Developers held onto their completed developments rather than selling them; partially this was a response to the tax system, as tax was payable on the trading profit but there was no tax on the surplus created by the developer until the property was sold. Some new funding was achieved by the floating of the property companies on the Stock Exchange in the late 1950s and early 1960s. These flotations achieved cash for new development without the developers having to sell the properties. Developers at this time let their buildings on leases without review and were not concerned with the effects of inflation on their income stream but instead concentrated on income from development profits. Fixed interest financing by financial institutions was standard practice by the 1960s and linked to shareholdings, options and conversion rights taken up in development companies by the institutions. Inflation rose in the early 1960s and the institutions providing finance as mortgages or debentures began to take a share of equity initially by conversion rights and then eventually by establishing joint companies with the developers. The insurance companies were especially active at this time. Developers who wanted to retain properties had to give away some equity to ensure finance at lower rates. Sale and leaseback, where the developer offered to sell the proposed building subject to the investor leasing the building back, became the dominant form of funding arrangement. This approach had many advantages, including not falling under the Government's credit control measures of the time (Savills 1989, p. 2).

By the early 1960s recession affected demand and credit squeezes made short-term financing difficult. The office development boom in London was eventually brought to an end by the Labour Government in 1964 with the Control of Office and Industrial Development Act 1965. This so-called 'Brown Ban', named after George Brown, who initiated the legislation, in fact artificially restricted the supply and sowed the seed of the next boom in the 1970s (Fraser 1993, p. 342).

The financial boom 1967–73

A renewed Stock Market boom commenced in 1967 and lasted until the crash in 1974. Institutional finance was being provided to the property companies in the form of leasebacks. Pension funds in this period joined the insurance companies in buying out completed developments and they dominated the investment market (Cadman and Catalano 1983, p. 12). New forms of indirect investment such as property bonds and property unit trusts were established. The market was characterised by a series of takeovers in the late 1960s and this activity continued in the early 1970s. By March 1972 property shares had risen more than fivefold from the low point of 1967 (Brett 1983, p. 109). The assets of existing property companies were becoming more and more valuable because of the effect of the shortage of investment properties. The value of property companies was thus increasing because of the scarcity of space rather than because of accumulated development profits. Because of inflation in this period rent reviews were introduced, initially on a 14 yearly basis; these reduced to 7 yearly reviews and then to 5 yearly reviews. Between 1964 and 1974 there was a reduction of 40% in the number of quoted companies due to amalgamation and liquidation (Ratcliffe 1978, p. 47).

To summarise, in the post-war era in the 1950s and 1960s the modern property developer had emerged and property companies had established themselves. The stimulation to development was based on the shortage of property in a period of low inflation. This meant that the rental levels of developments increased dramatically during the period while building costs were static. The other major stimulants to the developers were the fixed interest rates and the lack of equity input. The growth of the property developers was on the basis of refinancing the development on a fixed interest mortgage for 20–30 years. The institutions were providing finance for the developments and there was some link-up between developers and institutions. Over this period the institutions, generally insurance companies, insisted on having a greater share in the equity returns available. They purchased shares in the property companies and then made mortgage debenture loans convertible to shares so that an increased equity stake could be obtained if the scheme were a success. However, the taxation structure in the late 1960s affected this arrangement, gross funds (not paying tax) suffered from the taxation of income and dividends, and new structures of finance emerged. In the late 1960s and early 1970s developers began using sale and leaseback; the property was financed in the development stage using bank finance and was sold on completion. As time wore on, a shortage of schemes became apparent and the institutions (the insurance companies and now pension funds) purchased development sites directly with a building agreement and agreement for lease with the developer. Developers borrowed short term for their developments or to finance acquisitions, because they thought rising asset values would counterbalance the deficit finance. They ignored cash flow and borrowed against the increased value of their properties to meet the income shortfall between rental and interest payments.

The crash of 1974–5 showed how the economic indications had changed since the 1950s and 1960s. High interest rates, lessened demand and inflation of costs meant that profit levels were not achieved because of increased capital costs and income voids during which interest arrears fluctuated. The highly geared property companies had been fuelled by debt finance provided under fairly lax lending criteria.

In the aftermath of the oil crisis of 1973, interest rates were raised to a penal level, and secondary banks were heavily committed to property and began to collapse. Accounting conventions of the time had disguised the sharply negative cash flow of most property companies with large development programmes. It thus became impossible to sell a property and it was not possible to borrow on it. Property shares collapsed, as did the direct market in property (Brett 1990, p. 234).

The investment boom (late 1970s)

In the late 1970s the institutions were keen buyers of property and values rose sharply during this period. Large institutions were undertaking direct development or using developers as project managers. Larger companies were borrowing in the hope that the cash flow would be positive at the first rent review.

The rental boom (late 1980s)

In the 1980s and 1990s the usual approach to funding was that the fund was invited to purchase the site and provide funds for the building contract. Interest would be rolled up during the development period and added to the development costs. On completion and letting of the building, the profit on the development would be paid over. On this basis developers built up a large turnover basically matching their site funding and project management skills with the institutional investors. Such approaches greatly reduced the risk exposure of the developer to the project. Forward funding meant that the project was financed in terms of the development at a keep rate but generally the capital sum at the end of the project was valued at a higher yield.

In the early 1980s the recession and rising unemployment had affected the demand for property: rental increases fell, yields increased. Property lagged behind the rest of the economy in its recovery. There was not another boom until 1986–7. The institutions were now less important as providers of funds for property and their net purchases dropped as they re-weighted their portfolios towards equities and gilts, disappointed with the performance of their property assets. A development boom, funded by the banks, had begun. The banks were prepared to lend on individual developments and roll up the interest until the property was disposed of. Thus, developers were traders rather than investment companies. By the beginning of the 1990s the rental growth had tailed off and the market was collapsing. There were no buyers for the completed developments. The banks had to extend their development loans beyond the development period because there were no institutional funders in the market. Development loans were thus converted to investment loans, committing banks to staying in the market. Innovative financial techniques in the absence of traditional institutional finance were the key developments of the 1980s.

The 1990s

The present players in the lending market include those shown in the following table:

Players in the lending market	Examples
Banks	Clearing banks
	Merchant banks (also providing an advisory role)
Institutions	Insurance companies
	Pension funds
Investors	Private individuals
	Overseas investors

At the beginning of 1990 there were 140 banks lending to property companies and developers in the UK; 40% of these were overseas banks. In terms of bank loans £30 billion was outstanding to property lending, which equates to 7.5% of all bank lending. Lending had increased 20% per annum from 1981 to 1990 and the Bank of England had become concerned. The lending banks' response subsequently has been to reduce loan-to-value ratios from between 75% and 80% to between 66% and 70% but they will still lend, as they have to make profits.

Some comparison has been made between the lending crisis of the 1990s and the property crash in 1974 but they are very different. In the 1974 crash, banks were unable to deal with unpaid loans and they had a weaker capital base. There was a weaker tenant demand at the time. The strong investor demand in 1974 was pushing yields down and thus trading profits were based on investor reaction rather than rental growth. The developers had poor covenants. There was poor research by banks and property companies. Nowadays there are better financial controls and banks are taking security (notwithstanding non-recourse deals). The property sector has been driven by tenant demand. Yields have moved but not significantly.

1.5 VOCABULARY OF FINANCE

At this stage the introduction of a few basic concepts could be useful. Some of the simpler terms are set out below.

Debt
Someone else's money, e.g. an overdraft, a term loan or debenture (loan secured on an asset)

Deep-discounted bonds
Deep-discounted bonds are a means of raising long-term finance with a low initial interest rate. Attractions include:

(i) interest payments can be stepped to rise every 5 years to equate to a property yield;
(ii) tax relief can be claimed on the implied annual interest expense over the life of the bond.

To date, these bonds can only be used by blue chip companies whose creditworthiness ensures marketability in the bond market.

Drop lock
Drop lock is a mechanism within a long-term floating rate facility which, when triggered, allows the borrower to fix the interest rate over the remaining period of the facility. The trigger is the reduction of long-term interest rates to a predetermined level.

Equity
Your money. Money put into a project. Company equity is ordinary share capital.

Interest rate margin
Sometimes this will be sub-LIBOR (depending on the strength of the lender in the case of ICI, say). Generally between 0.1% and 1% for a good covenant, 1–2% for a medium covenant and 1–2% for property transactions.

LIBOR
The London Interbank Offered Rate. The average interest rate that the banks will lend to one another. The credit quality of banks.

Loan-to-value ratio
The ratio between the amount a lender will lend and the total value of the asset used as a security. Usually expressed as a percentage. A 75% loan-to-value ratio will mean that a £100 000 asset will raise £75 000 of loans.

Risk
Banks are not in the business of taking risks, only making money. They would generally consider any loan in excess of 70% of value to be riskier and expect to be compensated by a greater return.

Security

When money is lent for the purchase of an asset, the lender will usually have the right to sell the asset in the case of any default. This is achieved by way of a legal charge. Security could be just related to a single project and have no recourse back to the parent. This is known as a non-recourse deal. When there is some partial recourse back to the parent company, e.g. rental guarantees, this is known as a limited-recourse transaction.

1.6 OVERVIEW OF THE PRESENT FINANCE MARKET

Over the last few years the market has been very difficult; Berkley (writing in 1991) blamed the poor position of property lending on four factors:

(i)   New lenders in the market, such as building societies and foreign banks, who had money to finance property but little expertise in adjusting the terms of the loans to the risks being taken.
(ii) The use of commercial indemnity insurance (CMI, covered later in this book) to increase the debt proportion of value from 70% to 85%, say. CMIs were abused, especially on developments loans, and insurers have had to face considerable claims. Insurers failed to differentiate between the risks involved in indemnifying comparatively secure investment loans and the top slice position in a development or trading opportunity. (The top slice is the slice of income which has the least priority of charge.)
(iii) There was pressure on lenders to evolve innovative schemes which dealt with high interest rates. These underestimated how high interest rates would go during the period. Even clearing banks allowed overdrafts to increase to reflect the higher interest rates and, as more overdrafts reached their limits, so there were directives to call in the loans and this put more pressure on the secondary bank market to lend.
(iv) In a good market it is easier to obtain a report to confirm the borrower's bullish projections; now valuers are very cautious. A satisfactory offer of finance will not be forthcoming from a lender without a suitable valuation to support it (Berkeley 1991, p. 524).

The activity in the present financial services market has developed recently in the areas of debt finance, joint ventures and mezzanine finance. The main criteria in these areas are indicated later to give an indication of the nature of the financial products and structures in the market; this really is a selective introduction for the extensive overview of debt and equity which is outlined later in the book.

Debt finance

Clearing banks and, to a lesser extent, merchant banks have been prepared to provide loans for property development. Generally the loans have been secured on collateral beyond the property to be developed. Interest is charged on a fixed or variable basis. Non-recourse finance is now more popular. It can be defined as loans on property unsupported by outside collateral. Finance is available from banks for up to 70% loan-to-value ratio without outside security being provided. Banks take first charge over the site and advance monies during the development phase. Interest rates are between 1% and 2% over London Interbank Offered Rate but this is reduced with pre-let or pre-sale.

Loans generally have limited recourse with developer undertakings to:

- pay cost overruns;
- inject equity stakes either up-front or side-by-side;
- pay interest post completion;
- complete within certain time limits; and
- complete within certain costs.

Banks will normally allow interest to be capitalised during the construction period and developers generally include this as a construction cost, thus not affecting profits during the development process.

The main types of debt finance available are as follows.

Commercial mortgages

These are straightforward loans where the interest rate is either paid currently or capitalised. The principal is either amortised over the term of the loan or repaid by a single payment at the end. The interest rate can be fixed or variable and other capital market instruments can be used, including caps (preventing interest rises over a certain rate) and floors (preventing interest rate rises over a certain level) and collars (restricting the movement of interest rates between a floor and a cap rate). These instruments are used to minimise interest fluctuations, thereby reducing risk and obtaining finer pricing. The length of loan will vary but the maximum for many banks is 5 years, although insurance companies and building societies may lend up to 25 years.

Equity participation or convertible mortgages

This structure allows the lender to share in the uplift of the value of the property for a reduction in the interest rate payable.

Mortgage debenture issue

This is a traditional method of raising corporate finance. It involves a loan raised on a debenture issue which is secured against the property or other assets and yields either a fixed or index-linked return.

Multi-option facility

In this structure a group of banks agree to provide cash advances at a pre-determined margin for a certain period.

Deep-discounted bonds

Deep-discounted bonds are a method of raising long-term finance with a low initial interest rate. Interest payments can be stepped to accord with a rent review and there are also tax advantages. Bonds can be placed with institutional investors and can be very finely priced. It is anticipated that bond issues will become increasingly used to finance major projects to overcome the need to refinance on completion of the development.

Joint ventures

There are a number of different types of joint venture; the concept involves the coming together of two or more parties to undertake a transaction. Joint ventures are a useful means of bringing parties together with different interests in order to complete deals. The reasons for increased use of joint ventures include: pressure from the Bank of England to reduce the level of bank debt in the property sector; increased risk in property development; lack of equity in the property market (and therefore property companies being unable to raise new funds in the stock market); and demand from overseas investors who have a preference for joint venture arrangements.
    Forms of joint venture structures are:

(i)   limited liability companies;
(ii) partnership (one party must have unlimited liability);
(iii) profit participation.

    The decision on creating a joint venture will depend on the purposes of the joint venture and will depend on whether this is one property project or one of a number of schemes, secondly on the tax situation of the parties and the venture, and finally there may be stamp duty considerations which will affect costs of transfer and which should be minimised under the structure agreed.

On negotiation of a joint venture agreement important points to consider are:

(i)   the level of funding to be provided;
(ii) the development period/time;
(iii) who will control the decision-making process;
(iv) how the profit is going to be distributed;
(v)   what the provisions are for dissolution in the event of failure;
(vi) how disputes are to be settled.

Joint ventures are considered in detail in Chapter 11.

Mezzanine finance

There is often a gap between the costs of development and limited-recourse loans and this is filled by a mezzanine loan. The amount of mezzanine finance varies but can take debt up to 95% of cost. Mezzanine funders require rates of return of 30–40%, secured on a subordinated (i.e. charged after the main loan) loan with a share of profit, normally side-by-side with a cap at an agreed level. Should the project run into problems, the priority return that the mezzanine financier seeks can quickly diminish any profit. Interest payable on the mezzanine finance can be capitalised, producing cash-flow benefits.

The lending market

Bank of England property lending figures are showing that there is too much debt and too little equity in the market. Banks have continued to lend on the basis that the institutions or foreign investors would be around to refinance the projects. 'Big Bang' (the deregulation of the Stock Exchange in October 1986) and the deregulation of the financial services market sparked an increase in property lending by the foreign banks; £35 billion of debt was outstanding in 1993. If restrictions on loans are introduced, the property sector could be in serious trouble.

Despite the slowdown in the economy, property transactions are still being financed and some international banks, especially the Japanese, have regarded the situation as an opportunity to increase their market share. American banks have reduced their exposure. Clearing banks are now taking a cautious approach and with property values falling they will have to be very careful not to cause a collapse through unwarranted liquidations. The problems arising from the Rush and Tompkins (a major building contractor) collapse and the domino effect triggered by the collapse demonstrate this.

Building societies have become increasingly active but the demise of one or two of their major investments has caused them to reappraise the situation. Few banks are now lending on speculative schemes and even pre-let schemes can only be financed where an exit route for the financier can be clearly demonstrated. The borrower must be prepared to provide guarantees for any cost overruns and interest during the cost period. Equity injections may be required by the developer and the bank will demand a substantial level of recourse. The amount of equity initially required has increased. Most banks are not prepared to lend above 70% of cost and often insist on a developer putting in equity up front. By comparison, banks are still keen to lend on good-quality investment property, although they are not comfortable about capitalising interest over long periods. This creates difficulties with reversionary properties. Loans of up to 80% of investment value are available and can be exceeded if mortgage indemnity policies are used or the bank receives a share of profits.

In terms of future prospects, there is clearly a need for further liquidity in the property sector through increased equity. More funds may enter the market through Authorised Property Unit Trusts but despite the tax transparency they are unlikely to be successful in the short term because of falling property values. The London Future and Option Exchange was established to introduce a property futures contract which would provide further liquidity; however, this has been abandoned. Using such an exchange, investors would have been able to increase their exposure to the property market by purchasing contracts which could be used to hedge the risk of a trading or investment portfolio.

In the market of the early 1990s any loan structure which capitalises interest will carry great weight because of the need to provide funds to refinance development facilities. In the last few years deep-discounted bond issues have increased in popularity. Convertible mortgages offer another alternative whereby the borrower provides the lender or investor with equity in the scheme in return for a higher loan advance and reduced obligation. Both discounted bonds and convertible mortgages have suffered recently because of higher interest rates in international markets.

To conclude, until new investments or investment products bolster the amount of equity in the market property loans on new transactions will be difficult to secure.

Recent surveys

Recent surveys have shown some encouragement in the sector; this is based in the main on property share prospects, where the discount to net asset value is now at a premium. Savills' survey on *Financing Property 1993* (Savills 1993a) suggests that the previous year (1992) had been dominated by events in September 1992 which led to the devaluation of the pound and the withdrawal of the UK from the Exchange Rate Mechanism. Since that time there has been the development of a yield gap between average property yields and borrowing rates, and between average property yields and the yields on gilts and equities. Property yields have remained higher over this period. The FTA Property Index fell to a historic level in September 1992 but has since recovered. The rise in property share values has resulted in the narrowing of discounts on share price to net asset value (see Chapter 10 for a definition and discussion of this measure of performance). The long-term average discount of 30% fell to 13% at the beginning of 1993, reduced to 7% at April 1993 and reached a 4% premium in June 1993 (Savills 1993a, p. 3). The trend has been further upwards with recent measures at 21% premium at the end of 1993.

The speculation and institutional interest in property shares in the market has meant that share prices have risen as indicated above but also this has enabled the property companies on their rerating (increasing their value on the stock market) to raise new capital. This capital has been used to improve balance sheets and enable them to buy into the weak property market. The direct property market has shown a slow but positive progress due to the weight of institutional and overseas money; this has led to a downward pressure on yields, as shown in Table 1.1, and also a general expectation of recovery in the sector.

Reports from DTZ Debenham Thorpe (*Money into Property 1993* and other research) confirm that the demand for property assets has strengthened and that, led by the major property companies, the potential demand in 1993 is the highest for 5 years. There is a prospective better balance between the demands of institutions and property companies and between the demands for debt and equity, and this balance may help to avoid the same destabilising effect which happened with the influx of bank property lending in the late 1980s (DTZ Debenham Thorpe 1993, p. 2). The institutions are thus finding themselves underweight with property in their portfolios at the moment and this combined with the cash raising activities of the property companies has led to a number of rights issues which are likely to be followed by debentures and long-dated funds. Banks have continued to reduce their exposure and the figures for loans at March 1993 were down to £36.8 billion, down 85% from 1991 (Evans 1993, pp. 75–7). DTZ Debenham Thorpe suggest that these present indications mean that the severe lack of liquidity experienced in the market since 1989 is now beginning to ease.

Table 1.1 *Movement of prime yields by sector 1992–3*

		%
Sector	1992	1993
Retail	5.25	4.75
Office	8.75	7.50
Retail warehouse	9.25	7.50
Industrial	9.00	7.50

Source: Savills 1993b, p. 4.

Figure 1.3 shows the flow of new money into property: note that there are negative figures for banks, −£1707 bn (1982) and −£1134 bn (1983), and for property companies, −£0.034 bn (1983). The figures for 1983 are for the first quarter only.

The Chesterton Financial/CSW Confidence Barometer has also shown a change of attitude in the market. The Confidence Barometer is an overall measure of confidence among commercial property lenders and is based on whether the respondents are pessimistic or optimistic in the future across a number of criteria. This biannual survey has run since July 1991. The measure of net confidence is the percentage surplus or deficit of optimists over pessimists and the survey noted a dramatic change in attitudes from January to July 1993 (Chesterton Financial/CSW 1993). For the first time since the Confidence Barometer was first launched all measures of net confidence were positive by 1993 (see Tables 1.2 and 1.3).

Respondents to the Confidence Barometer survey expect an improvement in the overall state of their property lending, less bad debt provisions, fewer borrowers in breach of loan covenants and a lower rate of receivership among borrowers as indicated by their responses.

Table 1.2 *Chesterton/CSW Confidence Barometer – next 6 months*

The measures of overall net confidence for the 6 month period following the survey were:

%	July '91	Jan '92	July '92	Jan '93	July '93
Optimistic	8	8	9	16	43
Pessimistic	−48	−49	−48	−39	−13
No change	44	43	44	45	44
Net confidence	−40.3	−40.8	−39.2	−22.6	29.7

Figures are rounded except for net confidence.

Table 1.3 *Chesterton/CSW Confidence Barometer – next 12 months*

The measures of overall net confidence for the 12 month period following the survey were:

%	July '91	Jan '92	July '92	Jan '93	July '93
Optimistic	31	27	22	36	62
Pessimistic	−31	−35	−26	−27	−8
No change	38	39	52	36	30
Net confidence	0.5	8.3	−3.5	9.2	53.6

Figures are rounded except for net confidence.

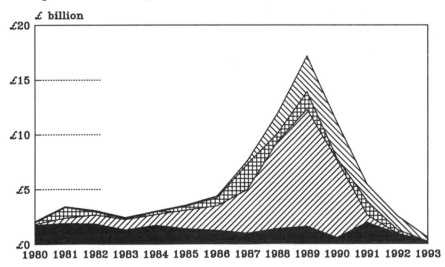

Figure 1.3 *New money into property. Source: DTZ Debenham Thorpe Research*

1.7   THE GLOBALISATION OF FINANCE

Financial, capital and money markets have moved from national to international dominance. These markets are globalised, deregulated and freer in which to operate. Thus, stateless finance, outside the jurisdiction of any one country and its regulatory institutions, can manipulate the market. Innovations in the finance of property have been a product of this globalisation. The traditional funding of development projects by short-term bank funding and long-term institutional finance has had to be replaced. Innovations in finance have also had to deal with the inherent illiquidity and lumpiness of property. Investor interest in liquidity, flexibility, the management of risk, yield analysis and portfolio management have been met by new advances of financing property (Pugh 1991).

The background to the finance of property in the 1980s and 1990s is the globalisation of the investment markets of the different asset classes which began to be established after the abolition of exchange controls for investment funds in the late 1980s in the UK. In the mid-1980s, banks became interested in the globalisation; they were following the needs of business occupiers as well as property investors. Property investment globalisation accelerated with the presence of Scandinavians, Japanese and other foreign investment which was having influence in the European markets in the late 1980s (Sieracki 1993).

1.8   SUMMARY

The late 1970s was a critical period for property investment, its performance out-performing inflation. By the early 1980s, average rental growth was under-performing inflation and returns from the capital markets were falling in certain sectors. According to the Richard Ellis Monthly Indices, only since 1986 has property begun to show significant real returns. In the early 1990s, wider performance measures, matched by increasingly sophisticated market research and analysis as property returns fell, produced a much keener understanding of the components of property investment of yield, rent and valuations methods, and by the mid-1980s property was being measured relatively as well as absolutely. In the late 1970s, capital growth was driven by falling yields; in 1987–8, capital growth was generated by rental growth. In 1988 Richard Ellis (Barter 1988, p. 7) tested the hypothesis that the property market moves countercyclically to equities and gilts and is thus a good prospect for the diversification of a portfolio. This study found:

(i) very limited similarity between property returns and equities (0.10 correlation coefficient);
(ii) no similarity between property returns and gilts (0.03 correlation coefficient);
(iii) gilts and equity returns were more in line (0.44 correlation).

If one takes away the sentiment of land and building, then a property investment is basically a flow of income arising from the property asset which can be distributed in many different ways to offer investors differing degrees of risk and thus differing yields and capital values. This is the basis of property securitisation and the innovative forms of property finance which have been developed; these new financial techniques attempt to overcome property's inherent illiquidity and inflexibility.

According to Barter (1988), the key concerns about property as an investment medium remain:

- *Illiquidity* Properties take 3 months to buy and sell. There is no certainty of price and terms until contracts are exchanged. This problem is acute for properties with capital values above £20 million because of the relatively small supply of potential single purchasers in the market, especially when there are no international purchasers. There are problems in appraising and financing the more substantial developments.
- *Inflexibility* There is a high unit cost with property purchases and little flexibility in the purchase; one needs to buy the whole. There are problems in portfolio diversification and management here. Property shares and property units offer some opportunity to diversify, but property companies are taxed in the same way as other companies and unauthorised property unit trusts are only available to pension funds and certain types of charities and cannot be listed on the Stock Exchange. Now there are authorised trusts for the general public but these may remain unlisted and have a corporation tax liability on the income. Some of the problems of illiquidity and inflexibility have been addressed by 'swapping' properties in matched deals. This avoids the exposure and bad publicity of putting properties up for sale in a poor market; a recent example was a swap valued at £35.35 m in which the Provident Mutual sold a mixed portfolio of six office, retail and industrial properties to Allied London in exchange for eight retail warehouses, valued at £21.6 m, together with £12.75 m in cash (*Estates Times* 1993, p. 24).

- *Growth of debt finance*   There has been a substantial increase in bank lending to the property sector in recent years. This has replaced new equity investment by institutions. This may pose a threat to the property market and is discussed later in the book, although the inflow of money into property from banks is now decreasing.
- *Valuation methodology and precision*   Conventional valuation methods are inflexible. The all-risk approach of traditional valuation methods is difficult to apply to more illiquid properties such as major shopping centres and substantial office buildings. Cases such as the Queens Moat Houses valuations confirm this. Conventional valuations also have difficulty in the valuation of over-rented property where rents are expected to fall on review.
- *The future role of the property profession*   The liberalisation of the financial markets and the increased importance of debt in property funding require new competencies for chartered surveyors. The demands of the Financial Services Act for those providing information on finance and funding will require different and greater competence in the financial area. In this area and others, the professional institutions are reorientating themselves to the market (Barter 1988, pp. 3–4).

Short-termism

Property is a long-term investment and cannot compete on similar terms with investments that pay off on a much shorter time horizon. Recent attitudes of funders and managers of companies in the UK indicate a short-term approach to investment and performance which may in most cases be a reflection of the recent difficult times that these companies have had to operate in. Companies may in some cases have opted for very short-term investment appraisals and rapid payback. The pressure to perform well has not only led fund managers to increase their activity in managing funds but also led to a short-term perspective of investment. This strategy focuses on the short-term performance of companies in arriving at the valuation of a company's worth with emphasis on current profit performance and dividend payments. This perspective, suggested by Pike and Neale (1993), has many consequences across the spectrum of companies, including:

(i) the neglect of the long term by management, leading to a failure to undertake important long-term investments in resources and research and development;

(ii) the volatility of short-term corporate results becoming exaggerated in securities markets, producing unacceptable fluctuations in share prices.

Because of their long-term production cycle, these consequences are likely to be very damaging to property and construction. A survey carried out by the Department of Industry's Innovation Advisory Board in 1990 concluded that City influence on corporate activity led to companies prioritising short-term profits and dividends at the expense of research and development and other innovative investment, and that practices of key financial institutions sustained these priorities. Researchers in the US have concluded that the increasing shareholder power of institutional investors has had a damaging effect on research and development expenditure among US firms. The City rejects this criticism by saying that much of the responsibility for the lack of long-term innovation investment is attributable to managers, to their preference for growth by acquisition, their poor record of commercial development and their reward systems based on short-term targets (Pike and Neale 1993, pp. 40–41).

The implications for property in this respect are very clear: property development and the development of its associated transport, social and services infrastructure is a long-term project. Development and refurbishment underpin the property investment market. Projects on difficult town centre sites or involving major infrastructure works encounter problems of risk and uncertainty as they extend into the future. Then there are the problems of high transfer cost and illiquidity in property, to force a sale of a development or investment property at an inappropriate time, e.g. halfway through a building contract, could cause a collapse in the price of the asset. This effect is accentuated because of the location attributes of property: markets are localised and imperfect. The problem of short-termism is that such an attitude is inappropriate to property finance, where long-term strategy and returns are the key to successful projects.

REFERENCES

Barter, S L (1988) 'Introduction', in S L Barter (ed.) *Real Estate Finance*, Butterworths, London.

Berkley, R (1991) 'Raising Commercial Property Finance in a Difficult Market', *Journal of Property Finance*, vol. 1, no. 4, pp. 523–9.

Brett, M (1983) 'Indirect Investment in Property', in C Darlow (ed.), *Valuation and Investment Appraisal*, Estates Gazette, London.

Brett, M (1990) *Property and Money*, Estates Gazette, London.

Cadman, D and Catalano, A (1983) *Property Development in the UK – Evolution and Change*, College of Estate Management, Reading.

Chesterton Financial/CSW (1993) *Property Confidence Barometer*, Chesterton Financial, London, July.

Debenham, Tewson and Chinnocks (1984) *Property Investment in Britain*, Debenham, Tewson and Chinnocks, London.

DTZ Debenham Thorpe (1993) *Money into Property*, DTZ Debenham Thorpe, London, August.

Dubben, N and Sayce, S (1991) *Property Portfolio Management*, Routledge, London.

Estates Times (1993) 'Swaps Not Cash', *Estates Times*, 19 November, p 24.

Evans, P H (1993) 'Statistical Review', *Journal of Property Finance*, vol. 4, no. 2, pp. 75–82.

Fraser, W D (1993) *Principles of Property Investment and Pricing*, Macmillan Press, London.

Pike, R and Neale, B (1993) *Corporate Finance and Investment*, Prentice Hall, London.

Pugh, C (1991) 'The Globalisation of Finance Capital and the Changing Relationships between Property and Finance', *Journal of Property Finance*, vol. 2, nos. 2 and 3.

Ratcliffe, J (1978) *An Introduction to Urban Land Administration*, Estates Gazette, London.

Riley, M and Isaac, D (1993b) 'Commercial Property Lending: Confidence Survey' *Journal of Property Finance*, vol. 4, no. 3.

Ross, S A, Westerfield, R W and Jaffe, J F (1993) *Corporate Finance*, Irwin, Boston.

Savills (1989) *Financing Property 1989*, Savills, London.

Savills (1993a) *Financing Property 1993*, Savills, London.

Savills (1993b) *Investment and Economic Outlook*, Savills, London, Issue 3, October.

Sieracki, K (1993) 'U.K. Institutional Requirements for European Property', *Estates Gazette*, July 17, p. 116.

2 Theories of Finance

2.1 INTRODUCTION

In the last 30 years a branch of applied microeconomics was developed and specialised in modern finance theory. It is important to understand some of the advances in this theory and how they underpin the principles for raising and pricing property finance. It is not within the range of this text to provide details of the theory or any extensive discussion and the reader is referred to one of the specialist texts. This summary, for instance, uses an approach from *Financial Theory and Corporate Policy* (Copeland and Weston 1988). The beginning of the separate development of modern finance theory was with Markowitz's work around 1958, when he was developing portfolio theory, which is now applied in the selection of investment portfolios. In addition, Modigliani and Miller were working on capital structure and gearing at this time. Modern finance theory emphasises the analytical and quantitative skills of management rather than a descriptive approach to the understanding of finance; however, you should appreciate that, in a text of this nature, a descriptive approach is appropriate at this level and thus the application of theory is limited.

2.2 FINANCIAL THEORY

Copeland and Weston (1988) suggest that there are six seminal and internally consistent theories on which modern finance theory is founded. These are listed below together with brief explanations. All these theories attempt to answer the common problem related to economics: 'How do individuals and society allocate scarce resources through a price system based on the valuation of risky assets?'

    (i)   Utility theory – the basis of rational decision-making in the face of risky alternatives: how do people make choices?
    (ii)   State preference theory.
    (iii) Mean variance theory and the capital asset pricing model.
    (iv) Arbitrage pricing theory.
    (v)   Option pricing theory.
    (vi) Modigliani–Miller theorems
    (vii) Market efficiency

Utility theory shows how people make choices. State preference theory, mean variance theory, arbitrage and option pricing theory describe the objects of choice. Combining the theory of choice with the objects of choice shows how risky alternatives are valued. If correctly assigned, asset prices should provide the appropriate indicators for resource allocation. Modigliani–Miller theory asks 'Does the method of financing have any effect on the value of assets, particularly the firm?'

Utility theory

In Figure 2.1, utility theory suggests that investors will maximise expected utility as their preferred outcome. This can be done by selecting the best combination of risk and return. The indifference curves for a number of assets (1–4) for a risk-averse investor are shown as functions of risk and return. $E(R)$ represents mean return. The standard deviation of return (often represented as σR) shows how expected return can vary and represents risk (see Figure 2.2).

State preference theory

Prices of investments represent the aggregate risk preference of individuals and firms. The development of state preference theory provides a means to determine the optimal portfolio decisions for individuals and the optimal investment rules for firms in a world of uncertainty. In a perfect capital market a set of prices for market securities can be derived. These prices are determined by:

   (i)   individual time preference for consumption and the investment
         opportunities of firms;
   (ii) probability beliefs concerning pay-offs which are dependent on the
         assumptions of the scenarios possible at the time of the pay-off
         (state contingents);
   (iii) individual preferences towards risks and the level of non-diversible
         risk in the economy.

Mean variance theory

Combines the theory of investor choice (utility theory) with the objects of investor choice (the portfolio opportunity set) to show how risk-averse investors wishing to maximise expected utility will choose their optimal portfolios. Measures of risk and return can be combined with probability to show the risk and return for a portfolio of risky assets, called portfolio theory.

Figure 2.1 *Utility theory*

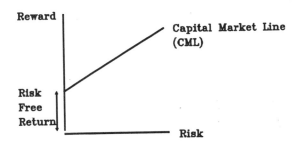

Figure 2.2 *The relationship between risk and reward*

From this theory two theoretical models can be derived that enable us to price risky assets in equilibrium; these are the capital asset pricing model (CAPM) and the arbitrage pricing theory (APT). In the CAPM the appropriate measure of risk is the covariance of returns between the risky asset in question and the market portfolio of all assets. The CAPM is a useful conceptual framework for capital budgeting and the cost of capital. Although the model is not perfectly validated by empirical tests, its main implications appear correct:

  (i)   systematic risk β (beta) is a valid measure of risk;
  (ii) the model is linear;
  (iii) the trade-off between return and risk is positive.

The CAPM is shown graphically in Figure 2.3, where R_F = risk-free return, $E(R)$ = mean return and β (beta) = risk. The CAPM says that the required rate of return on any asset is equal to the risk-free rate of return plus a risk premium. The risk premium is the price of risk multiplied by the quantity of risk. In the terminology of the CAPM, the price of risk is determined by the slope of the line, the difference between the expected rate of return on the market portfolio and the risk-free rate of return. The quantity of risk is called beta (β).

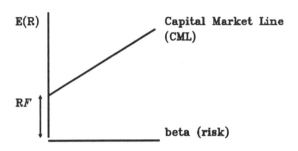

Figure 2.3 *The capital market line*

Arbitrage pricing theory

The arbitrage pricing theory (APT) is more general than the CAPM discussed above. It suggests that many factors, not just the market portfolio, may explain asset returns. For each factor the appropriate measure of risk is the sensitivity of asset returns to changes in the factor. For normally distributed returns the sensitivity is analogous to the beta or systematic risk of the CAPM. APT can be applied to cost of capital and capital budgeting problems.

Option pricing theory

The theory assumes that all financial assets are contingent claims. For example, ordinary shares are really a call option on the value of the assets of a firm. Similarly, other securities may also be thought of as options.

Option prices are functions of five parameters: the price of the underlying security, its instantaneous variance, the exercise price of the option, the time to maturity and the risk-free rate. All variables are observable except the instantaneous variance; this is the variation of the rate of return on the underlying asset – the holder of a call option will prefer more variance in the price of the stock, as this will increase the probability that the price of the stock will exceed the exercise price and this will thus be of some value to the call holder. The option price does not, in this theory, depend on either individual risk preferences or the expected rate of return on the underlying asset. Options are discussed further in Chapter 6.

Modigliani–Miller theorems

The cost of capital is used as a basis for a rate of return. This rate needs to be defined so that a project's returns can be assessed against required criteria. For a firm the main criterion is usually taken as whether the project improves the wealth position of the current shareholders of the firm. The original Modigliani–Miller theorems have been extended using the CAPM, so that a risk-adjusted cost of capital may be obtained for each project. When the expected cash flows of the project are discounted at the correct risk-adjusted rate, the result is the net present value (NPV) of the project.

In a world without taxes the value of the firm is independent of its capital structure. With the introduction of corporate and personal taxes the firm is unaffected by the choice of financial gearing. However, although no completely satisfactory theory has yet been found to explain the existence of an optimal capital structure, casual empiricism suggests that firms behave as though it does exist. Thus, the estimated weighted average cost of capital can be calculated using a target capital structure. Empirical evidence suggests there is a gain from being geared.

Market efficiency

The hypothesis of capital market efficiency says that the prices of securities instantaneously and fully reflect all available relevant information. Capital market efficiency relies on the ability of arbitrageurs (dealers who capitalise on dealing in assets which are over- or undervalued on the market) to recognise that prices are out of line and to make a profit by driving them back to an equilibrium value consistent with available information. In an efficient market securities will be traded at correct prices. This provides confidence to investors and the best allocation of funds.

For a stock market to be perfect, the following conditions need to apply:

(i)   The market needs to be frictionless without transaction costs and taxes. No constraining regulations limiting freedom of entry and exit for investors and companies seeking funds. All shares should be perfectly marketable.

(ii)   All services in the market should be provided at the average minimum cost, with all participants price takers.
(iii) All buyers and sellers should be rational expected utility maximisers.
(iv)   There should be many buyers and sellers.
(v)   The market should be efficient from an informational point of view; information should be costless and received simultaneously by all individuals.

No market satisfies all these conditions. It is possible to relax some of the assumptions and still have an efficient market. The assumptions of costless information, a frictionless marketplace and many buyers and sellers are not necessary conditions for the existence of an efficient capital market.

The capital market approach used in finance theory is important in respect of financial decisions made; the approach is only tenable if markets are efficient. If markets are efficient, then the market prices will reflect the effects of decisions made in the market. The market price is the present value of future returns expected by the participants in the market discounted at a rate which reflects the risk-free rate and an appropriate risk premium. The stock market is essentially a secondary market – a place to buy and sell established securities. The influence of the market on sources of new capital is very high. The conditions necessary for efficiency in the capital markets are not as stringent as those defined by a perfect capital market.

The efficient market requires:

(i)   dealing costs not to be too high,
(ii)   the relevant information to be available to a largish number of participants;
(iii) no individual dominating the market.

If people disagree on individual judgements on future returns, this will lead to transactions. The sum of the transactions process will produce unbiased valuations in an efficient market. Such a market is a 'fair game' one. If it is a fair game, then ex-*post* gains or losses cannot be predicted ex-*ante*.

2.3 THE THEORIES DEVELOPED

Capital market theory

Capital market theory relates to the capital asset pricing model and to arbitrage pricing theory. The theory is about discounting risky cash flows.

The theory has a number of important aspects which are covered point by point:

How is risk measured?   The risk is related to an asset (we can use a company stock for ease of understanding). It relates to the variability of returns, measured by their variance or standard deviation. This is applicable to a single asset or security.

How is risk measured in a portfolio of securities?   Investors generally hold diversified portfolios; we are thus interested in the contribution of a security to the risk of the entire portfolio. Because a security's variance is dispersed in a large diversified portfolio, the security's variance/standard deviation no longer represents the security's contribution to the risk of a large portfolio. In this case, the contribution is best measured by the security's covariance with the other securities in the portfolio. For example, if a stock has high returns when the overall return of the portfolio is low and vice versa, the stock has a negative covariance with the portfolio. It acts as a hedge against risk, reducing the risk of the portfolio. If the stock has a high positive covariance, there is a high risk for the investor.

What is the measure of diversification? β (beta) is the appropriate measure of the contribution of a security to the risk of a large portfolio.

What is the criterion for holding an investment?   Investors will only hold a risky investment if its expected return is high enough to compensate for its risk. There is a trade-off between risk and reward. The expected return on a security should be positively related to the security's beta:

expected return on a security = risk-free rate + [beta × (expected return on market portfolio − risk-free rate)] (Ross *et al.* 1993, pp. 233–4)

The term in brackets is positive, so the equation relates the expected return on a security as a positive function of its beta. This equation is the basis of the capital asset pricing model (CAPM). Arbitrage pricing theory (APT) also derives a relationship between risk and return but not in this form. The APT draws basically the same conclusions but makes assumptions that the returns on securities are driven by a number of market factors.

Capital asset pricing model

$$\overline{R} = R_F + \beta(\overline{R}_M - R_F)$$

where $\overline{R}_M$ is the expected return on the market, $\overline{R}$ is the expected return on the security, R_F is the risk-free rate and β is the measure of risk. Beta (β) is a measure of the security's sensitivity to movements in an underlying factor, a measure of systematic risk. Systematic risk affects a large number of assets and is also called market, portfolio or common risk. Diversifiable risk is a risk that affects a single asset or small group of assets; this is also called unique or unsystematic risk.

The total risk for an individual security held in a portfolio can thus be broken down:

total risk of individual security = portfolio risk + unsystematic or diversifiable risk

Total risk is the risk borne if only one security is held. Portfolio risk is the risk still borne after achieving full diversification. Portfolio risk is often called systematic or market risk. Diversifiable, unique or unsystematic risk is that risk which can be diversified away in a large portfolio.

Gearing and the cost of capital

The expected return on any asset depends on its beta (β). If a project has a beta risk similar to the firm's, then it can be used in the CAPM. If a project's beta is different, then it should be used in assessing the return for the project or else the average beta of similar projects in the industry. The beta of the company is determined by the revenue cycle, operating gearing and financial gearing (Ross *et al.* 1993, p. 350).

The cost of capital is the weighted average of the firm's cost of equity and debt. If the cost of equity is r_S and the cost of debt is r_B, the total cost of capital is

$$\frac{S}{S+B} r_S + \frac{B}{S+B} r_B$$

where S is the percentage of equity to total capital and B is the percentage of debt to total capital.

Operating gearing is based on the differences between fixed and variable costs: one cost alters with the quantity of output and the other does not. If there are higher fixed costs and lower variable costs, then there is a higher operating gearing defined as:

$$\frac{\text{change in EBIT}}{\text{EBIT}} \times \frac{\text{sales}}{\text{change in sales}}$$

where EBIT = earnings before interest and taxes. Operating gearing measures the percentage change in EBIT for a given percentage change in sales; operating gearing increases as fixed costs rise and variable costs fall (see Chapter 13 for a further discussion on operating gearing).

Financial gearing is the extent to which a firm relies on debt. A highly geared firm means it has to make interest payments regardless of the firms sale or income. So this is a fixed cost of finance. The risk (β) of an asset or of a company is reflected by its cost of capital and is determined by its capital structure, thus:

The firm's β = β of ordinary shares if the firm is only financed with equity. Otherwise:

$$\beta \text{ asset} = \frac{\text{debt}}{\text{debt} + \text{equity}} \times \beta \text{ debt} + \frac{\text{equity}}{\text{debt} + \text{equity}} \times \beta \text{ equity}$$

β debt is very low and in practice can be assumed to be 0. Thus (Ross *et al.* 1993, p. 348):

$$\beta \text{ asset} = \frac{\text{equity}}{\text{debt} + \text{equity}} \times \beta \text{ equity} = \text{equity gearing} \times \text{risk of equity}$$

Because $\frac{\text{equity}}{\text{debt} + \text{equity}}$ must be < 1 for a geared firm, it follows that β asset < β equity. β in an ungeared firm must be less than the β of equity in an otherwise identical geared firm.

Efficient markets

Efficient markets suggest that current market prices reflect available information. If valuations are a good proxy for prices, then valuations should reflect all known information (Brown 1991, p. 68). There are several forms of market efficiency: weak, semi-strong and strong. If markets are efficient, they can process the information available and the information is thus incorporated into the price of the security. Thus, systems for playing the market cannot succeed; abnormal returns cannot be expected. The definition of the types of market depends on the information the market uses to determine prices:

Weak form – incorporates the past history of prices and is efficient with respect to these prices. So stock selections based on patterns of past stock price movements are no better than random choice.

Semi-strong form – makes use of all publicly available information; this is reflected in the price of stocks, so investors will not be able to outperform the market by using the same information.

Strong-form efficiency – the market has available all information and uses all the available information that anyone knows about the stocks, including inside information, to price the stocks.

Evidence from different financial markets support the weak-form and semi-strong efficiency but not the strong-form. It is still not possible for the investor to use available information to beat the market; the share prices thus conform to a 'random walk'. Efficient markets enable us to say something about the way assets should be priced. If the market is a fair game, investors should be compensated for that part of the total risk that cannot be reduced by diversification. An efficient market implies valuers are doing a good job impounding information into valuations (Brown 1991, p. 69).

Capital structure

In a no-tax world, Modigliani and Miller suggest that the value of the firm is unaffected by gearing. But with taxes the firm's value is an increasing function of gearing.

The expected rate of return is related to gearing and before taxes:

$$r_S = r_0 + \frac{B}{S}(r_0 - r_B)$$

where r_S is the cost of equity, r_0 is the cost of equity in an ungeared firm, r_B is the cost of debt, S is the percentage of equity and B is percentage of debt to total capital.

Chaos theory

The efficient market hypothesis is based on the assumption that rational investors rapidly absorb new information about a company's prospects which then is impounded into the share price. Thus, the market has no memory; all price-sensitive events are random and independent of one another. The crash of 1987, possibly attributed to the market's realisation that shares were overvalued and triggered by the collapse of a relatively minor buy-out deal, has uncovered evidence that share price movements do not always conform to a 'random walk'.

A new branch of mathematics, chaos theory, has been used to explain these features. Chaos theory is based on the study of natural systems such as weather patterns and river systems. Observations of such systems give a chaotic impression of the elements lurching from one extreme to another. But chaos theorists suggest that these apparent unpredictable patterns are governed by sets of complex subsystems which react interdependently and can be modelled. Predictions of the behaviour of chaotic systems are very sensitive to the precise conditions specified at the start of the estimation period: a small error in the specification can lead to major errors in the model. It has been suggested that stock markets are chaotic in this sense: markets do have memories, are prone to major swings and do not behave randomly. In the UK some evidence has been found that today's price movement is influenced by changes in the past. If price moves were persistent, i.e. if previous moves in price had been upwards, then the subsequent price move was also found to be more likely to be up than down. Yet chaos theory also suggests that persistent trends are more likely to result in major reversals. Other observers of the market suggest that markets are essentially rational and efficient but succumb to chaos on occasions with bursts of chaotic frenzy being attributable to specific acts, which suggests some scope for informed insiders to outperform the market during such periods. The true nature of the market is still in debate but it seems likely that corporate financial managers cannot necessarily regard today's market price as a fair assessment of company value. However, the market may well correctly value a company over a period of years (Pike and Neale 1993, p. 39).

2.4 THE APPLICATION OF THEORY TO PRACTICE

Financial decisions

Financial management is concerned with answering three questions:

What specific assets should an enterprise acquire?
What total volume of funds should an enterprise commit?
How should the funds required be financed?

The study of finance is an extension to micro economic theory. Financial decisions are made within certain parameters, which are:

(i)   expected returns;
(ii) risk;
(iii) capital markets;
(iv) the firm's cost of capital.

The firm's cost of capital is used in assessing the expected returns and capital market conditions affect the firm's cost of capital. The fundamental model is the relationship between risk and expected returns. Thus, financial decisions are a trade-off between risk and return.

Profit and wealth maximisation

The firm's operating objective is generally taken simply as the maximisation of profit. Wealth maximisation is more satisfactory or, more specifically, the maximisation of shareholders' wealth (for a corporate entity).

The objections to profit maximisation criteria are:

(i)   The future is uncertain. It is not possible to express objective probabilistic distributions of the various returns possible. It is not possible to maximise the unknown.
(ii) Financial decision making concerns the trade-off of risk and return. The concept of profit maximisation cannot embrace this view of decision making.
(iii) The conditions of uncertainty are such that decisions of profit maximisation cannot be made. Companies tend to a level performance that satisfies rather than maximises objectives. The satisficing goal is consistent with the behavioural theory of the firm and is also consistent with wealth maximisation. The decision maker will satisfice in situations where the costs of searching for a better solution are thought to be equal to or greater than the benefits to be had from the possibly submaximal course adopted.
(iv) The view of profit maximisation is a narrow one. There are a number of external constraints to this approach. Wealth maximisation is unrealistic but maximisation could mean the maximum possible difference between the value of the input of resources into the firm and the value of the output of goods and services.

If a wider viewpoint is taken and the ultimate decision is a trade-off between risk and reward and decision-maker attitudes towards these will vary, then utility maximisation is the goal of financial decision making. Profit maximisation and wealth are subsumed under utility maximisation.

The cost of capital is important in these decisions. The firm will embark on projects which offer the prospect of a return greater than the firm's cost of capital. The firm's cost of capital will be determined by the finance markets. Market participants assess the performance of the firm and a collective judgement is made on the market. This assessment is a significant factor in pricing the firm's equity and rate of interest on debt.

Significance of capital markets

Finance uses the capital market approach as the basis for decision making. Such an approach is only useful if the capital markets are efficient.

The point made by the theory discussed previously on efficient markets is that in efficient markets investors cannot consistently achieve above-average returns other than by chance. In October 1987, on 'Black Monday' there was a sudden and dramatic fall in share prices on most of the world's stock markets, with share prices falling by 30% or more. Had this been triggered by a particular event, shareholders' reaction could have been explained as the efficient market reacting to new information. However, this collapse was not due to external events but was rather a recognition that the bull market had ended and the speculative share price bubble had burst. The equity returns in US markets were out of alignment compared with returns on Government stocks and there was a sharp international adjustment starting with this realisation and accentuated by futures dealing and 'program trading' which triggered sales of stocks and shares automatically as prices fell. This crash brought into question the validity of the simple efficient markets hypothesis and a view developed that there may be not a single 'true' value for the level of shares but a range.

Pike and Neale (1993) suggest that there are a number of implications for managing finance which arise from market efficiency:

(i) Investors are not easily fooled by glossy financial reports or 'creative accounting' techniques which boost corporate reported earnings but not underlying cash flows.

(ii) Corporate management should endeavour to make decisions which maximise shareholders' wealth.

(iii) There is little point in bothering with the timing of new issues. Market prices are a 'fair' reflection of the information available and rationally evaluate the degree of risk in shares.

(iv) Where corporate managers possess information not yet released to the market (termed 'information asymmetry'), there is some opportunity for influencing prices. Release of this information can be done strategically, as when an unwelcome takeover bid occurs (Pike and Neale 1993, pp. 38–9).

Capital structure and gearing

Money lent to the business by third parties is debt finance or loan capital. Most companies borrow money on a long-term basis by issuing stocks or debentures. The supplier of the loan will specify the amount of loan, rate of interest, date of payment and method of repayment. The finance manager of a firm will monitor the long-term financial structure of the firm by examining the relationship between loan capital (where interest and loan repayments are contractually obligatory) and ordinary share capital (where dividend payment is at the discretion of the directors). This relationship between debt and equity is called gearing (known in the USA as leverage). Strictly, gearing is the proportion of debt capital to total capital in the firm (Pike and Neale 1993, p. 8).

The capital structure of a property company is a key factor in how a company is viewed in terms of its attractiveness for an investor or lender. The property sector is characterised by a high level of gearing due to the availability of fixed interest finance during the first post-war boom from 1954 to 1964. This availability led to many property companies being highly geared.

High gearing is of benefit when property values are rising ahead of interest charges but can be dangerous if the real rate of interest is rising at a greater rate than property values. A simple example of gearing applied to house purchase is shown in Box 2.1.

2.5   THE COMPARISON OF PROPERTY RETURNS WITH OTHER INVESTMENT MEDIA

The relationship of property yield movements to interest rate changes is an interesting one. Short-term interest rates (bank base rates) or yields on long-term stocks generally move in the opposite direction to property yields. This is so whether prime yields are considered or even average yields. Secondary property, where rental yields are higher and likely to provide a greater proportion of overall return than with prime property, may have yields which may be more related to interest rate movements. In 1978–9 average yields fell but interest rates rose sharply. In 1982 and 1983 property yields began moving up while interest rates were falling. In 1988 the average property yield fell as short- and long-term interest rates increased (Brett 1990, pp. 227–8). Logically one would expect yields to decrease as expectation of rental growth increases.

GEARING
Example of the effect of gearing in house purchase

House is purchased for £100 000
The growth rate in house prices is 20%
70% is borrowed on mortgage
The interest rate on the mortgage is 10% p.a.
The house is sold after 1 year

---

1. What is the equity return?
2. What is the return if you borrow 50%?

1.	Sale price		£120 000
	Less mortgage	£70 000	
	Plus interest	£ 7 000	
	Balance		£ 77 000
	Profit		£ 43 000

$$^*\text{Return on capital} = \frac{£43\,000}{£30\,000} \times 100\% \;=\; 143\%$$

$$= 43\% \text{ profit}$$

2.	Sale price		£120 000
	Less mortgage	£50 000	
	Plus interest	£ 5 000	
	Balance		£ 55 000
	Profit		£ 65 000

$$^*\text{Return on capital} = \frac{£65\,000}{£50\,000} \times 100\% \;=\; 130\%$$

$$= 30\% \text{ profit}$$

Box 2.1 *Example of the effect of gearing in house purchase*

In theory, returns on different kinds of investment should have impact on others. If yields on government stocks are high, then one expects a higher return on shares. Interest rates and yields have three elements: a time preference element, an inflation element and a risk element (Isaac and Steley 1991, pp. 42–3).

Time preference element

This exists as a compensation to the investor who now cannot spend the investment monies immediately but will need to wait until the investment can be liquefied. The compensation stems from the premise that people prefer to have money now and not later – the money, after all, may be put to use either in consumption or in alternative investment, and thus immediate satisfaction or alternative investment opportunities are obtained. The interest rate needs an element to entice people to part with their monies and delay consumption or to compete with alternative investment. From the analysis above, the rate on index-linked Treasury stock is a measure of this. Ignoring redemption, the interest rate has the elements of risk (none) and inflation covered; it thus represents an indication of the time preference element. This rate varies with market conditions, but for ease of calculation we have assumed a 3% allowance in the following calculations.

Inflation

It is important that this element used in interest rates is a reflection of investors' anticipation of the inflation rate, which may differ from the expectations of the rate used by the Government, first because various financial advisors may be using different economic models to advise the Government, and second because the investors' index of inflation may differ from the one used by the Government. Our calculation of a possible inflation allowance can be assessed for the investors' view of the difference between index-linked gilts and ordinary undated Treasury stock. The calculation uses the relationship between market rates of interest which are inclusive of inflation and real rates of interest which exclude inflation:

$$i = \frac{(1 + e)}{(1 + g)} - 1$$

Here let us use i as the inflation-proof yield rate (index-linked, say 3%) and e as the inflation-prone rate of undated ordinary Government stock (say 10%). Thus, to find g (the rate of inflation):

$$0.03 = \frac{(1+0.1)}{(1+g)} - 1$$

$$(1+g) = \frac{1.1}{1.04} - 1.0577$$

so g = say 5.8%. The returns on index-linked Government stock are shown in financial newspapers, as is the rate for undated stock; the latter is listed as consols, being an abbreviation of consolidated loan stock (the Government national debt).

Risk premium

Much work has been done in the property and other investment sectors on this question of risk premium. This is the addition to the risk-free interest rate to take into account the risk of the investment. This risk may relate to the inability to predict the level of return and perhaps the likelihood of payment.

The relationship between risk and return is direct — for instance, the monetary rewards of university lecturers may be low to reflect the security of their position (this is probably an historic analysis), while a market maker in the City of London may obtain colossal earnings if successful in trading but runs the risk of being made redundant if earnings fall. A person investing in a building society will not expect very high rates of interest, as the investor believes the investment to be secure; on the other hand, couriers running drugs into Singapore may request large returns to cover the risk of a potential early end to their careers.

This relationship between risk and reward is called the capital market line, being the price on the market for raising capital given different risk rates. This line can be represented diagrammatically as shown in Figure 2.2, but note that the relationship between the two may not be a simple linear one (that is, not a straight line function) (Isaac and Steley 1991, p. 43).

Conclusion

Yields on different kinds of investment may influence those on others, but rental growth in property is more likely to be determined by supply and demand and the general economic situation. Inflation and risk attitudes may differ between investors in the different asset classes. Property yields do react to rental growth but with delay and in a haphazard fashion;

property cycles drive rental growth. Property values do not always rise as a result of inflation. In the long run inflation has an effect on building costs and profit which leads to expectations of higher costs and rents but growth in rents and capital values has taken place in periods of relatively low inflation (1978–88) and the property crash of 1974–6 took place while inflation was at its highest level (Brett 1990, pp. 229–30).

REFERENCES

Brett, M (1990) *Property and Money*, Estates Gazette, London.
Brown, G R (1991) *Property Investment and the Capital Markets*, E & F Spon, London.
Copeland, T E and Weston, J F (1988) *Financial Theory and Corporate Policy*, Addison-Wesley, Wokingham.
Isaac, D and Steley, T (1991) *Property Valuation Techniques*, Macmillan Press, London.
Pike, R and Neale, B (1993) *Corporate Finance and Investment*, Prentice Hall, London.
Ross, S A, Westerfield, R W and Jaffe, J F (1993) *Corporate Finance*, Irwin, Boston.

3 The Structure of Finance

3.1 INTRODUCTION

The cash-flow approach to the firm and the balance sheet model were discussed in Chapter 1. These approaches, besides looking at the application of company funds for the purchase of assets, also differentiated between the sources of the funds – in particular, the difference between long-term debt and shareholders' equity in the firm. An understanding of the difference between equity and debt is fundamental to an understanding of how finance works. The structure of finance can be analysed in two different ways: debt versus equity; project versus corporate funding.

In the past most interest in property concentrated on project finance, but with the size of schemes increasing and innovatory techniques of funding derived from the USA and other economic sectors, there is more interest in corporate finance. Generally, firms offer two basic types of securities to investors. Debt securities are contractual obligations to repay corporate borrowing; equity securities are shares of common stock and preferred stock that represent non-contractual claims on the residual cash flow of the firm. Issues of debt and equity that are publicly sold by the firm are then traded on the financial markets. These distinctions are clarified below.

Debt versus equity

Equity is money and resources provided by the developer, partners, investors and funds who participate in the risk and profit of the scheme. Debt finance basically consists of loans raised from banks and other sources against the project (project-specific) and non-project-specific loans raised in the market. This is not always a useful distinction, as corporate funding, the raising of finance against the assets of a company, can be based on equity as well as debt.

Project versus corporate finance

Project finance is finance provided where the principal or only security for the finance is the property itself, although supporting guarantees and additional collateral may also be requested. Corporate finance is finance raised on the back of the corporate entity rather than the project. Traditionally property and other companies provided funds for new projects from retained earnings, the issue of new shares and borrowings. In the post-war era, fixed interest mortgages and debentures were also used. Nowadays there may be a complex corporate package of different types of funds.

	CORPORATE FUNDING	PROJECT FINANCE
EQUITY FINANCE	Share issues	Partnership funds Single asset unitisation
DEBT FINANCE	Loan stock Fixed interest debentures	Bank overdrafts Short-term funds for development

Box 3.1 *Funding matrix*

Using the parameters above, the funding matrix can distinguish among the financing methods available and this is shown in Box 3.1.

Capital structure

Financing arrangements determine how the value of a company is sliced up. The persons or institutions that buy debt from the firm are creditors. The holders of the equity shares are shareholders. The size of the company's balance sheet will determine how well the company has made its investment decisions. The size of the firm is its value in the financial markets:

$$V = D + E$$

value of company = value of debt + value of equity

(Ross *et al*. 1993, p. 6)

Corporate securities issued are a contingent claim on the value of the company. The shareholders' claim on the value of the company is a residual after payment to the debtholder; they get nothing if the value of the company is equal to or less than the amount promised to the debtholders.

Figure 3.1 *Payoffs to debt and equity. Source: Ross et al. 1993, p.12*

In Figure 3.1, F is the promised payoff to debtholders. $X-F$ is the payoff to equity shareholders if $X-F > 0$; if not, then payoff $= 0$.

Financial markets

The financial markets are composed of the money markets and the capital markets. Money markets are the markets for debt securities that pay off in the short term (usually less than 1 year). Capital markets are the markets for long-term debt and equity shares. Primary markets are used when governments or companies initially sell securities. Companies offer their shares through public placings or public offerings and this is discussed in greater detail in Chapter 6 on corporate finance. Secondary markets come into operation for the resale of securities. Debt and equity are traded in the security markets. There is a distinction between auction markets and dealer markets: equity securities tend to be sold in auction markets (stock exchanges); debt securities are sold in dealer markets. Auction markets differ from dealer markets in two ways:

(i)   Trading in an auction exchange takes place at a single site on the floor of the exchange or with a centralised screen system. In October 1986, the Stock Exchange changed its system of trading, post 'Big Bang' (the deregulation of the Stock Exchange), from trading on the floor of the Exchange to an electronic market place. The Stock Exchange Automated Quotation System (SEAQ) moved the system of trading into dealing rooms equipped with computer screens.

(ii) The transaction prices of shares traded on the auction exchange are communicated almost immediately to the public by means of computers and other devices; this is not so in dealer markets (Ross *et al.* 1993, p. 23).

Direct investment versus property vehicles

The concept of project versus corporate finance can be looked at from a different perspective, that of direct investment in property as against investment through a property vehicle. Venmore-Rowland (1991) has considered the advantages and disadvantages of investment by these two approaches and these are shown in Box 3.2.

DIRECT PROPERTY

Advantages	**Disadvantages**
low risk relative to equities	illiquid
diversification benefits	management intensive
hedge against inflation	minimum portfolio size required
good for matching inflation-prone	
long-term liabilities	

PROPERTY VEHICLES

Advantages	**Disadvantages**
liquidity	loss of control
divisibility	tax slippage
management expertise	short-term, relatively poor
specialisation of vehicle	performance
gearing	high correlation to stock market
can shift weight/exposure	
income benefits from the discount	
to net asset value	

Box 3.2 *Direct property and property vehicles*

Two factors are working in opposite directions. These are correlation to other investments and liquidity. Correlation is important to obtain a diversified portfolio of investment and therefore spread risks. Direct property has a relatively low correlation to equities but is more illiquid. Property vehicles are liquid but are more highly correlated to equities (Venmore-Rowland 1991, p. 7).

3.2 CATEGORIES OF FINANCE

This section is based on a suggested classification by Brett (1990, pp. 147–51) and is summarised in Box 3.3.

CATEGORIES OF FINANCE

Debt or equity
Project finance or corporate finance
Loan or traded security
Secured or unsecured
Fixed rate or variable rate
Long-term or short-term
Recourse, non-recourse or limited recourse

MAIN CRITERIA

Debt or equity
Project or corporate finance

FINANCE MATRIX

	Debt	**Equity**
Project Finance		
Corporate Finance		

Box 3.3 *Summary of categories of finance*

Debt or equity

The distinction between debt and equity depends on whether the money is borrowed (debt), and here the lender has no direct involvement in the project, or whether the money has been invested on the basis of sharing both the risk and the returns of the project (equity). Borrowed money needs to be repaid and interest will be paid on the outstanding amount until the debt is repaid. The equity return for the person who puts up the money is determined by the success of the enterprise. The person shares the profits, and if there are none, then there is no return.

The most obvious form of equity is ordinary share capital. Equity shares can also exist in development situations where a financier is entitled to a share in profits of the scheme. There are also deferred forms of equity such as convertible loans, which start as debt instruments paying a fixed rate of interest but later the loans may be converted into equity shares.

Project finance or corporate finance

Project finance is the money borrowed for a project, usually a development project. The loan is based on the project itself and this becomes the main security. A larger company may be able to borrow on the strength of the assets of the company itself rather than its individual projects; this is asset-based or corporate finance. Interest will generally be lower for corporate loans than for project loans because there will be more collateral available for security rather than relying on the risk of a single project. Many companies are undertaking developments of such a size that they dwarf the company's own resources and the developer may then be concerned that, if anything went wrong with the project, the lenders might have recourse to other assets of the company, which then might undermine the company's financial position. In this case each development may need to be financed separately on a project basis and the developer may try to make the project 'off-balance-sheet' if possible.

Loan or traded security

Borrowed money may simply be a simple loan or a bond in the form of an instrument (a negotiable piece of paper) which is transferable. This is a form of IOU note and is called a security rather than a straightforward loan, and this can be sold on to other investors. The purchasers receive interest each year and also have the right for the original cost to be repaid at the end of the agreed duration of the security. If the purchasers do not wish to wait for this repayment date, they can sell the rights to other investors, who then become entitled to receive the interest and the eventual repayment monies. Securities of this kind are bought and sold on the stock market.

Secured and unsecured

Lenders will normally require security for the money they provide: they want collateral (security) for the loans and thus will charge assets to cover the loan, either the specific assets of a business related to the project or the assets of a business as a whole. If the borrower fails to pay the interest or capital repayments as required, then the lender can put a receiver into the company and the receiver will repay the loans from the proceeds of the sale of the company's assets or other available revenues. A secured loan is safer than an unsecured loan but well-established companies may be able to raise unsecured loans because the safeguard for the lender is the company's established profit record out of which the interest can be paid. Most borrowings in the euromarkets are unsecured, as are borrowings in the commercial paper market. The company's name and standing are the main guarantees.

Fixed rate or variable rate (floating rate) interest

Sometimes the rate of interest is agreed at the outset of the loan and remains unchanged over the life of the loan. With other loans the interest rate will change according to movements in money market rates or other rates agreed. For large-scale floating rate borrowings, the most common yardstick of interest rates is the London Interbank Offered Rate or LIBOR. This is the rate of interest at which the banks themselves are prepared to lend to each other. It is agreed at the outset, say, that the company will pay a margin over the LIBOR rate, say 2.5 percentage points (or 250 basis points, which is the same thing, as a basis point is 0.01%) over LIBOR. One can choose a LIBOR floating rate and then fix it. Short-term borrowings are most likely to be at the floating rate of interest. Long-term borrowings such as mortgage debentures are more likely to be at a fixed rate. The borrower can buy a cap for floating rate borrowing. This is a form of insurance policy which means that, whatever happens to interest rates in general, a maximum limit is set to the interest rate that a borrower will have to pay.

Long-term or short-term

Loans are usually over a period between 0 and 30 years. This range marks the difference between short- and long-term loans but the intermediate area is not defined. Many people consider 1–2 years to be short-term, equivalent to the development period for most projects, 2–7 years as medium-term and more than 7 years as long-term. Overdrafts are technically payable on demand and thus are short-term borrowing, but many companies have an overdraft outstanding almost indefinitely. With a multi-option facility (MOF), a company might technically be borrowing for 3 months at a time. At the end of 3 months it repays the original loans and takes out new ones for another 3 months. If the facility runs for 5 years, effectively it has the use of 5 year money by 'rolling over' (Brett 1990, p. 150).

Recourse, non-recourse or limited-recourse loans

If the loan for a particular project or for a particular subsidiary company is guaranteed by the parent, the lender has recourse to the parent, so can claim on the assets of the parent. If the only security for the lender is the project itself, as in a pure form of project-based finance, and the parent company has given no guarantees, the loan is non-recourse. A non-recourse loan is very unlikely to be granted in practice; banks would generally require the loans to be limited-recourse. The parent may have guaranteed interest payments but is under no obligation to repay the loan itself in these circumstances. A limited-recourse loan would still depend on the reputation of the borrower and the track record of the company as well as the quality of the project itself.

Domestic or euromarket loans

Loans can be raised in the UK or in the euromarkets. Euromarket loans can be in sterling abroad (eurosterling) or other currencies (eurodollar). A company may well raise monies in the euromarkets in different currencies and then swap to sterling if sterling is not popular at the time of raising the funds. The terms and conditions of operation in the European market can be different, e.g. euroloans are often unsecured.

3.3   THE FINANCE MARKET

The types of finance are shown with examples in Box 3.4 and these are discussed in detail in later chapters. Types of finance and the terms and conditions are going to vary depending on the purpose of the finance. The key areas for finance will be:

- finance for investment;
- finance for development;
- owner-occupier finance for property;
- structured finance based on the corporate structure.

	EQUITY	DEBT
Project funding	Unitisation/securitisation Loan with profit share Mezzanine finance Forward funding Venture capital Sale and leaseback	Mortgage Syndicated loans Bank loans Project management fee
Corporate funding	Authorised unit trusts (APUTS) Shares Warrants Options Futures Convertibles Venture capital	Bonds (deep-discounted bonds) Debentures Loan stock Multi-option facility (MOF) Commercial paper Euromarket

Box 3.4 *Types of finance*

Examples of the terms and conditions for these types of loans follow.

Development finance

Amount of loan:	75% total costs, perhaps 85% with profit share.
Loan period:	For construction period and void period before letting.
Interest rate margin:	1% (pre-let)–3% (speculative) above LIBOR or base rate.
Interest rate payment:	Variable, quarterly but rolled up to end.
Repayment of loan:	On sale of project or long-term mortgage.
Security:	First charge on property, recourse to borrower.
Comments:	Speculative finance might be difficult in the present market and the lender would be looking for a pre-let. Loan advances are determined by the level of security offered and can be increased to 100% of cost in some cases. Pricing is dependent on the level of security offered, type of building contract and profitability of the scheme.

Investment property finance

Amount of loan:	Up to 85% of cost or 75% of value, whichever is the lower.
Loan period:	Up to 15 years.
Interest rate margin:	0.25–2.5% above LIBOR or bank base rate. Long-term finance is priced off gilts and is available through the insurance companies. A maximum loan would equate to 75% of value.
Interest rate payment:	Fixed or variable rate interest payments. Part of the sum can be deferred and paid as a capital sum at the end of the facility.
Repayment of loan:	Most facilities are interest only and will require repayment through sale of the asset or by re-financing.
Comments:	The quality of the tenant is crucial to these transactions together with adequate levels of security.

Owner-occupied property

Advance:	Up to 100% of cost.
Loan period:	Up to 10 years.
Interest rate margin:	Between 0.5% and 3.0% over LIBOR or bank base rate.
Interest rate payment:	Fixed or variable.
Repayment of loan:	Full amount at the end of the facility or principal amortised over the term of the loan.
Comments:	Owner-occupiers are able to obtain a much higher loan-to-value ratio where it can be demonstrated that they can service the interest charges out of their business cash flow.

Joint ventures

A variety of joint venture partners, including banks, finance houses, insurance companies, pension funds, contractors and other developers, can be accessed in today's market. The structure of the transaction is dependent on what the parties bring to the venture by negotiation. Many financial contacts are passive investors enabling the developer to get on with the job. Joint venture arrangements are discussed in Chapter 11.

Structured finance

This can commonly use the following methods:

(i) Bonds, which enable interest rates to be rolled up, with payment at the end of the life of the bond.

(ii) Finance leasing – this enables the client to sell a property to a finance company, pay a market rent and have the option to repurchase the building at the original purchase price plus any deferred interest.

(iii) Off-balance-sheet financing – many clients reduce their exposure on their balance sheets by structuring loans outside of their group holdings.

(iv) Capital market instruments, including interest rate caps, interest rate floors, interest rate swaps (from variable to fixed interest rates) and swaptions (an option to swap in the future).

3.4 GLOSSARY OF FINANCIAL AND PROPERTY TERMS

Cap
A means of providing an interest rate ceiling for a variable rate loan by the use of an insurance policy.

Collar
Provides a ceiling and floor for interest rate movements for a variable interest loan.

Covenant
The financial status of a party involved in a property transaction.

Deficit financing
The financing of a project in such a way that the cash flows in the early years of the project are insufficient to cover the interest on debt payable.

Discount
Bonds with below-market coupons (interest rate payable) trade at a discount below par (the nominal value).

Finance lease
This involves the sale and leaseback with a financial institution; there may be tax advantages in such an arrangement without loss of control over the asset.

Gearing
Strictly this is the proportion of debt capital to total capital but commonly in property it is used as the ratio between interest-bearing debt and the shareholders' funds: basically the ratio between debt and equity, which gives an indication of the financial standing of the company. A highly geared company has a high proportion of debt.

Ground rent
An annual payment for the land element in a development proposal.

Interest capitalisation
The process of rolling up interest on a project and adding the interest to the costs of the project, the total being shown in accounts as the asset value.

Joint venture
Two or more parties, working together, sharing the rewards and risks of the project.

Loan-to-value ratio
The level of the loan expressed as a percentage of value.

Margin
The interest rate payable over a base rate to reflect the risk of the project or the parties involved. Commonly used as a margin above LIBOR.

Mezzanine finance
Above a conventional loan-to-value ratio of, say, 70% certain lenders will lend additional monies known as mezzanine finance. This is priced at a higher rate than the senior debt (the initial advance) and may include profit-sharing to reflect the increased risk.

Overage
The growth in capital value over the development period which is available to be shared between vendor and developer.

Pre-let
The letting of a development before the completion of the project. This reduces the risk of voids and improves the funding position.

Ratchet basis
Used on profit participation transactions; whereas the overall profit increases, the proportion of profit received can increase or fall.

Recourse
The ability of the lender in a loan situation to have recourse to the assets of the company receiving the loan in the event of default. These assets are in addition to the assets immediately involved in the project for which the loan was made. In a non-recourse situation the lender can only have recourse to the project and its underlying assets.

Rental void
The period of time a completed development is unlet and thus not income producing. During this period it is also not usually possible to sell the completed project.

Swap
An interest rate swap is an agreement between two parties to swap their interest rate obligations, normally from a variable interest rate to a fixed one. A swap option is an option to change to a fixed rate in the future at pre-set terms.

REFERENCES

Brett, M (1990) *Property and Money*, Estates Gazette, London.

Ross, S A, Westerfield, R W and Jaffe, J F (1993) *Corporate Finance*, Irwin, Boston.

Venmore-Rowland, P (1991) 'Vehicles for Property Investment', in P Venmore-Rowland, P Brandon and T Mole (eds), *Investment, Procurement and Performance in Construction*, RICS, London.

4 Property Lenders

4.1 SOURCES OF FINANCE

The main lenders in the market are:

(i) high street/clearing banks;
(ii) foreign banks;
(iii) building societies;
(iv) merchant banks;
(v) insurance companies;
(vi) finance houses.

In their latest report on the sources of money flowing into property, DTZ Debenham Thorpe gave the figures shown in Table 4.1 (Evans 1993, p. 76).

Table 4.1 *New money into property (Evans 1993, p. 76)*

	£ million					
Year	Pension funds	Insurance companies	Banks	Property companies	Overseas	Total
1980	908	855	72	147	100	2082
1981	843	1073	469	97	70	2552
1982	797	1059	822	263	120	3061
1983	680	845	934	83	85	2627
1984	997	744	963	237	65	3006
1985	590	815	1691	344	90	3530
1986	434	821	2224	737	150	4306
1987	240	755	3998	2300	290	7583
1988	312	1102	7954	761	1897	12 026
1989	92	1510	10 622	1647	3267	17 138
1990	−491	1080	7066	164	3269	11 088
1991	467	1483	678	1270	1551	5449
1992	349	600	−1708	334	1232	807
1993 Q1	134	74	−1134	−34	399	561
1993 Q2[a]				−23	356	333

Sources: Department of Trade and Industry; Central Statistical Office; Bank of England/ DTZ Debenham Thorpe Research.

[a] Not including pension funds, insurance companies and banks.

High street clearing banks

The big four are Lloyds, Barclays, National Westminster and Midland. These are probably the first port of call for people looking for loans, especially if they have established relationships. However, they are conservative and may view new transactions related to property in a cynical way. Smaller high street banks such as the Royal Bank of Scotland, the Bank of Scotland, Yorkshire Bank and the Clydesdale Bank may be more useful potential funders. The smaller banks are likely to have less of a bad debt problem and may want to increase market share. The larger banks are burdened at the moment by overexposure to the property sector; the emphasis at the present time is on debt repayment rather than new lending. British clearing banks' exposure to the property sector at the critical period to the end of the 1980s is shown in Figure 4.1.

Figure 4.1 *British clearing banks UK property lending (note: no figures for Lloyds 1986–8). Source: IBCA/Scott 1992, p. 348*

Foreign banks

The foreign banks tend to be more aggressive sources of property finance, or were in the early 1990s, but by 1993 they were showing less interest. They are useful sources of funding, particularly for quality and corporate transactions. The collapse of BCCI may make borrowers wary of dealing with foreign banks. The collapse of a bank half-way through a development may mean that it could take years to unwind the legal problems and thus would put the borrower's own financial position at risk.

Building societies

The building societies fared badly in the recent slump in the property market. In the late 1980s, their inexperience and desire for market share in commercial property lending led to substantial bad debt. They are now putting their respective houses in order with more qualified staff and are likely to be an important source of commercial finance in the future.

Merchant banks

Merchant banks rarely lend their own money but act as advisers and especially concentrate on large corporate transactions. They are unlikely to be interested in ordinary debt transactions, because there would be little opportunity to use their expertise and add value to such a transaction.

Insurance companies

The insurance companies are limited providers of funds. They do, however, offer the attraction of long-term, fixed rate funds priced over gilts, which can be useful in certain transactions.

Finance houses

In essence, the finance houses have been the principal providers of funding to the secondary leisure and retailing markets, providing finance for the purchase of freehold shops, pubs, restaurants and hotels. Their small trader exposure has made them particularly vulnerable to this latest recession, which has resulted in most of them leaving the market.

4.2 LENDING CRITERIA

The cost and availability of lending is a function of the value of any particular project and the amount of cost to be financed. The nature of the development is important: the design, mix, location and likely demand. The letting conditions are important, as are whether or not the investment is pre-let or speculative. The quality of the tenant, who will be providing the cash flow to the investment, will also be important. Other important criteria are the track record of the developer and the strength of security. Finally, the duration of the loan will be important as well as the details of repayment, e.g. the anticipated regularity of repayments and the size/amount of repayments prior to redemption.

Most lenders look for the same aspects of a lending proposal, which in simplified terms are the 'four Cs':

- character,
- cashstake,
- capability,
- collateral.

Character

This relates to the trading history or development experience of a borrower. In respect of a property developer or an investment company, the lender will want to know whether the borrower has the experience to complete the development, manage the investment or run the business, if applicable. The lender will also be interested in whether the client is respectable and trustworthy. The lender may also cynically wonder why the borrower's own high street bank will not lend the money.

Cashstake

This relates to how much equity (the borrower's own money) is going into the transaction. In addition, the bank will want to know where the equity has come from:

(i)   Is it lent from someone else?
(ii)   Is it from other profitable activities?
(iii) Is it simply a surplus which has arisen on the revaluation of property?
(iv)   Is it already pledged as security?
(v)   Is it legally acquired money – not laundered money?

Capability

Does the borrower have the capability to service the loan — that is, to pay the interest when it arises and the capital as and when repayment is required? Does the borrower have accounts or a business plan to show his/her present financial position and any estimate of future cash flow?

Collateral

The lender will want to know what security will be offered for the loan, its value and its saleability. The lender will want to know who valued the security and on what basis. The lender will need to assess the extent of the loan which would be exposed to the value of that security. Finally, will personal guarantees be given by the borrower?

General criteria

These are the general principles of underwriting but the most important aspect is the borrower's capability to meet loan repayments. Lenders will want the borrower to be a successful, well-respected individual or company who can comfortably afford to repay the proposed borrowing. There is a concern about the quality of the loans in the present market. Quality for the principal property sectors means:

Development: Profitable schemes pre-let to blue chip tenants with a full guarantee from the developer for cost over-runs.

Investment: Prime investments with blue chip tenants on long, full repairing and insuring (FRI) leases.

Commercial mortgages: Well-established companies with good-quality accounting information which clearly establishes their ability to service the loan.

4.3 DEVELOPMENT AND INVESTMENT LENDING

Development lending

Because of the recent rerating of property companies in 1993 (increased value on the stock market), the property companies have gone to the market to raise capital; this new injection of capital may act as a catalyst to the property market (DTZ Debenham Thorpe 1993, p. 3). There are, however, considerable difficulties in lending in the development market; speculative schemes are almost impossible to fund. However, this should be balanced by saying that if the development were being carried out by any of the principal UK developers, then there are still institutions who would look at funding schemes.

Speculative development

Funding is very difficult for speculative development. However, it may be possible to arrange loans where:

(i) The borrower is very strong and has accounts which prove an ability to repay the loan without any real need to achieve property sales.

(ii) The scheme is exceptionally profitable. This usually means that the borrower has been able to obtain the land for little or no cost.

(iii) The borrower is putting in an exceptionally high level of equity, thus ensuring the bank's exposure is kept to a minimum.

(iv) The borrower can prove that demand for the scheme is undoubted. There is, of course, only one way of proving such demand and that is to pre-let, but substantial evidence of demand may assist.

Pre-let/sold development

While a pre-let or sale makes the job of arranging finance substantially easier, it does, of course, depend who the scheme is pre-let or sold to. If there is a blue chip covenant on the other end of the contract, everything becomes that much more simple. If one has a covenant that no one has ever heard of, one may as well have a speculative development on one's hands.

While a pre-let to a blue chip covenant does make life easier, it still does not guarantee funding, as the banker will want to be satisfied that the borrowers, and/or contractor, could meet a completion deadline and/or liability for cost overruns, interest shortfalls, or losses on the sale of the investment. Should the scheme be pre-let to anything other than a blue chip tenant, this does not mean that finance cannot be arranged. What it does mean is that the banker will want to investigate the financial strength of the covenant, will probably wish to contribute less towards the overall costs of the scheme and will offer more onerous terms, such as a higher interest rate.

The lenders' view

The bank's view of speculative schemes can be fairly summarised in the expression 'why bother?' The banks currently have more unlet, unsold, uncompleted schemes on their books in 1993 than they know what to do with and are not eager to take on any more.

Conclusion

There is not a great deal of confidence in this sector at the present time but there are areas of opportunity, as follows:

(i)   Obviously, pre-let schemes. Any pre-let schemes that require funding, regardless of whether or not they are let to blue chip covenants, or less than 100% pre-let, are possible for funding.

(ii) Developments which are being undertaken by companies which are not solely developers, i.e. building contractors, who will have other sources of income without being reliant on property sales.

(iii) Residential developments. Development in this sector probably has the greatest upside potential in that an increasing number of sources will consider schemes in a more favourable light.

Generally speaking, funding for development properties can be arranged on the following terms:

- Land   70% loan to value;
- Construction   70% loan to cost.

For quality pre-let schemes, it may be possible to arrange the following:

either

- Land   80%;
- Construction   80%.

or

- Land   70% + 25% (mezzanine finance);
- Construction   70% + 25% (mezzanine finance).

Mezzanine finance will be explored in greater detail later. In exceptional circumstances, banks will provide 100% finance under joint venture arrangements. Interest rates for development loans will start at 1.5% above money costs, up to 5% above money costs for a straightforward 70% deal. A mezzanine lender would want a 30–40% return on this money, while a bank entering into a joint venture would probably want 50% of the scheme's net profit. So much for the theory. An example of a development loan is given below in Box 4.1.

DEVELOPMENT EXAMPLE

Background

- CLIENT
  Newly formed joint venture company owned –
  50% land owner (unencumbered site)
  50% building contractor (development experience)

- PLANNING

4 x 1 bed flats	£232 000
4 x 2 bed flats	£260 000
4 x 3 bed flats	£338 000
Total	£830 000

- COSTS/VALUE

Site	£220 000
Construction costs and fees	£420 000
Interest	£ 40 000
Sales costs	£ 22 000
Total	£682 000
Profit (22%)	£148 000

Requirement for finance

- The clients already had the land
- Needed 100% of the remaining costs
- Prepared to share in the risks/rewards

Offer for finance

- UK building society

75% land, i.e.	£150 000
75% construction and professional fees	£325 000

- *Total* £465 000

- 100% of construction costs, professional fees and interest
- 2% above GDMR (11.95%) at time of offer
- First charge on site
- Mortgage debenture
- Personal guarantees

(Note: GDMR is the Gross Domestic Mortgage Rate; see later in the chapter)

Box 4.1 *Development funding example*

Investment lending

The most notable change in the investment market, as far as funding is concerned, is the narrowing between the yield and interest rate gap. Rising property yields, and falling interest rates, now mean that many investments are close to self-funding. The difficulty for many funders is that there is not enough investment product to place with the banks, with most of the prime investments being snapped up by the institutions.

The lenders' view

There is a 'flight to quality' with investment properties. Increasing company failures have left banks with substantial problems in this sector, and they are now suspicious of anything but the highest-quality tenants. For any secondary investments, the banks will look very closely at the financial strength of the borrower and probably lend more onerously, reducing the loan-to-value exposure they are prepared to consider, and pushing up the interest margin they would expect the borrower to pay. An example of investment lending is given in Box 4.2.

INVESTMENT EXAMPLE: OFFICE PROPERTY

Background

CLIENT   Newly formed company owned 90% by overseas manufacturer and 10% by London property company. The property company was able to demonstrate a track record of previous successful transactions.

REQUIREMENT
- Client had the opportunity to acquire: newly built Birmingham office investment comprising a floor area of 3200 square metres let on 25 year term at £300 000 per annum to a blue chip tenant.
- The purchase price was £2.8 million – initial yield of 10.7%
- Independent valuation of £3 million
- The client wanted maximum advance at the lowest rate

OFFER
- Large British building society
- 85% advance, i.e. £2.4 million
- 5 year fixed rate (1.6% + 5 year SWAP)
- Bullet repayment (full repayment) after 5 years
- First charge on property
- Mortgage debenture
- 10% of loan guaranteed by the London property company shareholder
- £420 000 (15%) commercial mortgage indemnity

Box 4.2 *Investment funding example*

Banks are also looking at the level of interest cover provided by rental income. Previously, banks were happy for rental income to cover interest payable on a ratio of 1:1 or even deficit fund while rents were rising sharply. Today, however, banks will require rental cover more in the order of 1:1.2 or 1:1.25, taking the view that there may be little or no rental growth at next review. (1:1.2 means that every £100 of interest payable, say on a monthly basis, will have to be matched by £120 of rental income for the same month.)

Conclusion

The two main markets which are easier to find funding in are:

(i) Investments let to blue chip covenants where funding is arranged at 85% of the purchase price, at fixed rates of interest from 2 to 20 years.

(ii) Secondary investments bought on high yields with a good spread of tenants regardless of their covenant strength. In these instances funds can be arranged at up to 75% of purchase price and again on fixed rates of interest from 2 to 20 years.

4.4 PROBLEMS OF SECURITY

If a company can restrict borrowing to a few assets, there is much more flexibility in the financing strategy. The assets offered as security should make the borrowing cheaper by reducing the interest rates. If the debt is not secured on the company's assets, the investors will probably insist on restrictions on the company's overall level of borrowing.

The disadvantage of secured borrowing is that the company loses some flexibility in its handling of the properties within its portfolio that are charged as securities. One cannot sell the properties with the charge. Some flexibility will normally be built in. This flexibility might be an agreement between the borrower and lender that properties can be substituted from the pool of properties which constitute the security. The substituted property would, of course, have to be a equivalent property which may be acceptable. The property should be capable of maintaining the income and capital cover of the original portfolio. If, over a period of time, the value of the pool of properties rises, the capital cover for the debt may exceed the stipulated minimum and the borrower will probably be allowed to remove some of the properties from charge, provided that the capital and income cover requirements are still met. The alternative is for the borrower to use the excess security for further debt — for instance, in the case of debentures a further issue of the debenture can be made, identical with the original issue and ranking alongside it.

If the value of a property falls, the trustee could insist that the company top it up by putting further properties into the pool. The trustee can call for valuations to establish the value of properties that are charged.

Debentures offer good security but the 1986 Insolvency Act compromised this (Brett 1990, p. 184). Prior to the Act, if a borrower defaulted on the terms of a debenture with a fixed charge over specified properties, the trustee could sell the properties to recover the loss. With the 1986 Act, creditors with a floating charge have different rights from those with a fixed charge (a floating charge is one over the company's total fixed and current assets). If a company gets into financial difficulties but believes it may be able to get out of these difficulties or at least reduce them in the longer term, it can apply to have an administrator appointed. If this application is granted, then the administrator will provide a plan of action which may involve the continued running of the company or perhaps the selling off of assets over a period. Thus the creditor with the fixed charge, although still having a security for the loan, loses control over the security, as the administrator will decide how and when the security is sold.

The creditor with the floating charge can appoint an administrative receiver and block the appointment of an administrator by the company, and is thus in a more powerful position. Lenders are thus more likely to ask for a floating charge as well as a fixed charge in these circumstances. This approach is less likely to be popular with the borrower, as its charge is not limited to specified assets.

The alternative may be for the borrower to grant a floating charge over the assets of a subsidiary that owns the properties which would be subject to the fixed charge rather than charging the assets of the group as a whole. Investors would demand a higher yield on a debenture that does not offer a floating charge as well as a fixed one and the difference could be about 20 basis points (0.2%) (Brett 1990, p. 185).

Commercial mortgage indemnity market (CMI market)

There has been an explosion in the use of commercial mortgage indemnity policies. These top-slice policies involve an insurance company taking on the repayment risk on that part of a loan which the bank or building society could not lend. If the bank's normal loan-to-value ratio is 70% but the borrower needs 85%, then the bank arranges a CMI for the top slice of 15% and lends 85%. In the early years, Eagle Star wrote more business than the rest of the market. The downturn especially in the residential market had led to claims to support speculative developers. Other insurers have not suffered to the same degree as Eagle Star. The CMI market is now more cautious and informed. The CMI policy wording needs to be sufficiently broad and flexible to satisfy the banks while the insurers retain certain rights and controls. The underwriters are sceptical of highly geared financing where the investor claims to have bought cheaply.

In 1990 the mortgage indemnity charges were 7% on the 15% over 70% loan-to-value ratio, bringing the ratio up to 85%; for instance, on a £10m property, the premium was 7% of £1.5m = £105 000, about 1% of the value.

Underwriting property sales

The two inherent defects of property as an investment are illiquidity and the imperfections of the market. The disposal of property involves risks relating to the price achieved and the timescale of disposal. In a weak market delays make completion times uncertain. Underwriting Property Services (UPS) is a joint venture company established between the Bank of Scotland and Drivers Jonas, the property consultants, which provides a service in underwriting sales. The service in underwriting property sales aims to remove the uncertainty of the transactions and thus provide a more predictable outcome. The service is aimed at specific clients, for instance:

- investors wishing to change portfolios within a given timescale to maximise growth;
- unit fund managers wishing to meet redemptions;
- property companies who need to book a profit before the year end;
- owner-occupiers needing to raise capital in a given timescale; and
- public organisations tied to annual accounting and cash-limited budgets.

UPS contracts to buy a property if it has not been purchased at the end of a fixed marketing period. It works by granting the vendor an option to sell to UPS on a predetermined date in the future at a predetermined price. An underwriting contract is entered into by the parties at the outset (Armon-Jones 1992, p. 498). The underwritten price is in the region of 90% of open market value.

The scheme adds liquidity and certainty to sale and thus some stability to the market, although the scale of the operation is obviously limited. *Chartered Surveyor Weekly* (1991, p. 5) estimated to begin with that UPS would stabilise the market at £110m maximum.

4.5 PROPERTY LENDING SURVEY

Introduction

The *Property Lending Survey* is a survey of major property lenders which commenced in 1990 and has been carried out on an annual basis since. The survey is a joint project between Chesterton Financial, the financial services section of Chesterton International, and the University of Greenwich. A section of the *Survey* has looked repeatedly at the issues of interest rates and the security required. The 1993 *Survey* gave the following results.

The background to the 1993 *Survey* was a situation where there was £38 billion of outstanding bank loans to property companies according to Bank of England figures; this was a decrease from £40.7 billion at the peak in May 1991 (Evans 1993, p. 80), but these figures had risen from £6 billion in mid-1985 (see Figure 4.2).

Figure 4.2 *Outstanding bank loans to property companies (as at August). Source: Bank of England and Evans 1993, p. 80.*

The 1993 *Survey* had responses from 76 banks and financial institutions; this was an increase in the total sample of 50% from the previous year, but in some cases because of lack of commitment to lending in the market the information provided was limited. This *Survey* was the fourth in a series following on from those carried out in 1990, 1991 and 1992. In the sample replying, the UK banks made up 49% and the rest were foreign banks made up of North American (10%), European (20%), Japanese (9%), Middle Eastern (3%), Far Eastern (excluding Japan) (4%) and others (5%). In 1993 there were more UK lending institutions in the survey compared with 1992 and less response from North American banks. The increase in the UK response was especially noticeable in the non-banking institutions such as building societies. Terms remained comparable with 1992; the range of advances was practically the same but the average maximum advance fell; rates increased slightly. As a location for lending on property, Central London has become increasingly unpopular.

The *Survey* found that the average size of a property loan book was £418m, which is double the level that the previous surveys found; the range of the loan books had increased. What was more significant, in 1992 over half the respondents (53%) expected to increase their loan books by an average of 40%. This confidence followed the trend of the previous 2 years. In 1993, although the same proportion were thinking of increasing their loan books, this was by a much lower average (25%). It should be noted that the number of respondents prepared to put a figure to their expansion intentions was low compared with the sample.

The average split of property portfolios in the loan books in the 1993 *Survey* was 21% development and 79% investment; this continues a trend of reduction of development properties in portfolios (25% in 1992, 32% in 1991 and 43% in 1990). The reasons for this reduction are due to the ongoing completion of existing developments and the shelving of new developments together with lack of finance for speculative schemes. These comments are shown in the decreasing proportions prepared to undertake development lending in general (48% in 1993 compared with 63% in 1992) and the few still available to lend on speculative development in particular (down to 12% in 1993 from 22% in 1992). In fact, when asked their views on speculative development lending, only 7% of respondents in the 1993 survey would lend under given conditions; the remainder would lend only in exceptional circumstances or not at all. Lenders appeared in 1993 to be as cautious as in the last 2 years and again few were looking for additional involvement on the property sector, although slightly more than in 1992 (7% compared with 3%).

Investment

Most lending institutions still appeared keen to lend on good-quality investment property but this fell from 1992. The proportion lending on investment property was 70% in 1993 compared with around 95% for 1990–92. On the other hand, the proportion lending to owner-occupiers had gone up to 64% in 1993 compared with 48% for 1992, 74% for 1991 and 66% for 1990. The lending term for investment loans ranged from 1 to 30 years in 1993, although the average was 13 years, as for 1992. Bridging loans were provided by 23% of the lenders in the 1993 survey, a reduction from 1992. The amount that lenders are prepared to lend as a proportion of value has remained steady at 71% average, from a previous fall from 73% in 1991 and 75% in 1990. The average price margin over base rate or LIBOR a borrower will have to pay is 2%, which has increased slightly from 1992 (1.8%) but is in line with 1991. The lenders increased their average maximum advance from £18.5m in 1991 to £25m in 1992 but this fell to £15m in 1993.

Development

Forty-eight per cent of the lenders provided development finance in 1993, compared with 63% in 1992, 74% in 1991 and 94% in 1990. Only 12% would undertake loans for speculative developments in 1993, again down from 1992 (23%) and from 1991 (44%), although the major reduction in lenders had been from 1990, when 77% would provide monies. The term of loan in 1993 was on average 8 years, up from 1992 (6 years). Only 11% provided mezzanine finance and 18% provided finance on a limited-recourse basis in 1993; the latter has fallen from 1991 by half. In terms of interest capitalisation over the period of the loan, 69% of lenders responding in 1993 will provide this and, as a protection, 26% will use mortgage indemnity policies. These figures compare with 79% and 41% in 1992 and 87% and 46%, respectively, in 1991.

The range of advances in 1993 was narrower than the previous year; the average minimum/maximum loan was £2m/£17m and the range maximum had reduced to £60m. Loan-to-cost ratios remained steady at 77% for construction costs but had fallen as an average to 67% for land costs. Loan-to-value ratios in development property were also steady at 71%, from 73% in 1991 and 75% in 1990. The sectors in which lenders were interested to lend were commercial properties (65%) rather than leisure, residential or mixed development and this mirrors feelings from 1992. There did, however, appear to be an increased interest in the residential sector.

Location

The location preferences for development lending in 1992 were different from those for investment lending. In 1993, the preferences were broadly similar and this reflects the experience in the *Surveys* prior to 1992. The main aspect to note is that in 1993 there was a broad range of interest for investment and development lending locations, whereas in 1992, for development lending, Central London took precedence.

	Investment (%)	Development (%)
Central London	19	18
Outer London	20	19
South-east	19	21
Rest of England	25	26
Scotland	16	15
Europe (France and EU)	1	1

Overseas investment loans as a percentage of the total portfolio averaged 15% in 1993, down from 25% in 1992, but note that only 22% of lenders responded to this question.

Future

Thirty-seven per cent of respondents were more cautious about property lending in mid-1993 than they were 6 months previously. Fifty-six per cent said that their criteria for lending were unchanged from 6 months ago. These proportions are similar to the 1992 findings. Only 7% of the total respondents were ready to lend on speculative developments in the future, given certain conditions, while a further 12% would lend on speculative property only in exceptional situations. Half the respondents (53%) were expecting to increase their loan book in the forthcoming year, the same number as in 1992 but down from 69% in 1991. The typical increase based on a limited return is 25% on average compared with 40% in 1992.

The main criteria for judging a loan have remained the same according to the sample. The most important factors are cash flow and ability to repay, the quality of the tenant, the quality of the investment or development, the location and, finally, the security and financial status of the borrower.

4.6 MARKET PLAYERS

In the 1990s property came to be regarded as an investment like any other investment and there was a need to compare the characteristics of property with other investments such as Government stocks (gilts) or ordinary shares (equities). There was a need to compare the returns on these various investments. There was thus a realisation in the property profession that to enable financial specialists to compare these returns they will need some understanding of property and, in turn, the property adviser will need to be able to analyse returns from other investments. The idea was created, following the deregulation of the financial markets in the 1980s, of a one-stop shop, where the City security houses could merge with surveyors and the same company could provide property expertise and banking and stock market advice.

The idea of the one-stop shop has not really materialised but the smaller and medium-sized surveying practices have been taken over by financial institutions. This is in reference to commercial rather than residential practices. In respect of the latter, there was a major take-out of the private residential estate agents by the financial institutions and building societies, who generally paid expensive prices and with the slump in the property market found that returns did not justify the investment. The institutions and building societies are now selling off these agents, often to the original owners. The development in the commercial area has rather been that the financial groups in the city have tended to develop in-house expertise in commercial property, sometimes by acquisition (Brett 1990, p. 238).

Larger estate agencies have set up financial services subsidiaries employing ex-bankers. The banks have now begun to apply the innovative techniques of financing derived from applications to corporate bodies in the trading area and also those techniques introduced from the US. The traditional institutions, the insurance companies and the pension funds, have become less important as a source of finance for commercial property and the banks have become more important. Traditionally in development property, the surveyor has been the intermediary between the property developer and institutions. The combination of the factors above have deprived agents and surveyors of their most profitable business: the securities and bank markets.

The insurance companies and pension funds are traditional long-term owners of commercial investments. The life assurance and the general funds both have control of long-term investment monies and, in this respect, property appeared to be a suitable home for it. Both are investing their own funds rather than borrowed funds. So, for these funds, the element of capital appreciation as opposed to income generation is important. There are no problems of an income deficit, which may be a problem, for instance, to property owners reliant on borrowed money. In the traditional approach to property development the property developers relied on bank lenders for short-term finance during the development with a buyout by the institution enabling repayment of the short-term bank debt. Now the institutions are taking out a much smaller proportion and there has been a change to other more innovative forms of finance.

To summarise, the main actors in the property finance market are:

- the institutions,
- the property companies,
- private individuals,
- construction companies,
- industrial and commercial companies.

The financiers are:

- banks,
- specialist property lenders,
- building societies,
- insurers and brokers.

4.7 LOANS AND INTEREST RATES

Examples of interest rates which can be applied to the most common transactions are now set out. The example of a mortgage is used but these terms and structures can be applied to other instruments. The interest rates are analysed on the basis of the term, the repayment arrangement and the rates of interest.

Term of loan

Depending on the type of transaction, a client may borrow money on mortgage for terms ranging from 3 months to 30 years. This decision will depend on a number of criteria as follows:

Short-term (3 months to 2 years)	The client may only want a bridging loan, pending sale of an existing property. The client may wish to turn a property very quickly at a profit, or the scheme may only be a small development.
Medium-term (2 years to 7 years)	The client may be acquiring a reversionary investment that will be sold after the first rent review. The client may have a larger, phased development.
Long-term (7 years or more)	The client basically wants the security of a long-term mortgage facility and has no ambition to move in the immediate future, or the client may have a prime investment that is not intended for disposal, or is an owner-occupier.

Repayment structures

There are also a number of repayment structures that clients may wish to consider:

Bullet repayment	Commonly used in short- and medium-term loans, whereby the client repays interest only for the duration of the loan, repaying the capital in a lump sum at the end of the term. This structure is more commonly used by developers, but is available for investors as well.
Capital and interest	The most common type of mortgage, where capital and interest are repaid over a longer period of up to 30 years. This structure is used by those sectors referred to in the commercial mortgage market and by investors.
Capital holiday	Interest only is payable during the first 2–5 years after which capital and interest is re-payable over a further 15–25-year term. Particularly useful for investments where rental income will only service interest until first review or for businesses which are establishing themselves.
Deferred interest	Where interest is rolled up for an agreed period. Particularly useful for developers who have no income until sales or lettings are achieved on their scheme. Note that banks are not particularly happy to roll up interest in the current climate.

Rates of interest

The analysis above relates to loan structures, but the nature of the interest rates also has to be considered. A client may elect to borrow either *floating* or *fixed rate* funds, given the constraints of the loan facility.

Floating rates

Generally, developers and clients borrowing less than £1m will only have the option to borrow floating rate funds. In the case of the developer, it is impossible to predict what the outstanding balance will be at any point in the future, while the term of the loan will be governed by the speed at which the scheme is built and sold. For loans under £1m, the banks simply find it uneconomic to arrange fixed rate funding. The facility is priced, i.e. the interest rate is agreed at a level over a yardstick rate; this is commonly the base rate and the interest rate is referred to as 'so much per cent over base'.

Bank base rate

The bank base rate is simply the minimum level at which any bank may offer floating rate funds to the market as determined by the Bank of England from time to time. Each bank has its own base rate, so one may see documentation which states 2% over Barclays or Midland base rate. Essentially, each bank's base rate will be that which has been set by the Bank of England, but one should beware that some secondary banks who are struggling to maintain profitability have left their base rates up to 3% higher than the norm!

London inter-bank offered rate (LIBOR)

This is simply the price at which banks sell money to each other. LIBOR rates are quoted daily by the banks over 3, 6 and 12 months. If the client elects to borrow over 3 month LIBOR, then effectively he fixes his borrowing costs for a 3 month period. At the end of 3 months, the client's cost of borrowing is re-fixed for a further 3 month period and so on to the end of the loan term. To give some idea of the difference between LIBOR rates and bank base rate, the following are market quotes from the *Financial Times* dated 21 December 1993:

bank base rate	5½%
3 month LIBOR	av. 5³/₈%
6 month LIBOR	av. 5½%
12 month LIBOR	av. 5³/₁₆%

LIBOR can either be above or below bank base rate, depending on the market's view of future interest rate movements. Twelve months is effectively the longest period of time the banks would be prepared to gamble on fixing interest rates. Whereas LIBOR is the rate at which the banks themselves will lend to one another, the lower rate at which they are prepared to borrow is termed LIBID, the difference between LIBOR and LIBID thus producing the margin or profit on the operation. The middle rate between the two is termed LIMEAN. LIBOR rates are quoted on different terms, depending on the length of time from the transaction to repayment, i.e. 3 month LIBOR. Interest rates are usually quoted as being so many basis points above LIBOR or LIBID. A basis point is one-hundredth of a percentage point, so 50 basis points above LIBOR is LIBOR plus 0.5%.

Finance houses base rate (FHBR)

The FHBR is charged by the finance houses, such as Mercantile (Barclays) and Lombard (National Westminster), and is a 2 month average of 3 month LIBOR. It tends to lag behind bank base rates and is, therefore, higher as rates are falling and lower as rates are rising.

Gross domestic mortgage rate (GDMR)

GDMR is charged by the building societies and effectively is dictated by the largest society, the Halifax.

Fixed rates

These rates are generally available to investors and anyone borrowing over £1m. There are two main sources of fixed rate money, which are the *gilt* and *swaps* markets.

Gilts

Gilts are simply commercial paper issued by the Government to finance their public spending programmes. In the 1980s, the Government was a net repayer of debt, but more recently has started to borrow money again. They will, therefore, issue gilts with a variety of maturity (repayment) dates and yields (interest rates). The insurance companies will set aside some funds to invest in the property market and will offer borrowers fixed rates, based on a margin over a rate of return that they would otherwise be able to achieve in the gilt market. Their terms will be anywhere from 5 to 25 years.

Swaps

Given that banks will not offer fixed rate options over 12 months, how can borrowers gain longer terms on fixed rate? The only borrowers who can effectively borrow fixed rate money are large corporations such as ICI. To do so, they will issue commercial paper or bonds to private and commercial investors at fixed yields (interest rates) with a promise to repay the face value of the bond on a given date.

One will sometimes see references to convertible or euro-convertible bonds, which simply give the investor the option to take shares in the company issuing the bond at a predetermined share price, instead of taking cash. On occasions, it suits the large corporations to offer their fixed rate money to the open market at a premium. So, where they have been able to borrow from the bond market at 10%, they may be able to lend that money to the banks who operate swap options at 11%, thus generating a profit. The banks may then be able to offer that money to borrowers on a further margin of 2% over swap rate. Swaps are actually a little more complicated than described, but this outlines the basic principles by which clients can borrow fixed rate money.

The swaps market is an example of interest rate hedging where interest rates are controlled to an extent to reduce volatility. Swaps and capital instruments which reduce the movement of rates in a floating rate situation are the two common approaches to this, and aspects of capital instruments are discussed later in the chapter.

Advantages and disadvantages of different types of interest rate

In summary, floating rates may fluctuate wildly during the term of the borrowing. The cost of borrowing may, therefore, increase or decrease substantially. Fixed rates give certainty but can prove expensive if borrowing costs drop. Fixed rate finance can also be inflexible with substantial penalties for repayment. Capital instruments (caps) offer the benefits of floating rates with the comfort of fixed rates. They are also flexible and do not penalise the borrower for early repayment. Capital instruments are also tradeable commodities and can be sold on the open market, although their value will depend on the current level of interest rates and the length of term the cap has remaining. Their disadvantage is the cost of the up-front premium. The advantages and disadvantages of variable and fixed interest rates are summarised in Box 4.3.

Variable rate

Disadvantages:

1. Interest rate rises would result in increased costs and mean that the maximum loan amount is reached more quickly.
2. The term of the loan generally is shorter and therefore you will need to refinance earlier, which will result in increased costs.
3. The value of the property may fall at the time of refinancing and therefore a further cash injection may be necessary.
4. Banks are cautious about rolling-up interest and will reduce the loan to 75% value.

Advantages:

1. When interest rates fall, you will have to pay less interest.
2. You are able to sell the property at any time without breakage costs (costs on breaking the agreement).

Fixed rate

Disadvantages:

1. When interest rates fall, fixed rate money is more expensive.
2. Should you wish to sell the property and repay the loan, if interest rates fall you will be liable to breakage costs.

Advantages:

1. Certain of interest costs.
2. Interest rate is significantly below current variable rates.
3. Banks feel more confident to lend on this basis.
4. If interest rates increased, you would gain a significant advantage and there would be no breakage costs if you sold the property.

Box 4.3 *Advantages and disadvantages of variable and fixed rate interest rates*

4.8 MARKETS AND MARGINS

The basic pricing of a construction facility usually involves the following elements:

Arrangement fee This covers the cost of all preliminary investigations and internal reports and approvals, and a valuation fee if an in-house valuer is used. There is also an element reflecting risk if this element is higher than may be expected in the circumstances.

Management fee This covers the cost of monitoring the project and is usually payable on an annual or semi-annual basis.

Commitment fee This is usually a small fee which recompenses the bank for making the commitment and is charged on the amount of the facility that remains unutilised from time to time. The facility amount will be drawn down in stages over the life of the loan. This fee reimburses the bank, which has an obligation to provide the facility amount and therefore cannot utilise those funds for other lending opportunities.

Interest margin The margin above the cost of funds that is charged to pay the bank for its risks in lending the project funds. The loan is drawn down in stages. Any amount undrawn may attract charges.

Repayment/cancellation penalty fee

4.9 INTEREST RATE MANAGEMENT AND HEDGING

Hedging arrangements are different interest rate strategies and can include options, futures, caps, floors, forward rate agreements (FRAs), swaps, etc. Traditionally bank loans were repaid as instalments of interest and capital in much the same way as a traditional mortgage. The interest rate was calculated at a margin above a yardstick rate based on the minimum cost of borrowing, the base rate or LIBOR rate described above. New hedging techniques complement new financial approaches and can adjust cash flows to suit the borrower but also minimise exposure from the point of view of the lender.

If interest rates change, borrowers need protection from the wider swings of interest rates. This is very important in property, where a lot of money is borrowed. Businesses often work on very fine interest margins; cash flows can be severely damaged by unexpected rises in interest rates, so it is possible to fix interest rates in advance, relative to a common yardstick such as LIBOR, but this is still variable. The simplest way to protect against rising interest rates is to borrow at a fixed rate rather than a variable one. The Government has been a net repayer of debt rather than a borrower in the late 1980s; there is thus a shortage of long-dated Government bonds, and with a fair bit of competition the prices remain high and the yields low.

Companies take advantage by issuing long-dated bonds at interest rates above those on Government bonds but well below the short-term interest rates prevailing at the time. By 1990 long-term borrowing rates had moved right up and looked less attractive. Very long-term fixed interest borrowing may suit property investment companies with revenue-producing properties that they are intending to hold onto indefinitely with long-term borrowing matching a long-term asset. This type of borrowing is not possible for smaller concerns with a less established cash flow.

Fixed rate money has a drawback in that one may lock into a high rate of interest for a long period. For some companies, the best compromise is to borrow short or medium term at variable rates of interest but to 'hedge' the risk that interest rates will rise further.

Interest-only payments

This means that no repayment of capital is made until the end of the period of the loan. This can assist developers who may not have any income arising from the project during the currency of the loan — for instance, where the project is the development of a building which is to be sold on or refinanced at the end of the development period. This is also known as a deferred capital payment or bullet payment.

Deferred interest payment

Rolling up or interest rate holidays means that no interest charges are paid during the currency of the loan or are significantly reduced. The interest thus compounds over the time period before repayment.

Variable and fixed rates

Rates can be fixed at the outset but this is risky in the longer term; otherwise they can be variable but perhaps changing monthly or quarterly or even with some home loan mortgages changing on an annual basis.

Fully floating rates

These are related to bank base rates or LIBOR rates and can change from day to day, depending on the change in the yardstick rates. Euromarket issues may be fixed rate or may be floating rate notes (FRNs).

Drop-lock loan

This is a hybrid between the fixed and variable rate. The initial rate is variable but when triggered fixes to a fixed rate over the remainder of the loan period. The trigger is usually caused by the fall of the variable rate to a predetermined level, after which the rate fixes to protect the lender's margin. For example, a loan may be fixed at a margin of 2% over LIBOR; assuming this is, say, 6% at time of agreement, then the variable rate will commence at 8%. If LIBOR falls, the variable rate will fall but perhaps the loan will lock in at, say, 6% to a fixed rate.

4.10 HEDGING INSTRUMENTS

Interest rates have been extremely volatile over the last two decades and lenders need to be able to reduce their interest rate exposure. Interest rate exposure arises when:

(i) floating rate financial commitments create uncertainty in respect of future cash flows; or
(ii) assets and liabilities have a mismatch in their maturity or interest basis.

There are three categories of exposure – cash flow, portfolio and economic. Some companies adopt a full hedging policy if they are risk-averse but they are then unable to benefit from favourable movements in interest rates. Active risk management involves selective hedging to minimise costs and hedge costs simultaneously (Mitchell and Peake 1991, pp. 533–4).

Hedging instruments consist of:

- forward rate agreements,
- interest rate swaps,
- interest rate swaptions,
- interest rate options:
  - caps
  - floors
  - collars
  - floor/swap combinations
- futures.

These are covered in the following sections.

Forward rate agreements

A forward rate agreement (FRA) enables companies to hedge a future interest payment or receipt, and can be used to change a floating rate to a fixed rate and vice versa. No money is exchanged; the difference between the rates is discounted back to the beginning of the agreed period. A 4 x 10 FRA would start in 4 months and terminate in 10 months (Figure 4.3).

Figure 4.3 *Forward rate agreement (4 x 10 FRA). Source: Mitchell and Peake 1991, p. 535*

Interest rate swaps

There is a market for trading and exchanging fixed and variable interest rate debt arrangements. The type of loan required by a lender will vary according to market rates, the completion of projects and the cash flow and risk profile of the debt; thus, fixed rate or variable rate funding may be suitable according to the risk–return trade-off. The transaction takes place through a bank. By fixing some money, the lender can minimise exposure to changes of interest rates, especially in volatile periods. They enable balance sheets to be restructured and allow access to a wider range of markets.

The swap is an agreement by two parties to exchange interest payments on a specified principal amount in an agreed currency. The difference between the agreed rates exchanged is settled at the end of each rollover date. Swaps are used to change the floating rate to a fixed rate and vice versa. Companies with a 3 month LIBOR rate could exchange it for a 6 month rate. Companies with investments can use swaps to fix a future rate of return. The maturities of swaps can be up to 10 years and are available in most currencies. A swap is shown in Figure 4.4.

Figure 4.4 *Interest rate swap. Adapted from Mitchell and Peake 1991, p. 536*

Interest rate swaptions

An interest rate swaption is an option (see next section) to enter into an interest rate swap at an agreed rate exercisable on a certain date in the future for an agreed duration. The option is normally purchased with a view to being exercised for a cash settlement. Theoretically, it may also be exercised into an interest rate swap at the agreed rate. However, as the latter involves a credit exposure for the bank providing it, most swaptions are exercised for a cash settlement. At the end of the option period, if the fixed rate for an interest swap for the equivalent period is higher than the given rate for the swaption, a compensatory payment is due to the purchaser or the purchaser may convert the swaption into an interest rate swap. If the fixed rate for an equivalent interest rate swap is lower, the swaption is abandoned and the premium forfeited. Swaptions have been used as a hedge against the possibility of the election of a Labour Government in a forthcoming election on the assumption that such an election victory might lead to a sterling crisis. It is ironic that it was the Conservatives rather than Labour who found themselves in this position in September 1992 (Goldsmith 1992, p. 316). This type of hedging is useful in:

(i) purchase situations to offset fears of rising interest rates before finance is finalised;

(ii) sale situations where a hedging structure is in place, to protect against a fall in interest rate before sale which may lead to additional termination costs arising from the lifting of the hedge;

(iii) situations where property companies are negotiating new loans and hedging structure: a swaption will protect against rising interest costs and a more expensive hedging structure.

There are two types of swaption, based on the difference between US- and European-style options. European options are exercisable at the end of the option period only; US options can be exercised at any time during the option period. The normal swaption duration is 2–10 years. At the end of the option one is 'in the money' if the swaption strike rate is below the LIBOR rate it is protecting. If the LIBOR rate is less than the strike rate, the option is abandoned and there is no value (Goldsmith 1992, p. 317).

Example of a swaption

Initial swaption:	notional principal	£5 000 000
	option period	3 months
	underlying swap duration	2 years
	strike rate	10.5%
	interest rate basis	3 month LIBOR
	2 year swap rate on transaction date	10.31%
	premium cost	£18 000

On exercise date: equivalent 2 year swap rate   12%
borrower receives cash settlement of   £125 000
= net present value of 12%–10.31% for 2 years' duration.
If the equivalent rate swap = 10%, the swaption would be abandoned without value (Goldsmith 1992, p. 318).

Interest rate options

Options in general are discussed in Section 6.4. Options give the holder a right to sell or buy shares of common stock at a given exercise price. A call option is a right to buy and a put option is a right to sell. Option features can be found in many areas of finance, e.g. in convertibles and warrants, insurance, capital budgeting and currency and interest rate management (as here). Pure options are financial instruments created by exchanges (i.e. stock markets) rather than companies. Where the value of a company's assets fall below the value of its borrowings, shareholders may not exercise their option to repay the loan, but prefer the company to default on the debt (Pike and Neale 1993, p. 512). Options are the most versatile of hedging instruments, as they offer companies the right to 'walk away' if rate move favourably, yet provide protection if rates move against the company.

Capital instruments (caps)

An insurance policy which guarantees a certain rate for a certain period for an up-front premium is commonly called a cap (Figure 4.5). It places a ceiling on the floating interest rate. This is done by the payment of a single insurance premium at the commencement of the loan to protect the borrower against increases. The borrower still benefits from falls in the interest rate. This means that the borrower is benefiting from a partially fixed rate; certainly, if the rate exceeds the capped rate, then it is in effect a fixed rate at the capped rate for as long as this is the case. If a client borrows, say, £1m at a margin over base rate, that base rate can go up or down. For every 1% the base rate goes up, the client will have to pay an additional £10 000 in interest. Obviously, should interest rates go down, the client will make a similar saving in interest costs. If base rates are 11% and the client believes that they will rise over the next 5 years, the client can effectively fix the base rate at 11% by the purchase of a cap. The cap is effectively an insurance policy which pays out should the base rates rise above the capped level. So, if interest rates rise by 1%, and one has to pay one's bank an additional £10 000 in interest each year, the cap will compensate by the same amount. If, however, interest rates fall, one still gets the benefit of lower interest payments. To purchase a cap, the client will have to pay a one-off, up-front premium.

Figure 4.5 *Interest rate cap. Source: Mitchell and Peake 1991, p. 536*

To summarise, the simplest form of interest rate protection is the cap. The cap involves the borrower paying up-front a fee or premium for a guarantee that interest will not increase beyond an agreed limit. The fee payable will be determined by:

(i)   the interest rate of the cap relative to the market rate (the lower the rate of the cap the higher the fee payable); and

(ii) the duration of the cap.

The borrower will be recompensed for any difference between the agreed level bought through the cap and LIBOR on the prescribed dates, if on those dates the rate is greater than the level of interest rate bought. The lender on the other side of the guarantee finds counter-parties with opposite requirements to hedge the costs. Caps are quoted against 3 month LIBOR but depend on underlying funding and can be quoted against the base rate. The difference between the base rate quoted and LIBOR is fixed when fixing takes place.

The LIBOR cap is based on the 3 month LIBOR rate and this is checked against the base rate and the difference paid to the borrower. The base rate cap rate is checked daily from the fixing date to compare with the cap rate; the difference is paid 2 weeks after the calculation date. At present the smaller players are offered no more than the choice between a floating or a fixed rate. Caps for loans of less than £0.5m are rarely available. The cap thus sets a limit on the borrowing cost; if the interest rate rises, the company is reimbursed for costs above the ceiling ('strike rate').

Floor

Let us assume that at the same period as the cap mentioned above, you wanted to fix your base rate at 10% because the investment you were buying would not self-fund at a higher rate. In such circumstances, the cost of the cap is not cheap. Provided that the investment property has a suitably strong tenant, the cap provider may be prepared to purchase a floor from the borrower. This is precisely the opposite of a cap, whereby you guarantee that if base rates fall below, say, 9%, you will compensate the bank for their loss of interest. For this benefit, the bank pays the borrower a premium. Floors thus protect a company if LIBOR falls below the selected rate. Premiums vary according to the rate. See Figure 4.6.

Collar

This has a ceiling and a floor rate between which the floating rate operates. The collar limits the increases and falls in the interest rates; thus, the range of the interest rate is known by the borrower. The combined effect of a cap and a floor is known as a collar, which is effectively a corridor within which the borrower's base rate can fluctuate. Thus, the simultaneous purchase of a cap and the sale of a floor will provide a collar. The company offsets the premium payment for the cap by selling the floor and establishes a band in which interest rates can fluctuate. See Figure 4.7.

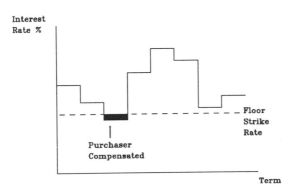

Figure 4.6 *Interest rate floor. Source: Mitchell and Peake 1991, p. 537*

Figure 4.7 *Interest rate collar. Source: Mitchell and Peake 1991, p. 537*

A zero cost collar is where the cap premium and the floor receipt cancel one another out. This has a disadvantage in that it is likely that a narrow band would be established in these circumstances. With a stepped collar the company has a narrow band initially and then it is more flexible. It is possible to have a zero cost for this.

Floor/swap combination

The combined purchase of a swap and the sale of a floor in situations of high interest rates can reduce the costs of hedging.

Futures

A futures contract is a legal agreement between two parties, one to make and the other to take delivery of a specified amount of a commodity or a financial instrument on a certain date in the future at a price fixed on entering the contract. Futures markets are claimed to be the most efficient markets because of their liquid characteristics and standardised investments (Dent and Weeks 1993, p. 132).

Futures are a less expensive hedging instrument than forward rate agreements (FRAs) or swaps. The disadvantage is that futures are bought only in standard sizes and to match certain dates and they require the maintenance of a broker. The market involved generally in interest rate hedging by future is the London International Financial Futures Exchange (LIFFE). In May 1991 London Fox introduced a property futures market in London, based on four indices:

(i)   commercial property values, using the Investment Property Databank indices;

(ii) commercial property rents, using the Investment Property Databank indices;

(iii) house prices, using the Nationwide Anglia house price index;

(iv) mortgage interest rates, using the London Fox mortgage interest rate index.

Initially property futures were aimed at developers to hedge their development risk. Futures are a zero sum game with one winner and one loser. A developer who takes out a futures contract would be expected to settle in cash at the end of the contract. This may not be simple, as the developer may be illiquid at this stage. Property futures are more suitable for property investors to hedge the risk of portfolio investments (Venmore-Rowland 1991, p. 4). The problem with London Fox's operation arose from the alleged manipulation of the market, probably to create an impression of volume. The market was trading at low levels and problems arose because the concept was new and had been launched on a market in recession (*Chartered Surveyor Weekly* 1991). The market closed in October 1991; a total of 11 000 commercial and residential contracts had been traded in the market in the 5 month period (Goodman 1991, p.11).

Deals were done on the London Fox by 'betting' on the movement of the indices – for example, if the IPD (Investment Property Databank) index stands at 100 and property values move up 20%, then the index moves to 120. Each point of the movement is worth £500 for the capital values contract, so a move from 100 to 101 is worth £500. If you think prices will fall, for instance, then you sell a contract; if the index is at 95, then the cost is £47 500 (£500 per point × 95 points). Assume the index falls to 75 on sale; then profit is 20 points × £500 = £10 000. Thus, on a larger scale this income could be used to offset the falling value of a property asset you are holding.

So, to bet on a fall in values you sell a contract; to bet on an increase you buy (Brett 1991, p. 71). If you are buying or selling where the index is at 95, you do not need to put down the full price of £47 500, but a small deposit of, say, £600 is sufficient. Futures markets thus require only a small proportion of the face value of the contract to be paid up-front. Changes in the value of the contract can be settled on a daily basis. The uses of the market are for speculation, hedging and portfolio management (Richard Ellis 1991).

REFERENCES

Armon-Jones, C H (1992) 'Underwriting Property Sales', *Journal of Property Finance*, vol. 2, no. 4, pp. 497–500.

Berkley, R (1991) 'Raising Commercial Property Finance in a Difficult Market', *Journal of Property Finance*, vol. 1, no. 4, pp. 523–9.

Brett, M (1990) *Property and Money*, Estates Gazette, London.

Brett, M (1991) 'How Property Futures Work', *Estates Gazette*, 18 May, p. 71.

Chartered Surveyor Weekly (1991) 'Editorial: Crisis at London Fox Leaves Futures Uncertain', *Chartered Surveyor Weekly*, 10 October, p. 5.

Chesterton Financial (1993) *Property Lending Survey*, Chesterton Financial, London, February.

Dent, P and Weeks, C (1993) 'Is there LIFFE after FOX?', *Estates Gazette*, 9 October, pp. 132–6.

DTZ Debenham Thorpe (1993) *Money into Property*, DTZ Debenham Thorpe, London, August.

Evans, P H (1993) 'Statistical Review', *Journal of Property Finance*, vol. 4, no. 2, pp. 75–82.

Goldsmith, G C (1992) 'Sterling Interest Swaptions', *Journal of Property Finance*, vol. 3, no. 3, pp. 315–8.

Goodman, T (1991) 'Property Futures Idea is Still Alive – Just', *Chartered Surveyor Weekly*, 10 October, p. 11.

Mitchell, C and Peake, J H (1991) 'The Management of Interest Rate Exposure', *Journal of Property Finance*, vol. 1, no. 4, pp. 530–38.

Pike, R and Neale, B (1993) *Corporate Finance and Investment*, Prentice Hall, London.

Richard Ellis (1991) 'A Look at Commercial Property Futures', *Investment Research Review no. 2*, Richard Ellis, London.

Riley, M and Isaac, D (1993) 'Property Lending Survey 1993', *Journal of Property Finance*, vol. 4, no. 1, pp. 43–8.

Scott, I P (1992) 'Debt, Liquidity and Secondary Trading in Property Debt', *Journal of Property Finance*, vol. 3, no. 3, pp. 347–55.

Venmore-Rowland, P (1991) 'Vehicles for Property Investment', in P Venmore-Rowland, P Brandon and T Mole (eds), *Investment, Procurement and Performance in Construction*, RICS, London.

Wyles, M (1990) 'Mortgage Indemnity – A Risk/Reward Arbitrage', *Journal of Property Finance*, vol. 1, no. 3, pp. 378–86.

5 Project-based Funding

5.1 INTRODUCTION

Project-based funding is where the funds are secured against the property being acquired or developed. Project finance is especially important for smaller unlisted property companies to whom stock market sources are unavailable. In these cases the existing assets may be fully charged against previous loans. The financial status of the companies may also not provide sufficient security for the financier.

Traditionally project finance was involved in two distinct operations:

Short-term, interim or bridging finance This is the finance raised to pay the development costs incurred during the development period for site purchase and payments to the building contractor and fees, for instance.

Long-term finance or funding This is required to repay the short-term finance on completion of the project. Long-term financing is not financing for project development but financing the retention of the project as a long-term investment. If the developer sells on completion, then long-term funding is unnecessary, as short-term debt can be repaid from the sale proceeds. If the developer wishes to retain ownership or an interest in the completed development that requires funding, then long-term finance will have to be arranged.

Types of finance typically available for project funding are:

- bridging finance;
- forward sale;
- mortgage;
- sale and leaseback;
- project management fee;
- general funding (these facilities are really based on the asset backing of the company or developer and are discussed later in Chapter 6).

In the past, when the market was more buoyant and funds were more easily available for project development finance, developers would try to observe the rules for seeking finance set out in Box 5.1.

---

1. Never use your own money in a development; try to arrange full external funding.

2. Never give a personal guarantee or personal collateral for any loan.

3. Roll up interest in the development period.

4. Keep as much equity as possible.

5. Fund in the local currency.

6. Avoid 50:50 ventures; someone has to be in control.

7. Avoid tax liabilities; exploit tax relief.

8. Larger projects are more uncertain; allow for contingencies.

9. Read the funding agreement; consider the consequences of a worse than expected outcome if conditions change.

10. Secure the funding commitment from the outset.

Box 5.1 *Ten golden rules for developers seeking finance. Adapted from Darlow 1988, pp. 265–6*

5.2 EQUITY PARTNERSHIPS

These relate more to a method of funding a development than to a true joint venture, which is explored more fully in Chapter 11. These may include arrangements such as participation lending and forward funding. In participation lending, the lender will take a share of the proceeds of a scheme and this may occur where a lender is taking a higher risk, by lending more or at more advantageous rates of interest.

Forward funding is where the purchaser of a development assists the short-term funding of the development; this provides security for the purchaser by having some control as the development proceeds. It may be that the forward funder will fund the development at a lower rate of interest. The subsidy of the interest rate and the reduction of risk to the developer will thus lead to a reduced developer's profit payable and a higher yield on purchase of the completed development paid by the purchaser (because of reduced risk and reduced cost to the developer). Thus, the purchaser purchases at a reduced price.

The problem with equity partnership arrangements is that the interests held by the parties are going to be difficult to resell until the development is complete, so the partners involved have no security to offer to tenders.

5.3 FORWARD SALE

A contract for a future sale can encourage short-term funds because the funder will know that it will get its money back within a period of time. Alternatively, the party providing the future sale contract may also provide bridging finance. If the investment yield for the scheme was 6%, then the forward sale might take place at 6½%. A forward sale with bridging finance might be 7%.

Pre-funded projects usually involve a forward commitment from the institution to purchase the development on completion. The arrangement would be that the institution advances interim finance at regular intervals at a lower interest rate than the existing market rate. Once construction is completed or when the building has been let, completion of the sale takes place and the institution hands over the purchase price less the total development cost and rolled-up interest (Savills 1989, p. 14).

The contrast between forward commitment (that is to say, an end purchaser being signed up now, but the purchaser's commitment only being absolute once the present conditions as to the building and its letting have been met) and forward funding, where the fund purchases the site, advances the capital and takes over the completed project with its share of excess profits, can be seen in Table 5.1.

Table 5.1 *Comparison of forward commitment and forward funding*

	Forward commitment	Forward funding
Target rent	£20.6m p.a.	£20.6m p.a.
Capitalised @	6.5%	7%
Less costs		
Net value, say	£308m	£286m
Deduct costs of construction and site	£190m	£190m
Interest rate	13%	9%
Finance cost	£44m	£30m
Gross profit to developer	£74m	£66m
Profit/cost	31%	30%

Source: Orchard-Lisle 1987, p. 361.

There is no need for the disengagement of the developer from the funder in such an arrangement. By a joint venture or a side-by-side lease, where profits are shared, ownership can also be shared. Securitisation (see Chapter 12) offers an ideal way in which to enable the original developer to retain a percentage of income and future benefits. The funder may receive in such an arrangement a pre-agreed share of the overage, being the additional return received over the previous maximum estimate in the calculation for cost, return and developer's profit. The share may be subject to the retention of all the overage if the capping of the development return is agreed.

5.4 SALE AND LEASEBACK

In a sale and leaseback the developer sells a completed project to an investor and simultaneously takes back a long lease of the development at an agreed rent calculated on the basis of an appropriate rate of return applied to the purchase. The developer then sublets the project to occupying tenants and enjoys by way of a profit rent the difference between the rent paid to the investor and that received from the tenants.

In the UK, one of the early major sale and leaseback arrangements was a fund reserved for Town & City Property by the Prudential. The developers would ask the Prudential to buy a site, pay the building costs and lease it to Town & City for a return of 6% plus 20% of income growth at the 33 year rent reviews. Thus, a base rent is agreed beforehand; arrangements could be complex and are as for equity partnership situations, e.g. top-slice, side-by-side, etc. So freeholder takes a ground rent/base rent and participates in increases in income. Arrangements for payment of the base rent may include:

Lease guarantee   If the development is not let in 6 months, the developer receives a profit from fund but takes a leaseback guarantee at the base rent. The guarantee is extinguished on letting.

Profit erosion   The developer stakes his profit against voids; the guarantee is for 2–4 years and is useful if the developer is weak and unwilling to provide a leaseback guarantee.

Priority yield   The fund sets the return at 6½%, target is 7½% (1% for developer) and the return over target is split 50:50.

Case study: sale and leaseback

A recent example of a sale and leaseback involved Barclays Bank (Fox 1993). Its portfolio of operational freehold and long leasehold property stands at just below £1 billion. Its property arm, Barclays Bank Property Holdings, wanted a more balanced portfolio. In 1992 it was decided that the large number of secondary, suburban and retail premises which were required for operating needs created the imbalance in the portfolio, so a programme of sale and leaseback of 92 of the properties earmarked was commenced with a target of £40m for their sale. The details of the sale (Fox 1993, p. 9) were:

Average lot size:	£400 000 in a range between £200 000 and £1.23m.
Leaseback:	20 year lease with 5 year rent reviews. (Consultants had advised that the market would not bear 15 year leases but was indifferent between 20 and 25 years.)
Initial rents:	Current market level.
Methods of sale:	Private treaty and auction for comparison.
Package:	6–10 properties in a package or else individually sold.
Actual sales:	42 by auction, 5 by private treaty, 5 package sales.
Leases:	Standard institutional lease. Open user clause with qualified alienation provisions for assignment and subletting.
Yields:	8–10% on the packages, best individual yield 7.9%.

History of the sale and leaseback

Sale and leaseback emerged in the 1930s; examples were used by retail trading groups such as that led by Charles Clore (British Shoe Corporation) to raise capital while sharing in the revenues of their developments. Initially leasebacks had no rent reviews and thus the institutions purchasing the freehold could not share in the growth of the rent and capital value. The income arising from the development was thus shared on completion of the leaseback and revised at each rent review. The nature of the sharing was important from the point of view of the overall return, the opportunity for growth and the risk to be taken by the various parties. An income could be sliced at each review, making the top slice vulnerable and risky. If the slicing took place initially, then two options arose at subsequent reviews. The rental could be re-sliced and this could give rise to a geared return to one of the parties, i.e. an increased proportion of total income. However, once the initial slicing had taken place, the proportions to the parties involved could remain stable (that is, proportional sharing at subsequent reviews). A reverse leaseback emerged where the company leased to the financial institution on a long lease and took a leaseback, leaving a more mortgageable interest to the company.

5.5 FINANCE LEASE

A variation on sale and leaseback is the finance lease. This is basically a sale and leaseback to a leasing company, typically Hambros, Abbey National, Lloyds Leasing, etc. The leasing company, owing to the timing of tax payments and efficient use of capital allowances within a building, can reduce the interest element of the rental payment to below bank base rate. This structure only applies to the top 200 UK corporates and non-taxpaying bodies.

The basic mechanics

The structure requires a property to be sold to the leasing company, who leases the building back to the vendor at a market rent. This rent is fixed for 5 years and is then increased at a predetermined level. At each fifth year, the vendor would have an option to repurchase the property at an amount which is equivalent to the original sale price plus any capitalised interest. The facility can be designed so that it is off-balance sheet, although the final arbiter of this will be the company auditors.

Outlined below are more details of the structure:

(i) The leasing company purchases the freehold or long leasehold of the property for up to 100% of market value.

(ii) The leasing company then grants the vendor a lease for between 5 and 30 years.

(iii) The lease will have a break option every fifth year. At this point, the vendor or associate/subsidiary company will have the option to repurchase the property. If the option is not exercised, the property will remain in the ownership of the leasing company and, depending upon the initial yield, the rent may be increased.

(iv) The rental pattern can be fixed at the outset, by the leasing company obtaining fixed rate finance. Initially, the rent can be below the cost of finance and any shortfall will be capitalised and added to the principle which is payable should the option to repurchase be exercised.

(v) The lease can qualify as an operating lease and under current accounting rules does not need to be capitalised on the balance sheet. This is subject to the auditor's approval, but leasing companies believe that it can be demonstrated that the risks and rewards of ownership are substantially transferred.

(vi) Tax relief can be obtained, owing to the capital allowances in the building. These allowances can be passed on to the vendor through the rentals paid, or directly. Most new office buildings have between 20% and 30% of their costs in plant and machinery, and with 25% writing-down allowances a significant reduction in a company's tax bill is achievable.

(vii) Stamp duty will be charged on the transfer of the property, which will be payable by the vendor.

(viii) Detailed analyses of tax, accounting and regulatory position will have to be undertaken prior to devising a structure which is suitable for a particular vendor.

Advantages

Leasing company

(i) As owner of the building they can use the capital allowances to off-set taxable profits.

(ii) Leasing companies make money by lending money, and those transactions would be perceived as a good credit risk, owing to the asset backing and quality of the covenants involved.

The vendor company

(i) The market rent is typically below the variable interest rate normally payable.

(ii) The leasing company will pass some of the benefits back to the company via a lower rent.

(iii) The company can benefit from any capital appreciation by re-purchasing the property at each fifth year.

(iv) The transaction may give accounting benefits.

Summary

Sale and leaseback to a leasing company with rental payments linked to the interest rate and level of capital repayment. Other features and benefits than can be incorporated include:

(i) Option to repurchase at each fifth year.

(ii) May be classified as an off-balance-sheet structure.

(iii) Interest rates are charged typically well below market levels, owing to the efficient use by the leasing company of capital allowances, which reduce interest rates by between 2% and 3%.

(iv) A non-taxpayer who is unable to use capital allowances can pass these to a third party and obtain the benefit.

Target clients for finance leases

(i)   Non-taxpaying bodies.

(ii)   Top 200 UK companies.

(iii) Major international companies.

(iv)   Major property investors.

A finance lease is a real alternative to a straight disposal and can give the vendor an opportunity to repurchase the property and benefit from any capital appreciation.

5.6 TYPES OF DEBT

Debt for project financing can be divided up into three types, depending on the duration of the loan:

- short-term bridging finance;
- medium-term loans and senior debt;
- long-term mortgages.

These types are outlined in the rest of this chapter and in more detail in Chapter 7 on debt.

Refinancing debt

Refinancing problems in the present market have arisen out of a poor state in the investment market. Investment property is the primary security for refinancing. The quality and spread of tenants, the term and review pattern of the leases are all crucial in reassuring a bank that a company will achieve acceptable levels of cash flow from a property in the medium term. Uncompleted or unlet development property is almost unrefinancable unless substantial amounts of additional equity are available (Clarke 1990, p. 438).

5.7 BRIDGING FINANCE

This is up to 3 years loan. Interest is rolled-up until development is sold and thus the developer must be able to pay the interest and principal on completion of the development. This would be done by selling the scheme or refinancing the bridging finance with long-term loans.

Commercial banks would require:

(a) security over and above project, i.e. other assets which are not charged;
(b) an interest rate of 2–4% above base (LIBOR);

They are not interested in an equity stake. Merchant banks may only require the project as security, but will charge 4–6% above base and want an equity share (profits share).

Bridging finance can be provided as a complete funding package. The interim funding is replaced by a buyout. Interim funding is provided at a rate between the short-term borrowing rate and the investment yield.

Bridging finance is also used in the very short term, i.e. repayable in 6 months or less, to cover the period between buying one property and selling another, or as an equity release pending refinance or sale. The market is dominated by clearing banks and the specialist lenders. As the market for bridging loans grew, several consortium lenders entered the market – Home Bridging plc, Cavendish Group plc and Berkeley Bridging. The collapse of the property market in the late 1980s took its toll on these lenders (Freed 1992, p. 187).

Types of bridging finance (Freed 1992, p. 188)

Closed bridging

Here one property is bought and another sold but the dates do not coincide. Lenders have a first charge on the new property and a second charge on the old, subject to a total exposure of, say, 75% of all value.

Open bridging

This occurs when the existing property is unsold before exchanging contracts on the new property. This is useful for 'chain-breaking'. The security is not as good as for closed bridging. There is a lower loan-to-value ratio, say 60–70%.

Bridging for acquisition

This is need for a rapid acquisition. The bridging loan is used to complete while putting together a long-term loan at leisure. This is popular with developers and property traders where the purchaser expects to effect a sale in the bridging period.

Bridging pending sale

Where equity release is required, perhaps for business/accounts reasons, the same principle as underwriting, enables rapid refinancing.

Bridging for refinancing

This is required when the borrower is in arrears with a conventional loan or unable to release equity with an existing lender. A new long-term lender is found to replace the bridging loan.

Factors in granting a bridging loan

- The loan-to-cost ratio or loan-to-value ratio should be in the range 60–70%, depending on security and nature of borrower.
- The rate of interest to be applied, 2–5% over LIBOR, whether fixed and floating rates.
- The duration of the loan, whether for the whole of the development period or not.
- Whether interest is to be paid at intervals or rolled up (added at monthly or quarterly intervals to the outstanding loan balance).
- Whether additional collateral or guarantees are required, such as a personal guarantee.
- Whether additional charges need to be made by the bank, such as commitment or facility fees, service charges.
- What monitoring procedures are in place.

5.8 LOAN TERMS AND FINANCIAL AGREEMENTS

In structuring the financial arrangement, the funder will aim to control certain aspects of the scheme, including:

- the criteria by which tenants are selected and leasehold terms agreed;
- negotiations conducted and agreements concluded with third parties;
- entry by the developer into any legal agreements such as planning gains with the local authority and consequent liability if the developer defaults;
- the nature and level of indemnity policies and collateral warranties held or offered by the developer, his professional team, the contractor and subcontractors, so that, in the event of failure, the developer can be dismissed and the funder can assume full authority for the completion of the scheme;
- tax implications of the project;
- the method by which the final purchase price of the completed project is agreed.

Practical problems may arise from the wording of financial agreements, and some are listed below (Ratcliff 1994, p. 63):

- Design documentation attached to the agreement should clearly and precisely set out the objectives of the scheme.
- A developer is well advised to try to restrict the number of outside consultants whom the funder appoints to act – usually as advisers – on his behalf for the project; a single firm of surveyors should be enough.
- The need to obtain written approval for the appointment of sub-contractors should be avoided by agreeing a list of nominated sub-contractors.
- A clear understanding of the definition of the date of practical completion should be established; where possible, the site visits of the developer's architect and the fund's surveyor should be synchronised.
- The date when the funder finally values the scheme and payment is made should be explicit, and should not depend on the actions of third parties.
- Access to the site by the funder's surveyors, and facilities to inspect and test materials and workmanship, should be kept within reasonable bounds.
- A procedure for arbitration should be agreed.
- It may be necessary for the developer to consider the inclusion of a 'walkabout' clause so that he can approach other sources of finance if a top-up of funds is required.
- Some mitigation should be allowed for delays that extend the completion date beyond that agreed, especially where such delays are beyond the developer's control.

5.9 SYNDICATED LOANS

This is where a group of lenders combine on large loans which would be too expensive or too risky for one lender to take on. Thus, the lenders diversify their loan books in respect of a number of loans on various assets to restrict the risk of being too heavily involved in any one. The loan is arranged and then syndicated by the lead banks. The syndicating bank may not be involved in the actual loan but may charge fees for underwriting the loan.

A typical 'syndicated loan' has the following characteristics (Fielding and Besser 1991, p. 103):

(i)   The bank with which the borrower has developed his relationship underwrites the loan and, in most cases, actually lends the monies.
(ii) The loan agreement is drafted as an advance syndicated loan agreement, enabling the original lending bank to transfer to other banks tranches of the original loan.
(iii) The asset teams of the original lending bank then sell off tranches of the loan in the banking market, the original lender acting as agent bank.

5.10 MORTGAGES

In the 1960s, fixed interest mortgages were used to finance the expansion of many of the large property companies. Interest rates were low and repayments could be serviced from rents. Because of the difference between cost and value, projects could be 100% financed.

For instance, in a *new development:*

Rents	£ 100 000 p.a.
Yield @ 6½%	15.38
Capital value	£1 538 000
Max. mortgage @ 60% capital value	£ 922 800
Cost of development	£ 900 000

Mortgage repayments @ 8½% over 25 years on cost	£ 88 000 p.a.
Less rental income	£ 100 000 p.a.
Surplus income to developer	£ 12 000 p.a.

Notes:

(i)   Developer has 100% funding.
(ii) Developer has income surplus from day 1.
(iii) Developer takes *all* increase on review.

Nowadays, inflation has undermined the use of the mortgage funding. The position is very different now where developers indulge in deficit financing, where rents do not cover repayments until the first review. Mortgages are generally 10–25 years with an advance of up to two-thirds of the valuation. Interest rate is gilts plus, say, 1½%.

Repaying a mortgage

There are three common ways of repaying a mortgage and this applies to residential owner-occupier mortgages also. These are:

(i)   The equal instalments or annualised repayment method, which involves regular repayments comprised of part capital and part interest.
(ii) The capital and interest method, which requires equal annual repayments of capital plus interest on the diminishing outstanding debt. The instalments are higher in the earlier years than in the later ones. The initial net costs are high, allowing for interest relief, but they decrease uniformly over the mortgage period.
(iii) A non-profit endowment mortgage, which can be taken out so that, at the end of the loan period, the amount produced by the policy will be sufficient to repay the original loan. In the intervening period interest is paid on the debt and regular monthly premiums are invested in the endowment policy. The costs remain high through the duration of the mortgage period, as the outstanding capital remains constant, but tax relief may be allowable in the interest payment.

See Figure 5.1.

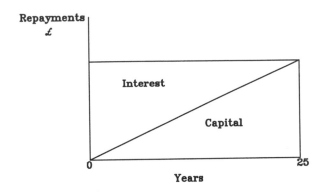

Figure 5.1 *Conventional mortgage*

If annual repayments cannot be serviced from income there may be a number of measures that could be taken:

- Interest-only payments could be made for a period (no capital repayment in this time).
- Interest holiday: the interest is rolled up (no capital or interest payment for period).
- Balloon repayment: interest-only payment; capital is all repaid at the end of the period.
- A variable rate of interest could be introduced which is stepped up as income increases, say from rental growth.
- Partial capital repayment is made in the period so that most of the repayment is interest.
- Have a smaller loan and extend the period of repayment.
- Give equity participation to the lender.

5.11   NON-RECOURSE AND LIMITED-RECOURSE LOANS

Here the loan is made solely against the security of a specific project and thus the lender has no rights to recourse to obtain other assets of the borrower if the loan goes wrong. This may be done by making a loan to a subsidiary of a company which holds the single property on its books. This property is the asset over which the lender takes charge. Because the loan-to-value ratio is less than 100%, the balance is made up by monies provided by the parent company. Limited recourse exists where the lender provides 100% finance but has some additional security or limited guarantee from the parent company. A non-recourse loan limits the liability of the parent company to the project by the extent of a cash investment or the extent of the limited guarantee. Full non-recourse is very rare and lenders will include clauses to cover interest and principal guarantees and obligations to refinance. Thus, the true non-recourse loan is given to a developer who has no other assets than those already committed to the development being financed. The costs of such loans can be 50% or more than that of a recourse loan. The advantages for a larger developer is that the loan is taken 'off balance sheet' but these opportunities are restricted by law. By doing this in theory, the debt ratio of the parent company is unaffected, thus enabling them to finance several schemes at once.

A new system of limited recourse funding which is off-balance-sheet was developed in the late 1980s. The *property* being developed in this case has again become the principal source of repayment, whereas in the past the property loan has been to a *developer but has been secured on the property*. If the outcome of the development is a successful one, then the bank lender would seek to structure a loan based on a percentage of value – typically 65–70%. It would then undertake to the borrower that it would only seek repayment from the refinancing or sale of the development and not from the borrower. The bank would expect 10–20% of development costs (the difference between the loan amount and the anticipated total cost of completing the project) to be contributed by the developer. The developer would contribute any additional costs incurred in excess of the loan amount in order that the development might be completed and let prior to refinancing. The amount of equity required to be injected by the developer would depend on the level of underlying risk. The bank lender believes that the 30–35% difference between the completed value and the total loan should provide a sufficient cushion.

The structure of a typical limited-recourse bank construction loan is as follows: The basic principles are accepted by all the main property lending banks. The bank will lend a hard core of the total development costs without recourse to the developer, but committing the borrower or third party if the developer is not strong enough to contribute all the other costs. It is prudent to ask for the injection of developer's equity at the start. With a strong developer, it may be possible to put some up at the beginning while guaranteeing to put up the rest at the end after the bank facility has been exhausted. There is a need to have some equity at the beginning or the developer could walk away if things get problematic.

5.12 PROJECT MANAGEMENT FEE

This is not very popular. Here the fund acquires the site and employs the development team. The developer acts as a project manager for a fee plus a bonus if the scheme is successful. The developer arranges all the finance to be provided from the start and this includes his bonus. The site is handed over to a funding institution, who then acquires the site, employs the professional team, with the developer acting as project manager for a fee, and provides all the development finance. The attraction to the developer is that the financial risk is minimised and instead an attractive fee is paid. The fee will reflect an element of commission or reward for introducing the project to the institution. The developer may also have carried out initial studies, with designs and costings from an architect and quantity surveyor operating on a contingency basis (no deal, no fee) but looking to be instructed by the institution if the development is taken up. There is very little incentive in a scheme like this to encourage the developer to maximise return, and thus an additional bonus may be added on, say a share of rental over the expected level (Darlow 1988). Project management can take many forms and it is outside the scope of this book to discuss these. In many cases a straight fee rather than an additional bonus is paid.

5.13 CONTRACTOR'S FINANCE

Construction companies are key operators in the property development process, as the companies actually construct the buildings in accordance with the form of contract and building procurement arrangement agreed. Construction companies will also undertake development themselves, usually through a development company subsidiary. Construction companies may also act as a source of finance for the developer. Often joint venture arrangements are organised between the developer and contractor.

REFERENCES

Clarke, R J (1990) 'Refinancing', *Journal of Property Finance*, vol. 1, no. 3, pp. 435–9.

Cohen, P (1992) 'Non-recourse Property Funding', *Journal of Property Finance*, vol. 3, no. 3, pp. 319–24.

Darlow, C (1988) 'Direct Project Funding', in C Darlow (ed.), *Valuation and Development Appraisal*, Estates Gazette, London.

Fielding, M and Besser, A (1991) 'Syndicated Loans – *Caveat* Borrower', *Estates Gazette*, 15 June, pp. 78 and 103.

Fox, J W W (1993) 'Sale and Leasebacks: A Case Study', *Journal of Property Finance*, vol. 4, no. 1, pp. 9–12.

Freed, N (1992) 'Bridging Finance', *Journal of Property Finance*, vol. 3, no. 2, pp. 187–190.

Orchard-Lisle, P (1987) 'Financing Property Development', *Journal of Valuation*, vol. 5, no. 4, pp. 343–53.

Ratcliffe, J (1984) 'Development Financing: Drawing up the Agreement', *Architects Journal*, 22 and 29 August, p. 63.

Savills (1989) *Financing Property 1989*, Savills, London.

6 Corporate Finance

6.1 INTRODUCTION

The two areas of corporate finance relate to debt capital (or loans) and equity capital (or shares). Equity finance is capital paid into or kept in the business by the shareholders, the owners of the business. It is long-term capital and carries the greatest risk and attracts the highest returns. Debt finance is money invested in the business by third parties, usually for a shorter period of time than equity and carrying a lower risk and lower return.

Corporate finance is related to the financial structure of the company itself. Choosing the right mix of debt and equity capital that meets the investment requirement of a business is a key financial management decision. There are four strategic issues here (Pike and Neale 1993, p. 274):

Risk There is enormous uncertainty in the business environment. Considerations about risk will consider how the firm would deal with a downturn in business or the economy.

Ownership The ownership of the firm is critical: it is important to know who exercises the current control over the company; a desire to retain control will affect financing decisions. The desire to retain control may mean that borrowing is preferred to raising equity capital.

Duration Finance should match the use to which it is put. Finance for investments with no returns in the early years should be raised so there are no payments in these years. One should not raise long-term finance for a short-life programme; the firm will be overcapitalised and will not generate sufficient return to repay finance.

Debt capacity The ability to borrow more depends on the existing level of borrowing. This also depends on the type of business and the sector of operation.

The balance sheet model of the firm can be used to analyse the sources of cash available to the corporate structure. The basic sources of cash for the firm are as follows:

Shareholders' funds The largest proportion of long-term finance is usually provided by shareholders and is termed equity capital. Share ownership lies at the heart of modern capitalism. By purchasing a portion of or share in a company, almost anyone can become a shareholder with some degree of control over a company. Ordinary share capital is the main source of new money from shareholders. They are entitled to participate in the business through voting in a general meeting of the shareholders and also to receive dividends out of the profits. As owners of the business, the ordinary shareholders bear the greatest risk but enjoy the main fruits of success in the form of higher dividends and capital gains.

Retained profits For an established business, the main source of equity funds will be internally generated from successful trading. Any profits remaining after all operating costs, interest payments, taxation and dividends are reinvested in the business (i.e. ploughed back) and regarded as part of the equity capital.

Loan capital Money lent to the business by third parties is debt finance or loan capital. Most companies borrow money on a long-term basis by issuing stocks or debentures. The supplier of the loan will specify the amount of loan, rate of interest, date of payment and method of repayment. The finance manager will monitor the long-term financial structure by examining the relationship between loan capital, where interest and loan repayment are contractually obligatory, and ordinary share capital, where dividend payment is at the discretion of the directors. This relationship between debt and equity is called gearing (known in the USA as leverage). Strictly, gearing is the proportion of debt capital to total capital in the firm.

The three sources of cash mentioned above are matched by three uses of cash in the firm (Pike and Neale 1993, pp. 8–9):

(i)   Cash is used to service (pay returns to) the main sources of finance. Dividends are paid to shareholders; interest is paid to lenders along with any repayment of the loan due. Tax is paid on the profits earned.

(ii) Cash is invested in long-term assets such as building and plant, to produce goods or services. The investment decisions made in respect of these long-term assets are critical for the success of the company.

(iii) Cash is also used to pay for materials, labour, overheads and costs incurred in producing the goods or services offered to customers. It is also used to purchase stocks of raw materials, work in progress, finished goods and debtors. In a property trading company these current assets would also include properties and developments in the process of completion held for trading. Current assets in a firm are offset by the current liabilities, which are amounts owing to suppliers of goods and services.

The main ways in which a property company could increase its capital include:

(i)   the issue of debenture stock;
(ii) the issue of loan stock;
(iii) preference shares;
(iv) ordinary shares.

These instruments are described later on; as a general introduction, it is important first to look at issues relating to the difference between debt and equity. Equity investments in a company usually come in the form of share ownership, and in this chapter types of share, including their issue arrangements, are discussed; in addition, there is a summary of debt approaches related to corporate finance. These sections need to be cross-read with the sections on equity and debt to obtain a more detailed picture. The use of different types of corporate finance can be gauged from the Savills Indicator, which relates to the amount of loans, bonds and rights issues over the period 1986–93, as shown in Figure 6.1.

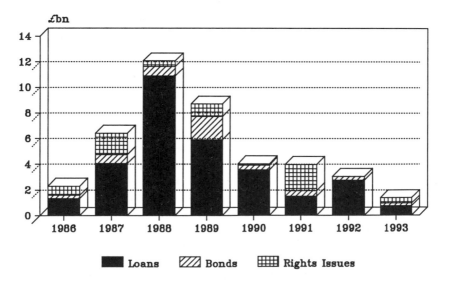

Figure 6.1 *Savills Indicator of loans, bonds and rights issues (Savills 1993a). (1993 figures are to April only)*

6.2 EQUITY FINANCE

Equity finance in the form of direct investment and partnership will be discussed in Chapter 8. The distinction between debt and equity is hazy when considered in the context of loans with conversion rights to shares and mezzanine finance, a halfway house between debt and equity. In this chapter, when dealing with corporate finance, the distinction is:

Equity	*Debt*
Ordinary shares	Debentures
Preference shares	Loan stock
Warrants	Bonds
Options	General facilities
Converted stock $\longleftarrow$	Convertible stock

6.3 ORDINARY AND PREFERENCE SHARES

The equity of a company consists of ordinary shares and shareholders participate in the profits of a company once prior demands have been met; these prior demands for payment will include creditors (trade creditors), holders of debt and preference shareholders. If a company finds that the total of accumulated and retained profits in the company's reserves have grown in relation to issued capital, then a scrip or capitalisation issue can be made.

Preference shares rank after debentures and loan stock but before ordinary shares in terms of a charge to the company. If profits are insufficient to pay the fixed rate dividend, then arrears can be carried forward if the preference share is a cumulative type. Conversion rights may be available to convert the shares to ordinary capital. This sort of share may be set up if the company is a new company and thus there may be a risk attached to the ordinary shares. If, for instance, the company is a management buy-out or start-up company, then it may attract 'venture' capital, i.e. risk-taking capital used to finance new business opportunities. In this case the investor may wait some years for the company and its cash flow to stabilise before converting the fixed return preference share to an ordinary share. Preference shares are unsecured, so, if no profits are made, no dividend will be paid, but if they are cumulative, they can carry forward the payment due, as indicated above. The characteristics of preference shares are thus:

(i) more secure than ordinary shares;

(ii) less secure than debentures or loan stock;

(iii) return is from a fixed rate dividend payable from profits;

(iv) unsecured;

(v)   can be cumulative or non-cumulative;

(vi) can be voting or non-voting shares but rarely are voting;

(vii) can be convertible or not convertible into ordinary shares.

The priority of charge against the profits of the company are simply:

(i)   debentures and loan stock;

(ii) preference shares;

(iii) ordinary shares.

6.4 ISSUES AND OPTIONS

Company shares, together with other securities such as Government bonds and stocks and the loan stock of public authorities, are traded on the Stock Exchange. The Stock Exchange arose out of the need to deal in the shares of joint-stock companies, which originated in the seventeenth century. By pooling of risk, combination of resources and the development of limited liability, these companies expanded and created the requirement of transferability of capital. Owners of shares or loan capital in the companies required a market to sell their holdings; otherwise the original investment would not have been attractive. The stock market is thus a secondary market for investment in the sense of reselling shares and securities, but it is also a primary market as a source of new funds.

The primary market operates for new issues, and where a company is seeking a listing on the Stock Exchange it will need to be represented by a broking firm. The broking firm will advise on the company's prospectus and the issue price. The Bank of England controls large issues to programme the timing of such issues. Underwriting is arranged, so that, if the stock is advertised but not fully taken up, the underwriters take up the undersubscription. This new issue procedure is called a prospectus issue, but other methods exist such as an offer for sale, a placing and a rights issue. In 1983, more than one hundred property companies were listed on the London Stock Exchange and at the beginning of 1983 the market value of the 42 major property companies monitored by brokers Rowe and Pitman exceeded £4.27 billion. By the end of 1993, 118 companies were listed by the *Financial Times* in their property section. The Datastream analysis of property companies in their sample had a total market capitalisation in excess of £13 billion; this figure appears to be the same quoted by Millman in 1988 (p. 169), although the sample may be different. The main features of a property company which would be considered by an investor would be: the quality of assets; the quality of management; sources of income; capital structure and financing. The quality of assets is dependent on the portfolio composition and the location, age and tenure of individual properties within the portfolio. The quality of management is very much a subjective judgement and may in fact be related to the persona of the founder or managing director of the company. Sources of income to property companies vary greatly between investment companies reliant on rent and development companies reliant on the capital gains from the sale of completed developments. Capital structure is important from the point of view of the investor, as a highly geared financial structure is more appropriate for established companies deriving a large proportion of revenue from rental income than for development companies dependent on less secure trading profits.

New public property companies created since the 1960s have rarely gone through the expensive process of obtaining a full listing on the stock market. A quoted property company may emerge from an existing company whose manufacturing or trading activities have declined or been sold off, or a company may be bought as a shell into which property assets are transferred. Another alternative which was popular was to obtain a quotation on the Unlisted Securities Market (USM); this, however, has been suspended at the time of writing.

The advantages of property shares lie in two general areas. First, equity investments generally provide a means of investing in very small units and denominations and thus risk can be spread. Equity investments can also be traded easily in the stock market at low costs of transfer. Thus, besides the liquidity advantage, trading takes place in a market characterised by almost perfect knowledge where share prices are known. The second area of advantage relates to the nature of property itself. The advantages of durability and its effectiveness as a hedge against inflation are clearly seen. As the shares of property companies are based on income arising from rents, these companies are perceived as providing a higher degree of income security than other equities (Debenham, Tewson and Chinnocks 1984, p. 45).

Raising corporate funds

The aim of this section is to analyse further recent developments in the property company sector and to understand why equity capital is important in the present state of the market. Historically, property companies grew in the post-war years because of the ability to obtain funds at low interest rates. It is important to recognise the relationship of low interest rates to higher inflation rates to understand property company growth. Basically, if the cost of a development was, say, two-thirds of its value, then the total cost could be covered by mortgage funds. If the mortgage interest rate was, say, 7% and the yield, say, 6%, it can easily be seen that from the completion of the scheme, using 100% borrowed funds, the developer not only owned one-third of the value but could retain this equity as his return (at 6%) covered his interest payments (at 7% on two-thirds of the capital, say 4.7%). Further, with growth, the value of the property and the level of rents increase, but as interest rates are static, the return to the developer increased dramatically over time because of the gearing effect. (With a 5% compound growth rate over 5 years the return to the developer would have increased to 7.66% on the original capital value.)

The purpose of the above analysis is to understand the position of present-day development funding. Because interest rates have been high relative to the rate of inflation, it is difficult to finance developments using long-term money. Real interest rates had been positive and over 4% for most of the mid-1980s, a state of events which had not existed for this long since the 1930s (Scrimgeour Vickers & Co. 1986, p. 2). Thus, in the late 1970s and early 1980s, many developers became 'merchant developers' and 'traders', using short-term monies and selling on the completed development to institutions. This analysis is a simplification of a number of different phases which have been evident in the market as institutional influence increased and property crashed in 1974–5. By 1983, because of the changes in interest rates a number of established property companies had provided for their financial needs by raising cash from their shareholders by the issue of ordinary shares or convertible stock. Land Securities raised £100m in 1980 and MEPC raised £30m of 35 year debenture money (Brett 1983, p. 102). After 1983, the debenture market continued to raise large sums and the latter half of 1985 alone saw £220m raised with coupons (interest) around the 10½% mark (Scrimgeour Vickers & Co 1986, p. 5):

		£m
Jul. 1985	Evans of Leeds	12
Aug.	Brixton Estates	15
Oct.	Hampton Court	10
Oct.	Peachey	20
Nov.	Haslemere	100
Nov.	Land Securities	40
Dec.	Rosehaugh Greycoat Estates	15
Dec.	Allied London Estates Agency	8
		£220m

In the late 1980s there was an ongoing need to raise corporate funds because of a shortage of funds in the markets due to institutional absence. The institutional lack of enthusiasm has been caused by the lack of performance of the property sector compared with equities since 1979–80 and limited evidence of satisfactory growth. Basically, the institutions had bid down initial yields on purchase to unrealistically low levels and the growth of the overall institutional portfolio was insufficient to provide the target return. Thus, there was an institutional oversupply of funds which moved yields to historically low levels because of the scarcity of new buildings (Cadman and Catalano 1983, p. 27). Study of the property price and yield relative to all shares for the period 1968–86 indicates how the institutions, as well as depressing direct yields, also had the same effect on property share yields. Other recent research has also shown that the yield of the pension funds' portfolio over the last 10 years has been depressed by the inclusion of property (Graham 1985, p. 22). By the early 1990s institutions were still avoiding the property markets.

While institutional finance is still important in the longer term, alternative sources are increasing in number, providing both equity and debt finance for the construction phase or medium-term finance, perhaps up to the first rent review. Investment trusts, venture capitalists and various corporate entities have provided finance together with short- or medium-term bank debt. Medium- and long-term financing has generally centred upon mortgages or debentures. This finance has been in the form of loans varying in term between 10 and 40 years with fixed rate, floating rate or 'drop-lock' interest options and capital repayment holidays. Traditionally, this form of funding has been applied more to income-producing property than speculative development, but in recent years medium-term mortgage and debenture arrangements have been used to redeem construction loans. The problems of replacing long-term institutional finance in the development buy-out is a difficult one. If there is a shortfall of rent against interest charges, then the developer will need to await rental growth for his return.

Issues and options

There are a number of different ways of issuing shares – for instance, a new issue can be introduced to the market, i.e. sold to existing shareholders; this does not create much of an interest to the public at large. As an alternative there can be a placing where shares are sold privately to a number of brokers. Finally, there can be an offer for sale. Companies are launched on the Stock Exchange, which is the main dealing area. The unlisted securities market which formed the secondary market is now defunct. A summary of different methods of issuing shares in the UK in shown in Box 6.1.

- **Public issue by prospectus**   Uses an issuing house as an agent and attempts to persuade investors to buy shares in the shortest possible time. Superseded by the offer for sale method.

- **Offer for sale**   Used when a large amount of capital is required. The issuing house, acting as principal, offers the shares at a fixed price. A detailed prospectus is issued and the offer is extensively advertised. In the event of an oversubscription, the issuing house allots the available shares to the applicants. To ensure that a ready market exists, as many applications as possible get some shares, so applications for large holdings usually obtain only a small proportion of shares applied for and small applications are settled in full.

- **Private placing**   Can be used by unquoted companies who require a small amount of funds with the minimum of issue costs. Normally, an issuing house agrees to purchase a number of shares in the company with the intention of placing them with institutional investors.

- **Stock Exchange introduction**   This does not raise additional finance but allows the company to obtain a Stock Exchange quotation.

- **Stock Exchange placing**   This is a combination of a private placing and a Stock Exchange introduction. The company will need both a quotation and a small amount of capital, which is raised from institutional investors.

- **Issues by tender**   These are used when there is some uncertainty over the issue price. A minimum price is set and the public bid for the shares. Allotments are made at the price that will just clear all the shares, known as the striking price.

Box 6.1 *Summary of different methods of issuing shares in the UK. Source: Asch and Kaye 1989, pp. 48–9*

An option gives the owner of the option the right to buy a share in the future at a price which is fixed at the time of purchase of the option. This is strictly a 'call' option which empowers the owner to do something. A 'put' option gives you the right to sell to someone else at a predetermined price. Options are traded on the Traded Options Market. To purchase an option, you need to take a view on how the value of the asset you have taken an option on will move over a period of time. For example, you may purchase an option for, say, 10p to purchase shares in A, say at 120p, on the basis that the shares are worth 100p now but you think they will rise to 150p. If the shares do not increase in price, then the option has no value. If the share price rises, then you will make a profit by purchasing under the option and reselling the shares. You would, however, need to clear 130p before making a profit. If the share price does not increase over 130p, then you have lost money. Traded options in the market usually have a life of 9 months.

Options are not created by the company; rather the market is created by the owners of the shares. A warrant is different because it is issued by the company who issued the shares. Instead of issuing shares, the company may issue warrants giving the rights to subscribe for new shares in the future. Thus, put and call options generally give the holder the right to buy or sell shares at a given exercise price. A call option is a right to buy and a put option a right to sell. American options can be exercised at any time up to and including the expiration date. European options are only exercisable at the expiration date. The valuation of the option depends on the price of the underlying assets, the exercise price, the expiration date, the variability of the underlying asset and the risk-free interest rate:

Value of share + value of put − value of call = present value of exercise price

(Ross *et al.* 1993, p. 645)

Finally, to clarify types of issue, we should distinguish between a new issue (by an offer for sale, introduction or placing) and a rights issue, where a company issues new shares for cash, offering them first to existing shareholders, perhaps on the basis of 'so many' shares to their existing holding. This needs to be compared with a scrip issue. A rights issue will increase the shareholders' funds and the issued capital. A scrip issue or capitalisation issue is an issue of shares from revenue reserves where the existing share capital is small to the shareholders' funds. So, accumulated profits have built up in the company and this is a process of distributing them. Note, however, that no new money is involved in the process, because the net asset value of the company is the same; this is merely a redistribution of the capital in the company and, while the shares are issued to shareholders free, pro rata on the basis of their existing holdings, the price of the shares will fall to reflect this (Brett 1990, p. 100).

Rights issues

For property companies quoted on the International Stock Exchange in London, it is possible to raise extra capital through rights issues, an issue of shares offered to existing shareholders in proportion to their existing shareholdings. In order to persuade the shareholders to buy the shares, they are offered at a discount to the current market price. Shares which are not subscribed to by the holders to whom they have been offered must be sold on the market for the benefit of those holders.

The concept behind a rights issue can be explained by the following example:

Company X has 1 million 25p shares in issue with a current market price of 150p. It makes a rights issue of one new share for every four held at 100p. A shareholder with four shares has an investment worth £6. If the shareholder takes up the rights issue, the ownership is:

4 shares at the original market value	£6.00
1 share at cost	£1.00
Total: 5 shares worth	£7.00

Thus, each share is worth £1.40.

This final price is called the theoretical ex-rights price, since it excludes the right to the next dividend.

Capital issues were very popular with the quoted property companies until the stock market crash in October 1987; the funds raised through such issues were very often used to repay short-term debt. Capital issues over the period 1980–88 increased from around £200m in 1980 to a peak of £1.6 billion in 1987 and this reduced to around £400m in 1988. In the current market, some property companies are financing their short-term debt through the issuing of debenture stock which is attractive to institutions given the continuing shortage of long-dated gilts (Savills, *Financing Property 1989*, London, 1989). Recent increases in share prices since September 1992 have led to the rerating of property companies on the Stock Exchange. Property company shares were, in 1993, standing at a premium to net asset value estimated on average to be 21%. This rerating has enabled new capital right issues to be issued, amounting to over £1 billion from March to October 1993. All the well-known property companies were involved in these issues in 1993, including MEPC, Hammerson, Brixton Estates, Slough Estates and British Land (Savills 1993b, p 3).

6.5 WARRANTS AND CONVERTIBLES

A warrant gives the holder the right to buy shares of common stock at an exercise price for a given period of time. Typically warrants are issued in a package with privately placed bonds. Afterwards they become detached and are traded separately. A convertible bond is a combination of a straight bond and a call option. The holder can give up the bond in exchange for shares of stock. Convertible bonds and warrants are like call options but there are some important differences (Ross *et al.* 1993, p. 669):

(i) Warrants and convertible securities are issued by companies. Call options are traded between individual investors. Warrants are usually issued privately and are combined with a bond. Warrants can usually be detached immediately after the issue. In some cases warrants are issued with preference stock, common stock or executive compensation schemes. Thus, convertibles are bonds (debt) which can be converted into shares. Call options are sold separately.

(ii) Warrants and call options are exercised for cash, but the holder of the warrant gives no cash for the warrant and receives shares for a further cash payment.

Thus, a warrant is an 'option' giving the lender of the money the right to subscribe for shares at a given price. Although the price of a warrant is a fraction of the share price itself, in combination with the subscription price it will exceed the current market value of the shares. Thus, a premium is being paid for the right to subscribe at a fixed price in the future. Warrants in themselves do not provide capital for the company; they are a trading vehicle for investors (Gibbs 1987, p. 348). Warrants are not often issued for cash but as a 'sweetener' to some other kind of issue, such as a fixed-interest bond.

Convertibles are basically debentures (see Section 6.7) which have a right to switch to ordinary equity shares at a date in the future at a fixed price agreed at the date of sale and normally at a higher price than the market value at the time. The attraction to the lender is that a lower coupon can be attached to the stock. If a convertible element is detached from the stock, it is bought and sold separately as a warrant.

6.6 DEBT

Debt can be applied to the corporate structure and can be seen simply in terms of the application of funds in a general funding situation where the criteria for the funding will be based on the status and assets of the borrower rather than for a specific project.

The lender will look at the borrower's accounts and will want to see:

- good-quality property assets on modern leases;
- a realistic development programme;
- a good portfolio mix;
- not all the assets pledged;
- a healthy proportion of equity.

A general funding facility may be negotiated where the agreed sum is secured on the developer's assets. This allows the developer to have access to predetermined amounts of money over a given period of time. These loans may be, say, 10–15 years in duration with an option to exercise in a shorter period, say, 5 years. This facility may be negotiated on the basis of an agreed interest rate. An example is given below of a drop-lock loan which may be used on such a facility, but you are referred to the section on interest rates and hedging in Chapter 4 for further information. In a drop-lock loan, the base interest rate is agreed and if the market rate of interest, which is assumed to be above at the commencement, falls to that level, it is locked in as a fixed rate; otherwise it will vary with the market rate. Two other conditions may also be imposed:

(i) If the market interest rate falls below the base rate agreed during the option period, the option can be exercised in reverse and the developer could be obliged to take up a tranche of cash at the rate which is locked for the term.

(ii) If the developer takes up the loan before the predetermined base is reached, then the borrower has to pay a variable rate linked to the base rate until it falls to the base rate, when the loan is converted to a fixed rate.

Overdrafts are common for companies; developers will borrow from the bank to finance such short-term requirements as the interim payments to builders in the construction phase of a development. Borrowing from a clearing bank is traditionally on a short-term basis with a variable interest rate tied to a margin over the LIBOR rate. Companies with a large amount of bank finance will be vulnerable to rising interest rates and short-term recall of the funds by the bank. Merchant banks and finance houses are normally willing to lend on specific terms for up to several years but obviously such sources are more expensive (Fraser 1993, p. 248).

6.7 DEBENTURES

Debentures, which are secured loans, are discussed in Chapter 7 in detail. They are the sealed bonds of a company acknowledging a debt on which interest is due until the principal is repaid. A debenture holder has a prior charge on the developer's corporate assets, although in practice property company debentures are secured on specific assets. Interest is paid half-yearly and there are often trustees appointed to look after debenture holders' interests. Debenture stock can be redeemable, non-redeemable or convertible.

Advantages of debentures are (Gibbs 1987, pp. 347–8):

to developer
- money borrowed is not tied to a single project;
- it is a charge against profits before tax.

to investors
- it gives a higher rate of interest than gilts;
- they are tradeable securities;
- there may be rights of conversion.

6.8 LOAN STOCK AND BONDS

These are the same as debenture issues but may not be secured. The coupon (interest rate payable) is generally high but allows smaller developers to raise non-project-specific funds. Interest is paid half-yearly. Convertible loan stock has a slightly lower rate of interest but can be converted to ordinary shares at a fixed price at a stated date. If the right of subscription is detachable from the loan stock, this is a warrant and can be traded separately.

Bonds may have a low or nil interest rate and these are basically loan stock which are tradeable; zero-coupon and deep-discounted bond issues are examples.

6.9 STRUCTURED FINANCE

Finance can be structured as appropriate to the capital structure, the assets, cash flow and activities of a corporate client. Structured finance could include the following options as an example:

(i) Bonds or loan stock, with a cumulative structure, which allows interest to be rolled up with the repayment at the end of the life of the bond.

(ii) Finance leasing, which enables the borrower to sell a property to a finance company, pay a 'market rent' and have the option to repurchase the building at the original purchase price plus any deferred interest.

(iii) Off-balance-sheet funding, which will reduce the lender's exposure on the balance sheet by restructuring loans outside of their group holdings.

(iv) Capital market instruments, including interest caps, floors, swaps, etc.

These options are considered in detail elsewhere; the intention of off-balance-sheet funding is to reduce the level of debt in the company accounts. This improves the gearing, the ratio between equity finance and total finance in the balance sheet, and thus makes the company look more financially attractive. A case study showing the application of deep-discounted bonds in structured finance is shown in Box 6.2.

The use of various financial instruments has been the subject of regular surveys by Savills, the property consultants. Since the mid-1980s the range of financial instruments used in corporate finance has decreased, perhaps a reflection of the general state of the market and a move back to funding based on fundamental criteria rather than elaborate derivatives. The graph in Figure 6.2 shows the usage of various debt instruments; see Figure 6.1 for the additional usage of rights issues.

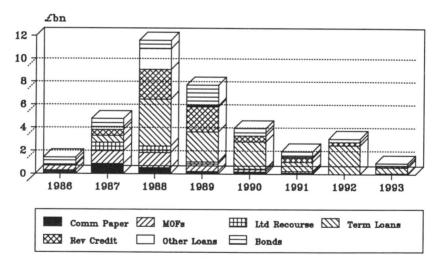

1993 to April. Rights issues excluded.
Comm Paper = Commercial Paper
Rev Credit = Revolving Credit

Figure 6.2 *Savills's indicator of debt instrument usage (Savills 1993a)*

A medium-sized private company has an existing relationship with a clearing bank but no other banking relationships. It sees falls in value on the property sector as an opportunity to buy high-yielding investments. Its clearing bank does not wish to increase its exposure.

Financial Information:

Various properties some let/some sites:

capital value	£54,000,000
income p.a.	£ 2,900,000
ERV p.a.	£ 3,800,000
Clearing bank loan	£15,000,000
Net Worth of company	£39,000,000

Problem:

This is one of cash flow; current income at £2.9m will only service say a loan of £18m. (Case study assumes rates in 1990.) Company overheads of £0.5m are not covered by the present income after interest on the existing £15m loan. Two of the properties are reversionary and thus would be good security for some kind of roll-up/deep-discount facility.

Solution:

On the basis that these reversionary properties account for say £30m of value and about £1.3m of current income, it should be possible to raise around £20m of initial loan with the interest shortfall rolled up and borrowings on a 5 year fixed or capped basis. This leaves £1.6m (£2.9m income less £1.3m for the deep-discount arrangement) to service overheads and additional debt. Assuming that the new properties purchased yield an initial 10%, the company should have the capacity to borrow an additional £26.7m and buy a further £31.7m of property as follows:

Analysis:

Available income	£1,600,000
Less overheads	£ 500,000
	£1,100,000

Available income + new income = new interest expense
$£1.1m + (0.10 \times (L + £5m)) = 0.16 \times L$
$L = £26.7m$, where L = loan amount and extra £5m comes from the extra proceeds of the £20m loan.

Box 6.2 *Case study in structured finance. Source: Clarke 1990, pp. 438–9*

6.10 HYBRIDS: DEBT WITH PROFIT SHARE

Development projects are funded generally by debt and equity. The senior debt will be the 70% of the cost of the project (or may be based on a loan-to-value ratio); the rest is made up by equity. If there is a shortfall, this is filled by mezzanine debt, which is exposed to risk, or else by profit sharing arrangements. The mezzanine debt may be provided by the same institution as the senior debt or may be supplied by merchant banks or specialist lenders. Mezzanine finance has been discussed elsewhere, as have loans with a profit share. Profit sharing is a complex area looked at in the debt section. Quasi-equity is a term given to convertibles and warrants. Convertible bonds and warrant bonds have been described in Section 6.5. These instruments can be issued in the euromarkets. Another example is convertible mortgages; these are looked at in Section 7.5.

REFERENCES

Asch, D and Kaye, G R (1989) *Financial Planning: Modelling Methods and Techniques*, Kogan Paul, London.

Beveridge, J A (1991) 'New Methods of Financing', in P Venmore-Rowland, P Brandon and T Mole (eds), *Investment, Procurement and Performance in Construction*, RICS, London.

Brett, M (1983) 'Indirect Investment in Property', in C Darlow (ed.), *Valuation and Investment Appraisal*, Estates Gazette, London.

Brett, M (1990) *Property and Money*, Estates Gazette, London.

Cadman, D and Catalano, A (1983) *Property Development in the UK – Evolution and Change*, College of Estate Management, Reading.

Clarke, R J (1990) 'Refinancing', *Journal of Property Finance*, vol. 1, no. 3, pp. 435–9.

Debenham, Tewson and Chinnocks (1984) *Property Investment in Britain*, Debenham, Tewson & Chinnocks, London.

Fraser, W D (1993) *Principles of Property Investment and Pricing*, Macmillan Press, London.

Gibbs, R (1987) 'Raising Finance for New Development', *Journal of Valuation*, vol. 5, no. 4.

Graham, J (1985) 'New Sources of Finance for the Property Industry', *Estates Gazette*, 6 July.

Millman, S (1988) 'Property, Property Companies and Public Securities', in S L Barter (ed.), *Real Estate Finance*, Butterworths, London.

Pike, R and Neale, B (1993) *Corporate Finance and Investment*, Prentice Hall, London.

Ross, S A, Westerfield, R W and Jaffe, J F (1993) *Corporate Finance*, Irwin, Boston.

Savills (1993a) *Financing Property 1993*, Savills, London.

Savills (1993b) *Investment and Economic Outlook*, Savills, London, Issue 3, October.

Scrimgeour Vickers & Co (1986) *United Kingdom Research, Annual Property Report*, Scrimgeor Vickers & Co, London.

7 Debt Finance

7.1 INTRODUCTION

The property company can raise debt capital through loans or equity capital through share issues. Share capital is restricted to the issuing of ordinary shares and this is considered in detail in the section on equity; in this section debt finance is considered. A large proportion of the bank debt currently outstanding is provided by the clearing banks on small to medium-sized properties throughout the country. It is useful at this point to compare the debt problems in the property sector in the early 1990s with the property collapse in 1973–4. The banking crises of 1973–4 put the reliance on institutional investment for recovery. The institutions provided attractively priced 100% fund packages for property development which they would commit to purchase in the future at a discounted yield on completion. While property provided satisfactory returns during the period of high inflation in the 1970s, property's performance began to look pedestrian compared with the more sparkling returns offered by the equity market during the prolonged bull market and low inflation of the mid-1980s. The problems of finance in property during the late 1980s and early 1990s cannot really be compared with the property collapse in 1973–4, the new developers are stronger, the lending banks have more expertise. The collapse of 1973–4 was affected by a rise in interest rates and generally the economy appears more sound now (Barter 1988, p. 16). However, the total debt outstanding in 1992 was in real terms three times that of 1974 and the surge of inflation which assisted in the debt repayment of the 1974 crash is not expected to occur in the 1990s. There is also a distinct difference in institutional attitudes. In the 1970s, institutional portfolios were weighted towards property, insurance companies commonly had 30–40% exposure and pension funds were acquiring property to build up portfolio to around the 20% level. The proportion of property in institutions is much less now, around 7% (see Chapter 9); thus, the institutional takeout is less likely (Scott 1992, p. 348). The banks are, however, heavily involved in the property sector; in June 1989 Debenham Tewson and Chinnocks found that property formed the most important lending security for banks and facilities secured against property accounted for some 35–40% of total loans. The number of banks with property loans had grown to 140 in 1989 and the combined property debt of the overseas banks accounted for 40% of loans. Corporate facilities may account for 50% of the loans to property companies outstanding at this time, with specific development funding another 30–35% and investment lending around 20%. Finally, 35–40% of total loans to property companies could be on a limited-recourse basis (Debenham Tewson and Chinnocks, *Banking on Property 1989*, quoted in the *Journal of Valuation* 1989, pp. 87–89).

In the late 1980s the investment and development boom in property was funded by debt capital. British and foreign bank loans grew by an average of 51% per annum. Bank lending to property companies reached £40.7 billion in 1991, a peak of 8.72% of total bank lending. Since then the amount has fallen. In 1992 the figure was £39 billion, but if loans to the construction sector are included, this reaches £55 billion or 12.2% of bank lending (Scott 1992, p. 347).

Overview of market

The debt finance market is very tough. To reiterate, the banks' exposure in the property sector peaked in 1991 at over £40 billion; this represents more than 8% of the total exposure of the banks, the highest since 1973–4. Bank lending problems are not just confined to the property sector and it is this fact that makes financing arrangement very difficult at the present time. There are major problems with retailers, leisure operators, construction and manufacturing industries, and banking itself. This makes it difficult for banks to lend at all without an improvement in economic conditions. There is a major problem to do with refinancing debt. The debt outstanding may exceed the value of the property; banks have the option of taking equity in the project or foreclosing on the loans and realising the property asset.

There are two important aspects of the dire problems of the debt market, in that, firstly, the banks need to lend money to make money and more so now. A bank which loses £1000 may need to lend £50 000 for 1 year to make up that loss. The banks have written off some £5 billion in the last couple of years and thus need substantial activity. Also, as finance becomes more difficult to obtain, so the importance of intermediaries grows as they provide the contacts.

Sources of debt finance

- High street clearing banks
- Foreign banks
- Building societies

7.2 CORPORATE VERSUS PROJECT-BASED DEBT

Debt finance can be project-specific or generally tied to the assets of the borrower. Project-specific and asset-based funding and the distinction between the two have already been considered. The principle of asset-based debt finance is that the borrower borrows a sum of money against a company's assets in return for which the company undertakes to make a 'bond' to pay interest on the loan until the principal is redeemed. The difference between a corporate bond issue and traditional bank finance is that borrowers are free to use the loans however they see fit and the loans are thus not project-specific.

Types of debt finance

Project-specific:

- project finance,
- mortgages,
- long-term loans,
- convertible loans.

Corporate finance:

- commercial paper,
- multi-option facility,
- debentures,
- loan stock,
- bond,
- deep-discounted bonds,
- junk bonds,
- euromarket.

The types of debt used can be seen from research carried out by Savills, as shown in Figure 6.2 in the previous chapter.

Overdrafts

An overdraft occurs when a customer of a bank draws an account into negative balance. Company overdrafts may be for any size, provided that the bank is satisfied by the asset backing and the credit risk of the company involved. The main disadvantage of an overdraft facility is that repayment may be called for without the bank giving any length of notice and could therefore come at any time, when the liquid reserves of the lender are very low, for instance.

Bank loans, syndicated loans and term loans

Since 1986 bank lending to property companies has risen dramatically, and sophisticated lenders have enabled property companies to reduce the cost and risk associated with interest rate and exchange rate fluctuations. Syndicated loans have returned to prominence, this means the loans are syndicated or spread around a group of banks so that the risk of the loan is also spread. Term loans provide a company with a facility to draw down a certain amount of borrowing from a single bank or a syndicate; the rate and timetable of the drawing down can be previously agreed. Additional charges may be made if the timetable is not adhered to or if the facility is not taken up. Term loans will specify the dates and manner by which the loan is to be repaid. They can also carry an option to convert into a limited-recourse loan where, for instance, the funds are for a project which will produce income soon after completion. Interest rates may fall once the property has been pre-let. Term loans cannot be called in before the pre-agreed date for repayment, unlike overdrafts. In their 1989 survey, Savills found most term loans were for less than £100m, although loans up to £300m were not uncommon. Maturities were between 1 and 7 years, but the 2–5 year range was most common (Savills 1989, p. 13).

Debt to equity swaps

Debt to equity swaps increase liquidity in the market and have been tried on a few occasions recently. Property companies such as Imry and Randsworth are now effectively controlled by their banks. Much of the debt outstanding in 1993 might be considered *de facto* equity because the loans will not be serviced and the choice would then be between the banks taking equity and foreclosure (DTZ Debenham Thorpe 1993, p. 30).

7.3 LONG-TERM LOANS

The main types of debt finance available at the moment which relate to long-term finance are:

• commercial mortgages,

- mortgage debenture issues,
- equity participation or convertible mortgages,
- multi-option facilities,
- deep-discounted bonds.

These types of loan are summarised below.

Commercial mortgages

Interest is paid currently or capitalised. The principal is either amortised over the term of the loan or capitalised. The interest rate can be fixed or variable and other capital market instruments can be used for the management of the interest rates:

- caps prevent interest rises over a certain rate;
- floors prevent interest rates falling below a certain level;
- collars restrict the movement of rates between the cap and floor level.

By minimising interest rate fluctuations you reduce risk and more accurately determine the cost of finance. The length of the loan varies but for banks is usually a maximum of 5 years; insurance companies and building societies may lend up to 25 years.

Mortgage debenture issues

This is a traditional way of raising corporate finance. The loan is raised against a debenture issue which is secured against the property or other assets. The issue yields either a fixed or index-linked return.

Equity participation or convertible mortgages

This structure allows the lender to share in the uplift in the value of the property for a reduction in the interest rate payable.

Multi-option facilities

In this structure a group of banks agree to provide cash advances at a predetermined margin for a certain period.

Deep-discounted bonds

This is a method of raising long-term finance with a low initial interest rate (Figure 7.1). Interest payments can be stepped to accord with rent reviews and there are tax advantages. Bonds can be placed with institutional investors. They are debentures on which the annual interest payable is less than the market rate.

Cash flow to investor

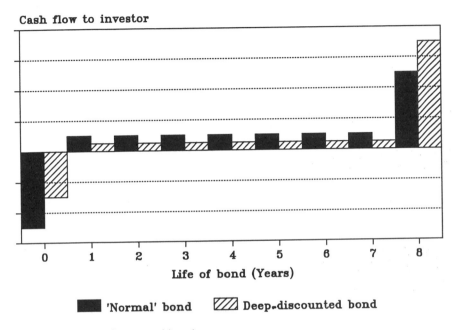

Life of bond (Years)

■ 'Normal' bond   ▨ Deep-discounted bond

Figure 7.1 *Deep-discounted bonds*

In order to make up for the interest shortfall, the bond is issued at a discount to its nominal value (the amount to be paid at the end of the term). The combination of the difference between the amount initially raised and the amount paid at the end of the term together with the interest is equivalent to the market interest that would have been payable.

7.4 COMMERCIAL MORTGAGES

Fixed rate institutional mortgages are advanced generally between 66.6% and 75% of the value of the property. In 1993, the ratio was likely to be at the lower end. The lender will require that the income produced by the investment will service interest costs at the start of the mortgage. The rate of interest attached to the loan is priced off the gross redemption yield of a comparable gilt security. Savills in 1989 quoted this margin as 1.25–2.25%. Interest is normally payable half-yearly in arrears. Institutions are unlikely to consider advances less than £250 000. The maturity dates vary between 5 and 20 years. It is possible to get a forward commitment to a mortgage so that funds can be made available on completion of the project or when a pre-let is in place (Savills 1989, p. 15).

Banks are still attracted by the commercial mortgage market, which is not considered as property lending. In most instances, commercial mortgage applications will be supported by historical accounting information, providing the bank with the comfort of knowing that they do not have to rely on the underlying property asset for repayment. The commercial mortgage market offers the financial services market the largest single growth opportunity because of its very scale and variety.

Example of a commercial mortgage

Status: Owner-occupier

Background: Client was originally a buyout with an institutional investor
                 Is a provincial manufacturer
                 Completed first year end 1991

Requirement: Needed to expand (£4m turnover)
                 Clearing bank would not lend further
                 Clearing bank were owed £600 000 (mortgage), £200 000
                     (overdraft)

Client's assets: 2000 m² factory   £1 000 000
                 Plant and machinery   £ 500 000
                 Debtors   £ 300 000
                 Client wanted another £200 000
                     to refurbish factory

Offer: French bank
                 80% mortgage   £ 800 000
                 80% debtor facility   £ 240 000
                 Loans at 2% above 3 month LIBOR
                 First charge on factory
                 Mortgage debenture

7.5 CONVERTIBLE LOANS AND MORTGAGES

This is a loan, bond or debenture in which the lender of the money has a right to switch the holding into ordinary shares (equity) at a stated date in the future at a fixed price. This price is normally higher than the current share price. The advantage to lenders is that they can partake in decision making and the growth of the company, while for the borrower they can attach a lower interest rate to the loan coupon and the cost of capital is lower, as the conversion rights are seen by the lender as advantageous. If the convertible element is 'detachable', it can be bought and sold separately as a warrant. This is considered under equity finance.

The conventional mortgage is the usual way of debt financing in the long term (more than 10 years). The lender usually takes first charge on the property being mortgaged and thus the position of the borrower is secure. No more that two-thirds of the value is usually lent (the loan-to-value ratio). The problem is that, for the borrower, the rental income from the property may not cover the interest repayments under the mortgage. The borrower is thus deficit financing, because the cash flow from the property may not cover the outflow. The borrower will still want to hold onto the property because in the long run there may be rental growth from rent reviews and at that stage the reviewed rent may amply cover the interest repayments; however, in the short run there is obviously a problem. If the borrower has income from other sources, such as income-producing assets which are not indebted, then this could make up the shortfall; if there is no additional income, then the borrower will need to roll up the interest deficit. The borrower may not wish to do this and this was unpopular with lenders in the 1990s. A possible solution to the problems may be a convertible mortgage. The convertible mortgage may be secured on one or more buildings. A lower interest rate is charged in return for participation in the equity of the building or in the rents received.

7.6 CORPORATE DEBT

Replacement of institutional funding by debt

A new system of debt funding has been developed to replace the traditional approach. The emphasis is on limited-recourse and off-balance-sheet funding. The importance is on the property being developed being the principal source of repayment, as opposed to the traditional position in the past, where the loan has been to a developer, which is then secured on a property.

The basis of the loan arrangement is that the bank will agree a loan-to-value ratio on which it will lend. Typically this may be 65–70%. It then undertakes to the borrower that it would only seek repayment from the refinancing or sale of the development and not from the borrower. The bank would expect two types of contribution from the borrower:

(i) An amount of equity from the developer, probably in the region of 10–20%, being the difference between the loan amount and the anticipated total cost of completing the project.

(ii) Payment in respect of any cost overruns not budgeted for.

Thus, the loan to the bank reflects perhaps 80% loan to cost but 65–70% loan to value. The essential point is therefore that the bank will lend the main element of development costs without recourse to the developer but commit the developer, or a third party if the developer is not strong enough, and requires a guarantor to contribute all the other costs (see Figure 7.2).

Figure 7.2 *Finance structure. Example of a project with a value of £10m, with a bank funding 70% of the value. Source: Wolfe 1988, p. 86*

Shorter-term corporate finance

Floating rate

LIBOR rate has a different rate for 3 months, 6 months and 1 year. The finance house base rate is the average of 3 month LIBOR and is reviewed every 6 weeks. The building society base rate is another measure.

Fixed price money

This is usually obtained from insurance companies and is priced off gilts. This can also be obtained from SWAP markets in the form of mortgages.

Mortgages

These can be interest-only with a bullet repayment or repayment of capital and interest. They can also be on the basis of part repayment and part interest only, leaving an amount payable at the end, known as a 'balloon'. The interest can be fixed or variable and can be deferred.

Revolving credit facility

This is mainly available for larger companies and is generally secured on assets. The minimum size is of approximately £30m. This is an ideal form of finance for many property developers and traders.

A line of credit

Large companies can borrow money from a bank within certain parameters, i.e. if income covers interest or the loan is less than 65% of value, etc.

Syndicated loans

Where large sums are involved, it is common for such loans to be spread among a syndicate of banks where one bank is taking the lead. Syndicated property loans have become increasingly frequent with banks keen to share both the risks and the rewards involved in large-scale property development.

Tender panel facility

A tender panel is a method of raising short-term floating rate finance as a long-term facility with a fixed interest margin. At present it is only available to blue chip quoted companies. What makes it different from other forms of finance is that although the maximum interest margin over the money rate is fixed, say 1% over LIBOR, the actual rate paid by the borrower may be less than the maximum. The banks underwriting the transaction guarantee the borrower that it will not have to pay more than the fixed margin but the actual cost of funds will be determined by the banks participating in the tender panel who bid for the opportunity to lend money to the company. Money is usually borrowed over a 3–6 month period, and should the tender panel fail to rise the required amount at the maximum margin or cheaper, the underwriting banks make up the shortfall to the maximum margin. At the end of each period the exercise is repeated until the term of the facility expires. This is discussed further in Section 7.8.

Equity kicker or earn out

This is a facility where a profit share or agreed figure is paid at the end of the facility in payment for a reduction in the effective rate of interest.

Why developers use debt

They are able to take all the rental growth over the development period. There is greater flexibility, greater speed, greater control. Especially used when the development product is not prime.

7.7 COMMERCIAL PAPER

Commercial paper is a form of IOU note. The issuer sells the paper to investors who are looking for a short-term investment. Bank lending has traditionally provided short-term finance but commercial paper is a means of tapping the money markets direct. Paper is issued in sterling or in dollars. There is currently a lack of investor confidence in the market and prospective borrowers need to have good-quality rated names. Security markets have virtually been untapped by UK property names in the period to 1991; better sterling pricing was achieved by issuing in US dollars and swapping to sterling (Beveridge 1991, p. 14). The sterling commercial paper market (Sterling CP) was launched in April 1986 to provide an alternative method for companies to raise short-term finance, which was previously restricted to bills of exchange, syndicated loans, advances and overdrafts (Savills 1989, p. 16). Commercial paper was initially restricted to use by large stock market listed companies but restrictions were relaxed in the 1989 Budget (Brett 1990, p. 152) and medium-sized companies were allowed to join the market.

Commercial paper does not bear interest but is sold at a discount rather like the sale of gilts by the Government. For example, £95 will purchase, say, £100 nominal value of commercial paper; thus, £100 will be repaid in 3 months. Thus, the interest rate is £5 ÷ £95 for 3 months. If the money is then reinvested, the annual interest rate can be calculated on the basis of a quarterly reinvestment of funds, i.e.

$$\left(1+\frac{i}{4}\right)^4 - 1,$$

where $i/4$ is the quarterly interest rate. The interest rate is quoted relative to the LIBOR rate.

The sterling CP market suffers from competition from the Bank of England eligible bill market. There is no secondary market for the paper; sterling CP issuers prefer the issues to be placed with investors to be held to maturity. Financial institutions, banks and other companies invest in commercial paper, usually for a maximum period of 1 year, although after the 1989 Budget this could be a maximum of 5 years. The average period of a commercial paper loan is 40 days but the minimum is 7 days. A commercial paper programme can be set up which effectively lengthens the life of the loan. The programme effectively makes commercial paper into a medium-term source of finance because, as one issue of commercial paper falls due for repayment, so there is a further issue and thus a rolling programme of issues is established.

To get into the money market, a bank will need to set up a programme for the company involved. The maximum amount of paper that the company may have outstanding at any one time is £50 million. The banks will act as intermediaries between the issuers and potential investors. The issuer will also need an agent to deal with the redemption of the paper and the banks provide this function. The commercial paper market is not for small issues or investors; the minimum denomination for sterling commercial paper is £100 000.

Commercial paper is unsecured and thus the financial standing of the issuer is very important. The original market was restricted to larger known firms, but now there are less familiar names in the market. The issuer therefore looks for an independent credit assessment for the paper being issued. Rating services can be provided by Moodys or Standard and Poors (see Section 7.11). These credit ratings assist investors who do not know the market in assessing the risk.

The procedure for issuing commercial paper is as follows (Brett 1990, pp. 154–6):

(i)   The bank that is arranging the issue will prepare an information memorandum to be circulated among investors. Some companies will have a constant amount outstanding in the commercial paper market; other companies will become involved in the market when rates become competitive. The traditional approach to this form of financing is through bills of exchange and acceptances; these are used to finance trade transactions and thus are not applicable to property. However, bills of exchange provide the main competition for commercial paper.

(ii) If conditions in the commercial paper market are unattractive for future issues at the time of redemption of the paper, then smaller borrowers may have a fallback facility for the renewal of their debt by a line of credit or a multiple-option facility (MOF) as a committed facility. A committed facility is where a group of banks have arranged to make a specified amount of funds available at a pre-arranged rate over LIBOR if the borrower cannot raise the finance more cheaply elsewhere. A MOF frequently provides backing for a commercial paper programme.

(iii) The costs of the programme set out in (i) and (ii) are £5000–£10 000 to set up. The borrowed money is spread in terms of pricing from LIBID (the lower rate to LIBOR at which banks are prepared to borrow rather than lend) to 12–13 basis points over LIBOR for small property companies, with medium-sized companies somewhere in between.

Very large property companies are not confined to borrowing in the sterling commercial paper market: there is a larger and longer-established domestic commercial paper market in the USA for those wanting funds in dollars or who are prepared to borrow in dollars and swap into sterling. This can provide cheap finance but an appropriate credit rating will be required for the borrower and a fallback facility for the borrower will be essential. There is also a euro-commercial paper market tapped by some larger property companies. This euro-commercial paper market (ECP or Euro CP) was started in 1983. There is a small secondary market. Swaps play an important part in the ECP market (Savills 1989, p. 17).

7.8 MULTIPLE-OPTION FACILITY (MOF)

The newer financing techniques are usually applied initially to the larger corporate borrower. The multiple-option facility (MOF) is a flexible method of tapping the money markets for short-term funds. As with commercial paper, money is borrowed for relatively short periods but can be rolled over to provide the equivalent of a medium-term loan. As one 3 month loan falls due, another is taken out to replace it. It is possible to arrange a multiple-option facility in excess of £25m, and large and medium-sized property companies have taken advantage of this.

The MOF should provide cheaper funds because it encourages banks to compete to provide the finance. The MOF can take a number of different guises. The most common form is in two parts, a guaranteed or committed facility, which ensures that the company will get its money when it needs it. Also, there is an uncommitted facility which may allow a company to borrow at more advantageous terms.

If a company requires an MOF, it will need to go through several stages. It will need to involve a bank to set up the facility. If the MOF is for £50m, then this means that the maximum outstanding at any one time is £50m. The arranging bank talks to other banks, who put together a syndicate of banks who agree that jointly they will provide up to the amount (£50m) required if called on to do so. The interest rate is agreed at this point – not as an absolute amount but as a margin over LIBOR. The agreed margin might be, say, 15 basis points or 0.15% over LIBOR. The borrowing costs will go up and down with the LIBOR rate but the maximum percentage margin over LIBOR remains constant. Note that this rate represents the maximum amount, but is not the real rate. The second stage of the MOF is for the arranging bank to put together a tender panel; the bank will arrange to add some additional banks to the original syndicate that agreed the committed facility. When the company wants to borrow, the tender banks are invited to bid to provide the finance. Those offering the cheapest rates will make the loans. If the banks in the tender panel do not bid the amount, the company will need to draw down funds under the committed facility instead. Either way it is sure of getting its finance.

The advantage of the system is, in theory, the competitive element of the tender panel. Banks which have a lot of money available can bid to put up the cash required. Others who have limited funds may not wish to bid. This part of the facility is thus uncommitted; the cost of the uncommitted funds will normally be lower than for the committed facility, because the tender panel banks are not entering into an undertaking to supply funds. The limit on the uncommitted facility may be the same as the committed. Sometimes, the uncommitted facility will be larger, though a company may organise a committed facility of £50m and an uncommitted facility of £100m. This means in real terms that although the maximum it can borrow is £100m, it is not guaranteed more than £50m. Recently, the tender panel mechanism has become less effective as the banks have been more aggressive on the profitability of such transactions. In these cases, the borrower has been thrown back on the committed facility. The multiple option in the facility refers to the fact that the company is able to raise its funds in more than one form. It can thus pick the loan which suits its requirement at the most reasonable price. The facility may also include bills of exchange facilities, i.e. acceptance credits. Bills of exchange are short-term IOUs, based on trade transactions and thus not available to property investors, but there may be facilities to offer the forms of short-term IOUs and raise loans in other currencies. The commercial paper programme may be included in the MOF or backed by a MOF (a committed facility).

To calculate the cost of an MOF, you need to allow for fees as well as the interest rate margin on funds borrowed. There are arrangement fees for the bank for setting up the committed facility and this may be an annual rate over the life of the MOF. There is an annual indemnity fee for the banks which provide the committed facility. This ensures that the funds will be available when required. The general hope of the borrower is that the tender panel will provide finance at a cheaper rate and thus will not need to draw heavily on the committed facility. There is thus a utilisation fee if the company does not draw down more than a contracted percentage of the committed facility, say 50%. If a company's credit rating falls, then the tender banks will not provide funds and the company will need to rely on the banks underwriting the committed facility (Brett 1990, p. 160).

Example of a multi-option facility (Gibbs 1987, p. 349)

Company:	Wates City of London
Facility:	£56m
Guaranteed ceiling:	LIBOR + 30 basis points
No of banks in tender panel:	19
Bids:	over 3–6 months, lowest bidder gets business

If the tender panel fails to raise the required amount at the maximum margin or cheaper, the underwriting banks make up the shortfall beyond the maximum margin. This exercise is repeated until the facility expires.

The advantages to the borrower are:

- fine pricing,
- loan can be unsecured,
- option to receive cash or notes (commercial paper),
- can be in currency (cash) or in promissory notes ($US).

An underwriting fee and arranging fee must be paid. The MOF offers a variety of financing options in one package, including facilities such as commercial paper and multi-currency arrangements. The loan size of MOFs in the 1989 Savills survey was between £50m and £300m, with an average of £120m. Maturity dates were 2–10 years, with 7 years the most popular (Savills 1989, p. 14).

7.9 LOAN STOCK

Loan stock is the same as a standard debenture issue. If the loan stock is unsecured, the lender has no guaranteed security other than the previous track record of the borrower. Thus, the coupon (return) is very high but it does allow smaller developers to raise non-project-specific finance. Also, loan stock can have a call option giving the borrower the right to repurchase the stock before maturity. The use of options in loan stock is evidenced by convertible loan stock, which gives the holder a combination of a straight loan arrangement or bond combined with a call option. On exercising the option, the holder exchanges the loan for a fixed number of shares in the borrowing company.

7.10 DEBENTURES

A debenture is a tradeable 'IOU' similar to gilt-edged securities (gilts) issued by the Government. There is a different terminology in the UK and the US. US debentures are unsecured borrowing but in the UK the borrowing is secured on the assets of the company. This thus differs from similar unsecured loan stock or bonds issued in the euromarket, which is generally unsecured. The mortgage debenture is the longest-term and most traditional way of raising finance by a security issue (Brett 1990, p. 173).

A debenture is the sealed bond of a corporation or company acknowledging a sum on which interest is due until the interest is repaid. A debenture is thus the description of a financial instrument, while debenture stock is the description of a debt or sum secured by an instrument. The lender holding a debenture has by right a prior charge on the developer's corporate assets, although in practice property company debentures are typically secured on specific assets. Properties up to 150% of the value of the loan are put up as security in the event of default. Interest on the loan is normally paid half-yearly and independent trustees are often employed to look after the debenture holders' interests.

A company can also issue debentures as convertible securities (secured or unsecured) containing an option entitling the holder to convert the debt at specific times to ordinary or preference shares at a prearranged rate. These can be issued at a low rate of interest because of the conversion rights. Debentures may also be issued with subscription warrants attached, which are the options to acquire ordinary shares in the company (Savills 1989, p. 15).

Debentures are advantageous to borrowers because:

(i) They can do what they want to with the money.
(ii) The interest paid is a charge against profits before tax.
(iii) Debentures can be a contract between single investors and the company or by a public issue or placing on the stock market. Private arrangements are more frequent.

Debentures are advantageous to lenders because:

(i) They are able to obtain a marginally higher rate of interest than for the equivalent gilt-edged stock.
(ii) Debentures are legitimate tradeable securities and therefore can subsequently be bought and sold at varying prices dependent on the prevailing market cost of capital.
(iii) Debentures are sometimes accompanied by rights of subscription or part conversion (see convertibles).

Issues relating to the Insolvency Act 1986 have already been considered in Section 4.4. This Act restricts the Trustee's powers of enforcing the security. Most large debenture issues are listed on the Stock Exchange and can be traded in the same way as Government stocks. Smaller issues are placed with a limited range of investors; this is called a private sale. Because a debenture is a debt security rather than equity, issuers are under no obligation to offer new issues to existing investors. In the domestic market, issues are available in the registered form, i.e. the owners are registered with the company who knows who owns the stock. In the euro-market, the stock is likely to be in bearer form, so the stock certificate is the proof of ownership. Debentures may be issued in a part-paid form, so that the price is paid in instalments over a period of time, as with some share issues.

7.11 DEEP-DISCOUNTED BONDS AND JUNK BONDS

A 'bond' is basically another term for a debenture or secured long-term loan. These are long-term borrowing facilities with the interest either rolled up or phased at a substantially lower rate than the market would expect (i.e. lower than the gilt rate, which is the rate on Government securities which is risk-free). The stepping up of the interest rate (coupon) can correspond to actual rent reviews. Thus, these bonds pay less as a coupon/ interest, but make up for it by paying a higher redemption figure. A zero coupon bond, for instance, pays no interest but the redemption figure should be sufficient to allow for this, so that, when interest is analysed over the period to redemption together with the redemption sum, a realistic yield will be obtained. In order to borrow on a deep-discounted bond, a company will need to provide a strong covenant. This facility has been used so far by owner-occupiers seeking to develop property and for whom property is not their main business. An example of this approach was the issue by Safeway Ltd (Gibbs 1987, p. 348).

Safeway Limited deep-discounted bond issue

Issue:	£100m
Date:	1986
Purpose:	Property expansion programme for owner occupation.
Redemption:	20 years with a defined 5 yearly uplift pattern.

The attraction of the deep-discounted bond is that it compensates for the reverse yield gap; money can be raised at low rates comparable to initial yields on a prime property. The phased uplifts are usually structured to ensure that the effective equated yield enjoys a clear margin over the prevalent gross redemption yields on gilts. These are tradeable instruments.

Example of a deep-discount bond refinancing

A joint venture company has successfully developed and let a property but has failed to sell it. How can it realise some cash and hold on to the property until the investment market recovers without substantial commitments to interest shortfall?

Solution

Existing income (p.a.)	£ 3 800 000
ERV (p.a.)	£ 4 750 000
Value	£48 000 000
Maximum loan at maturity	£43 200 000
Reviews through loan period	5 years
Interest rate	13.5% p.a. fixed
Initial drawdown (approximately)	£37 000 000

Notes: After the initial drawdown, the balance of the loan will be used to meet the interest income shortfall for the 5 year loan period. The estimates for rent passing during the period are based on appraised ERV, assuming no growth. The bank benefits from a CMI from an insurance syndicate on the first £7.2m of the loan – the additional cost to the borrower of £430 000 is paid on first drawdown. (Source: Clarke 1990, p. 438)

Deep-discount, zero coupon and stepped bonds are referred to generally as DDBs. The main characteristics can be summarised as follows:

(i)   The debt may be secured or unsecured.
(ii)   The value at redemption should exceed that on issue.
(iii) The interest rate is defined by reference to a coupon and this is usually priced off a floating rate LIBOR and the margin is known.
(iv)   The repayment date is a fixed, one-off date where the principal sum or nominal value needs to be repaid.
(v)   The discount may be likened to a rolling-up of interest and this has a compounding effect, creating a higher effective rate than the coupon, which is charged on the outstanding value of the instrument.
(vi)   The bond has a discount to nominal value at the time of issue.
(vii) A coupon is paid on an annual or some other periodic basis.

ZCBs (zero coupon bonds) are the same as deep-discount bonds except that the discount is greater and there is no coupon paid out. All interest is effectively in the discount, which grows until the date of redemption, when it is paid out. Stepped coupon bonds (SCBs) have a coupon which rises at fixed intervals by fixed amounts during its life. There can be variations, such as a zero coupon bond for 3 years, then a fixed coupon (see the example in Figure 7.3) (Shayle 1991, pp. 11–12).

Junk bonds

Junk bonds are not very relevant to property funding at the present time but they do provide a case study in the use of derivatives. They experienced a period of popularity, then notoriety in the US. They are linked to very risky investments and are highly geared and unsecured but may offer a high reward commensurate with the risk taken. They have been issued as a defence against takeovers in some instances by companies.

Term to maturity 9 years Initial roll up period 3 years
Coupon 10% Coupon payable/roll up on a
Amount on issue £2.0m semi-annual basis

Value at the end of year 3: £2,680,200*
Coupon payable:
year 3.5 = £134,010} Annual payment £268,020
year 4.0 = £134,010} Annual equivalent rate 13.4%

*Found by using the formula: $p(1+r)^n$
where p = issue price,
r = coupon rate,
n = number of periods
to be rolled up

£m

3 — Redemption value

Discount 25.4%

2 – – – – – – – – – – – – –

Issue price 74.6%

1

2   4   6   8   10 Years

Figure 7.3 *Example of a complex deep-discount bond. Source: Shayle 1991, p. 12*

The growth in junk bond financing can better be explained by the activities of one man than by a number of economic factors. While a graduate student in the 1970s, Michael Milkin observed a large difference between the return on high-yield bonds and the return on safer bonds. Believing that this difference was greater than what the extra default risk would justify, he concluded that institutional investors would benefit from purchases of junk bonds. His later employment on Wall Street, at Drexel Burnham Lambert, allowed him to develop the junk bond market. Milkin's salesmanship simultaneously increased the demand for junk bonds among institutional investors and the supply of junk bonds among corporations. Corporations were particularly impressed with Drexel's vast network of institutional clients, allowing capital to be raised quickly. However, with the demise of the junk bond market and with Michael Milkin's conviction on securities fraud, Drexel found it necessary to declare bankruptcy.

Junk bonds were important in their use to finance mergers and other corporate restructuring. Whereas a firm can only issue a small amount of high-grade debt, the same firm can issue much more debt if low-grade financing is allowed as well. Therefore, the use of junk bonds lets acquirers effect takeovers that they could not do with only traditional bond-financing techniques (Ross et al. 1993, pp. 600–1).

Bond ratings

In American texts the junk bond is defined as a speculative grade bond rated Ba or lower by Moody's or BB or lower by Standard & Poor's or an unrated bond. The junk bond is also referred to as a high-yield or low-grade bond. The bond ratings are very important to the status of an issue and thus the amount that can be raised. Firms in the US frequently pay to have their debt rated and the two leading bond rating services, as mentioned above, are Moody's Investor Service and Standard & Poor's. The debt rating will depend on:

(i)   the likelihood that the firm will default;
(ii) the protection afforded by the loan contract in the event of default.

Bond ratings are important because bonds with lower ratings tend to have higher interest costs. In the 1980s in the US, a growing part of corporate borrowing has taken the form of low-grade bonds (high-yield or junk bonds, see Table 7.1). Bond ratings are set out in Table 7.2 on p. 150.

Table 7.1 *Growth in junk bonds in US 1985–91*

Year	Par value of bonds outstanding ($billion)
1985	59
1986	93
1987	137
1988	159
1989	201
1990	210
1991	209

Source: Ross *et al.* 1993, p.600.

7.12   EUROMARKET LENDING

Larger companies can raise long-term unsecured loans in the international market. The international market or euromarket is a market of 'stateless' money, i.e. money held outside its country of origin. For instance, deposits of US dollars in a German bank are eurodollars; pounds sterling held in Holland are eurosterling. The market in eurocurrencies is not subject to the controls of any one domestic financial authority. London is the main centre for eurocurrency dealing but British banks are not the main players in the market, which is dominated by American and Japanese banks. There is no central marketplace, deals are arranged over the telephone and funds can be borrowed in most of the world's currencies The eurocurrency markets provide a parallel for most of the products and facilities available in the domestic financial market. Thus, money can be borrowed very short term called euro-commercial paper, and very long term like a 20 year euro-bond. The borrowing can be in the form of bank loans as well as security issues. There is a fundamental difference between the euromarket and the domestic market:

(i) Euro-borrowing is generally unsecured and thus, without security, the reputation and standing of the borrower is all-important. Thus, major internationally known corporations have no trouble in tapping the market but it is not accessible to smaller companies known only in their domestic markets.

(ii) Domestically, property investment companies have always been regarded as exceptionally secure because of the strength of their assets. In the euromarkets, investors are looking more at the cash flow and are less familiar with the structure of the British property company, which may not be rated so highly; thus, it will normally be the large companies that tap the euromarkets.

(iii) With changes in the rules for the issue of domestic sterling bond, the distinctions between domestic and euromarkets have largely broken down for sterling issues. The euromarket stands more for a issuing and trading technique than for a totally separate market. Most British banks and security houses will deal almost interchangeably in domestic and euro-issues of sterling bonds. Eurobonds are normally listed on a stock exchange, probably London or the lightly regulated Luxembourg market; most dealing is between traders rather than through exchanges.

The euromarket is not restricted to fixed interest money or the long term: bonds can be issued with a life of just a few years or, instead of a fixed interest bond, a company might issue a floating rate note (FRN) where the interest payment changes with a movement in a benchmark interest rate, usually LIBOR. Traditionally eurobonds in sterling denominations have not done well in the market but it has been possible to issue long-dated sterling eurobonds at maturities of 15/20 years and this has been done over the life of the market. The bonds are usually at a fixed rate, and if sterling is not popular at the time of issue, it is possible to issue in an alternative currency and then swap to sterling subsequently. In 1990 MEPC issued two separate Luxembourg franc issues and one euro-yen issue and subsequently both swapped into sterling at satisfactory levels. The issue of the bond can thus be linked to a swap subsequently (Beveridge 1991, p. 14).

Table 7.2 *Bond ratings*

Bond rating	Standard & Poors	Moody's
Very high quality	AAA AA	Aaa Aa
High quality	A BBB	A Baa
Speculative	BB B	Ba B
Very poor	CCC CC C D	Caa Ca C D

Junk bonds are speculative grade or below (Ross *et al.* p.599).

An example of a eurobond issue was the £100m issue by Hammerson, a major property company, in 1989. The bond was issued at £99.888 for £100 nominal stock at a 10.75% coupon. The bond was repayable in 2013. The bond was issued in denominations of £10 000 and £100 000 bearer bonds, so the owners were not registered with the company. A feature of the bonds was that UK income tax on interest paid was not deducted at source (Brett 1990, p. 189).

7.13 SECURITISATION OF DEBT

The securitisation of property loans (for a wider analysis and understanding of securitisation, see Chapter 12) by banks or their conversion into mortgage-backed bonds is a solution to the problems of loan turnover. Lenders can raise new funds by the sale of these financial assets, which can then bolster lending capacity. There is a problem here which relates to the risk of default by the borrowers, since, if the seller of the securitised debt continues to provide a guarantee or security of the debt, then that debt may still need to be shown in the bank's accounts (DTZ Debenham Thorpe 1993, p. 29). Another problem is that buyers of secondary debt can demand a high level of discount against the original value of the loan. Despite these difficulties, the secondary debt market has developed into a million-dollar industry in the US; Bank of America and First Chicago disposed of $3bn of real estate loans recently.

Recent moves by the Bank of England suggest a growing support for innovations in trading in debt, including debt-for-equity swaps, property-backed bonds and securitisation. The object is to break the log-jam in property loans and inject liquidity. The traditional financing approach of funding the development during the development period with loans that could be refinanced on completion and letting has meant that when these short-term loans become repayable, in many cases the level of debt outstanding exceeds the value of the property. The borrower at this point would normally be required to put further equity in, to take out the debt. As this is not possible in the present market, banks are faced with the choice of taking an equity stake in the project or foreclosing the loan, realising the property asset and making provisions to cover the loss incurred. As has been said earlier, much of the debt currently outstanding can be considered already as *de facto* equity (Scott 1992, p. 349).

REFERENCES

Barter, S L (1988) 'Introduction', in S L Barter (ed.), *Real Estate Finance*, Butterworths, London.

Beveridge, J A (1991) 'New Methods of Financing', in P Venmore-Rowland, P Brandon and T Mole (eds), *Investment, Procurement and Performance in Construction*, RICS, London.

Brett, M (1990) 'Property and Money', Estates Gazette, London.

Brett, M (1991) 'Property and Money: Mortgages which Convert into Property', *Estates Gazette*, 17 August.

Clarke, R J (1990) 'Refinancing', *Journal of Property Finance*, vol. 1, no. 3, pp. 435–9.

DTZ Debenham Thorpe (1993) *Money into Property*, DTZ Debenham Thorpe, London, August.

Gibbs, R (1987) 'Raising Finance for New Development', *Journal of Valuation*, vol. 5, no. 4, pp. 343–53.

Journal of Valuation (1989) 'Market Data', *Journal of Valuation*, vol. 8, no. 1, pp. 87–9.

Ross, S A, Westerfield, R W and Jaffe, J F (1993) *Corporate Finance*, Irwin, Boston.

Savills (1989) *Financing Property 1989*, Savills, London.

Scott, I P (1992) 'Debt, Liquidity and Secondary Trading in Property Debt', *Journal of Property Finance*, vol. 3, no. 3, pp. 347–55.

Shayle, A (1991) 'The Use of Deep Discount and Zero Coupon Bonds in the UK Property Market', *Journal of Property Finance*, vol. 2, no. 1, pp. 11–17.

Wolfe, R (1988) 'Debt Finance', in S L Barter (ed.), *Real Estate Finance*, Butterworths, London.

8 Equity Finance

8.1 TYPES OF EQUITY FINANCE

An equity investment is a financial interest in an economic venture where the return to the investor is residual in character and entirely dependent upon the financial profitability of the venture. The returns to equity are thus variable, volatile and insecure. The distinction between debt and equity is that in comparison debt is based on borrowing. The borrower offers the lender a guaranteed money return, expressed in fixed terms, usually over a finite period. The investment return is not related to the financial success of the company and is usually secured. Apart from the risk of default by the borrower, the investment return is therefore quite precisely predictable in money terms and is comparatively secure.

Up until 1991 property development expanded on the back of bank finance. This had grown to £37 billion or with committed loans around £40 billion; now new debt is shrinking. At the same time the amount of new equity into property has been around £2–3 billion per annum. The sources of equity have relied on institutional purchasing of building; in the past few years this has mainly been from overseas, institutional take-up of debt, mainly debentures and eurobonds, and small amounts of directly subscribed capital. At this rate it will take many years to replace the bank debt outstanding and for many years banks will be committed to 'rolling over' their current and outstanding positions. UK property is financed too much by debt and has been starved of equity for many years (Beveridge 1991, p. 13).

8.2 SOURCES OF EQUITY

In the market, the main sources of equity are:

(i) long-term institutions (pension funds and insurance companies);
(ii) property companies;
(iii) private investors;
(iv) others.

Institutions and property companies are examined elsewhere This chapter will concentrate on private investors and others, who can be owner-occupiers, overseas investors and construction companies.

Private investors are excluded from participation in many areas of the property market because of the large sums involved in purchase and transaction costs. Some funds have been established for groups of investors with a single specific purpose. Authorised unit trusts are one means of access and are discussed later. In the lower end of the market with high-yielding secondary and tertiary property, individuals do play a part; this is a significant sector. However, generally the role of the private investor in the property market in the UK is smaller than elsewhere.

Other sources of finance may be owner-occupiers. Commercial owner-occupiers are in operation to earn a profit and therefore will compare rental payments with the opportunities for owner-occupation. The benefits of purchase mean that the asset base of the company is extended and if the cash flows have been worked out correctly, there may be net savings in occupation costs. However, if the company has to borrow to purchase the property, the debt will need to be shown on the balance sheet. In the 1960s and 1970s, there were a number of sale and leasebacks where owners disposed of their freehold interests in land and took on occupational leases. There appears to be a reversal of this in recent years because of the disadvantages of the standard institutional lease. These disadvantages are:

(i) The length of lease and difficulties of assignments; privity of contract previously meant liability for the full term whether assignment takes place or not.

(ii) Because of regular rent reviews which may have been upward only, no equity can be built up in the property asset.

(iii) Lease terms, besides the rent review terms and length of lease, can be onerous in terms of repairing, use and other obligations, and damaging to the cash flow (Mallinson 1988, p. 42).

Construction companies may also provide equity. This is likely to be short-term finance and may be provided as a package to the developer to ensure a building contract. Some construction companies will participate over a longer period as partners or joint venturers, but these interests are usually held in property company subsidiaries.

Overseas purchasers are generally institutions, property companies or construction companies; they tend to deal in London and are cautious small players often seeking partnerships with UK developers. The scale of overseas investment was estimated at £1.5–£2 billion for 1993; this is down from £3 billion in 1989/90. The overseas investment is concentrated in central London. German investors have led the market with Middle Eastern and Asian investors following (DTZ Debenham Thorpe 1993, p. 3). Overseas investment is shown in Figure 8.1.

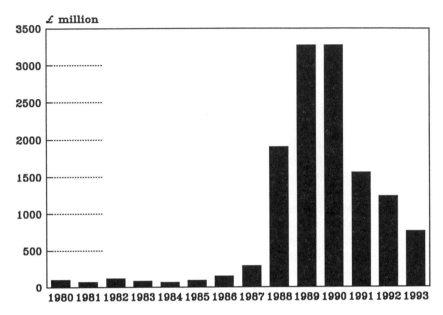

1993 first 2 quarters (Evans 1993, p 81)

Figure 8.1 *Overseas direct investment in UK property 1980–93 (1993, first two quarters only) (Evans 1993, p. 81)*

8.3 EQUITY IN PROJECT-BASED FUNDING

If equity finance is project-specific, it can take a number of forms, e.g.:

(i)   Finance from the developer's own cash and resources.

(ii) Partnership funds, where another party joins in to share the risks and rewards of the enterprise.

(iii) Financiers providing equity against which collateral or debt can be raised. The money is thus not used in the development nor is a joint company formed; a form of guarantee is provided.

(iv) Forward funding by an institution; the institution may meet the costs of development, including the acquisition costs of the site, construction fees, interest and letting fees. The institution may provide these monies at a lower interest rate but may require purchase of the completed development at a lower rate.

8.4 EQUITY IN CORPORATE FUNDING

The types of equity share and issues have been dealt with elsewhere. This section will concentrate on an overview. If the maximum debt gearing available to a certain project is 70% of cost or value, whichever is the less, then there is a substantial shortfall to make up with equity. In a development situation the offer from a lender may only be, say, 70% of the site cost plus the prime building cost, which may only perhaps equate to 60% of overall cost. In addition, such a level of funding may assume that a pre-let or pre-sale is in position at the outset. If a lender agrees a 70% loan-to-cost ratio, this may include interest and thus effectively the loan reduces to perhaps 50-60% of cost (Berkley 1991, p. 527).

The balance can be funded in a number of ways. Typically in the present market it may be funded from:

(i)   The lender's own resources.
(ii) Collateral security, but even with this the maximum gearing of, say, 70% applies.
(iii) A commercial mortgage indemnity (CMI) taking the loan-to-value ratio up to 85% (CMIs have been discussed in Chapter 4). This additional 15% cover is often used to service a shortfall on rental income until a review or to purchase a 'cap' to limit the interest charged by the lender to a figure that equates with the rental income.
(iv) Issues of shares if the company is a plc.
(v)   Equity/mezzanine participation finance.

Mezzanine finance is discussed in detail in Section 8.7. This mezzanine finance can come from the supplier of the prime debt but usually is provided by a specialist lender. The loan above the 70% level will attract a higher rate of interest than the prime debt because of the additional risk; alternatively, a single fee may be charged. This mezzanine debt may be used by borrowers to take the loan up to 85% of value where a cap is not available. The return reflects a share in anticipated profits. Some lenders take shares in the borrowing company; others prefer a second charge on the subject property and collateral security ranking behind the prime debt (Berkley 1991, p. 257).

8.5 AUTHORISED PROPERTY UNIT TRUSTS

The use of unit trusts to encourage investment in property has already been discussed as well as the difficulties related to setting up an authorised unit trust. On 15 July 1991, the Securities and Investments Board issued regulations enabling authorised property unit trusts (APUTS) to invest directly in property. Thus, APUTS will allow the investors to enter the commercial property market in exactly the same way as the unit trusts offer investors exposure to shares. Prior to the change in regulations, unit trusts were not permitted to invest directly into property. This meant that unauthorised property unit trusts were only open to exempt funds such as pension funds and charities.

There are tax advantages of investing in an APUT. Corporation tax is paid at the base rate level of 25% on net income instead of the full rate of corporation tax at 33%. A distribution made by an APUT to its unit holders will be treated for tax purposes as dividends. Individual unit holders will receive a tax credit of 25% on those distributions and will only be liable for higher-rate personal tax. Corporate investors who pay corporation tax at the small companies' rate of 25% will also have the whole of their liability to tax arising from APUT covered by the tax credit. An APUT, in addition, is entirely free from capital gains tax arising on the disposal of property. Unit holders will, however, remain subject to any capital gains tax arising from the disposal of their units unless, of course, they are tax exempt. Set against these tax advantages, APUTS will have to comply with many regulations imposed by the Securities and Investment Board (SIB) to protect non-institutional investors from the risks involved in property investment. These problems include the lack of liquidity of property, a unit price based on possible subjective valuations, changes in values and the actual market for the units themselves (Ryland 1991, pp. 163–4; Baring, Houston and Saunders 1991, p. 11).

The regulations are as follows.

Structure

The structure of an APUT is similar to that of existing unit trust schemes with a trustee and a manager. The manager is responsible for the day-to-day management of the scheme, with the trustee and manager owing a fiduciary duty to the unit holders.

Investment characteristics

(i) A fund must attain a value of £5m within 21 days. Thereafter between 20% and 80% of its funds must be invested in property or property-related securities. These investments can be in EU member states and a number of other countries, such as the US and Canada.

(ii) Up to 10% of the portfolio may be invested in unlisted property shares.

(iii) 20–30% may be invested in cash or near cash (Government securities or quoted property company shares).

(iv) It can only invest a maximum of 15% of the value of the fund in any one property. This maximum value may increase to 25% once the property has been included in the portfolio. No more than 20% of the gross rental income may come from the tenant and only 25% of the fund may be invested in vacant or development properties.

(v) APUTS may borrow against properties, up to a maximum of 30% of each property's value or 15% of the whole portfolio.

Valuation

The value of an APUT is strictly controlled with a full independent valuation once a year, carried out by a qualified surveyor in accordance with the Royal Institution of Chartered Surveyor's guidelines. In addition, to keep unit prices current, there will be an 'armchair' valuation at least once a month to review the last full valuation. Any new purchases must not exceed 105% of the valuation.

Redemptions

Units will normally be redeemed within 4 business days after the valuation following the request for redemption. In certain circumstances, a manager may suspend redemption rights for a period up to 28 days subject to trustee approval and the SIB being advised.

Potential

APUTs offer a good opportunity of gaining exposure to the property investment market. By the end of 1991 only two APUTs had been established, as substantial commitment is required from the institution or funder to establish an APUT. The APUT has achieved more acceptance in the market than securitisation vehicles (see Chapter 12), but APUTs are not a direct alternative to these vehicles. APUTs invest in smaller-sized properties which already have a broad market appeal among investing institutions, not large illiquid properties (Sexton and Laxton 1992, p. 468).

8.6 INVESTMENT TRUSTS AND UNIT TRUSTS

Investment trusts are companies which own shares on other companies; they suffer from the problems of discount on net asset value, which are described in the context of property companies in Chapter 10. As an example of a property investment trust, Banque Paribas announced in October 1993 the setting up of a £50m property investment trust on the Stock Exchange. The trust is called the Wigmore Property Trust and will concentrate on the shares of small companies with a market capitalisation of less than £250m. The trust will invest in mainly quoted ordinary shares and focus on investment companies. It may also have up to 20% of its net asset value in special situations, which could mean finance for corporate restructuring and acquisitions (Catalano 1993, p. 52). The Trust is a quoted company and closed-ended, unlike a unit trust. (For an explanation of closed- and open-ended trusts, see Chapter 10, Section 10.1.)

Exempt property unit trusts (PUTs) are designed for non-taxpaying investors such as pension funds and charities. The market in these units is illiquid. They are valued at the underlying net assets value with no discount. Exempt PUTs are open-ended.

APUTs, as discussed in the previous section, are also open-ended; the manager has to be in a position to liquidate part of the trust's investment at any time to redeem units that investors wish to sell. The market price of APUTs is again the net asset value without discount. The experience of Rodamco in Holland has shown the shortcomings of open-ended funds which invest in illiquid assets; this is treated as a brief case study in Box 8.1. There is a liquidity problem with APUTs (Venmore-Rowland 1991, p. 3).

Australian PUTs and US real estate investment trusts (REITs) are closed-ended trusts. The REIT market is a useful comparison for developments in unit trusts and securitisation. The REIT market started in the US in 1960; the laws allowed certain companies (REITs) to own property and mortgages and to pay dividends without prior deduction of corporate taxes. Of the REITs in existence in the US now, 50% are mortgage REITs and 40% are equity REITs (which derive their income from rent); the remainder are hybrids. There were some mistakes in the issues during the period 1985–6 which affected the confidence in the market; now there is better gearing in these companies and management is better trained to deal with investment decisions, especially in the specialist investment areas (Jennings 1993, pp. 14–15).

A property unit trust could be used with securitised property (SPUTs; see Chapter 12 for developments in the area of securitised property).

The Principle

Rodamco was established in 1979 as an open-ended fund. Rodamco forms one of the main investment vehicles within the largest Dutch investment fund management group. To investors, the vehicle appeared a safe and highly liquid exposure to direct property; it attracted the interest of institutional and private investors, who formed, initially at least, 80% of the shareholders. Such companies expand by issuing new shares when demand exceeds supply but as the company stands in the market it also has to repurchase shares when no other buyer can be found. The shares were thus considered a low-risk investment. Stock market transactions took place at prices close to the net asset value of the company and the net asset value was recalculated each day. This situation requires the company to maintain substantial cash balances, but at the same time there was little dilution of assets or earnings per share from share issues; this enabled the company to expand without the need for increasing bank debt to any significant level.

The Reality

The fund grew rapidly by way of share placings in 1980. This expansion led to a series of acquisitions, especially in the UK and US; in 1986 Haselmere Estates were acquired in the UK and Hexalon Real Estate in the USA. In 1988 it mounted a bid for Hammerson but was outbid by Hammerson's major institutional shareholder. The downturn in 1990 in the US and UK markets led to investors selling the Rodamco stock. This was easy for investors to do as the company stood in the market and bought in the shares offered at the daily quoted net asset value price. The company's shares were suspended in September 1990 and the company changed to being 'close-ended', i.e. to having a fixed number of shares in issue. On being relisted, the share price fell sharply (around 20%), prompting additional selling of the stock before settling at a more normal, in UK terms, discount to net asset value.

Box 8.1 *Rodamco, a case study of an open-ended trust. Source: Paribas Capital Markets 1993a, pp. 11–12*

8.7 MEZZANINE FINANCE

Mezzanine debt represents the additional finance that has to be put between the senior debt and the equity to complete the development costs. Senior debt is assessed as a proportion of loan to cost or loan to value, cost here being the total development cost and value the gross development value on completion. If the loan-to-value ratio is 70% and the gross development value is £10m, then the equity required is £3m. If the developer can only come up with £2m, then mezzanine finance will be required for the additional £1m. This is riskier than the senior debt and thus should attract a higher interest rate or the alternative would be to offer rights to convert into equity. The lenders can thus be provided with a profit-sharing arrangement, or options for equity, or they may get an additional proportion of the surplus profit. Possible returns are set out below:

Returns on debt and equity

	Percentage of cost	Gross return
Senior debt	0–70%	17%
Mezzanine debt	70–90%	30–40%
Equity	90%	40%+

An example of the application of mezzanine finance is shown in Box 8.2.

Residential Example

Development of 40 residential units

Appraisal: £

Net sale proceeds	3 490 000
less Total cost	2 600 000
Projected profit	890 000
Return on cost	34%

Funding:

Prime debt finance (70% of site and prime building costs)	1 400 000
Equity funds from borrower	500 000
Mezzanine finance required	700 000
Total finance @ 100% of cost	2 600 000

Profit share:

	Profit	Split	Return
Borrower	£534 000	60%	107%
Mezzanine	£356 000	40%	51%

Box 8.2 *Example of mezzanine finance. Source: Berkley 1991, pp. 527–8*

8.8 VENTURE CAPITAL

Venture capital is a specialist area but related especially to situations discussed previously under mezzanine finance. Venture capitalists invest in risky start-up operations or restructures. These would generally be in respect of commercial companies but may overlap with property in two areas at least:

(i) where the company is trading in the property or construction sector;
(ii) where the company has large property assets or where the cash flow is very dependent on its property assets (leisure, housing, medical).

Venture capitalists will introduce risky equity and use this perhaps to gear up or assist in restructuring a new venture. Restructuring may take place by a reverse takeover or an import of management skills or assets or technology. The common types of equity investment for venture capitalists are:

(i) management buy-outs (MBOs);
(ii) start-up companies;
(iii) restructuring of companies;
(iv) purchase of bankrupt operations;
(v) pump priming for new developments or infrastructure;
(vi) development of new technologies.

Needless to say, besides private sector monies, this equity may involve quasi-public sector monies (trusts, funds which are provided at subsidised rates) and public funds (development agencies). In the November 1993 budget, the Chancellor of the Exchequer introduced a Venture Capital Trust to encourage venture capital investment with tax concessions. The Venture Capital Trust Scheme will give tax-free dividends and capital gains for pooled investment schemes in unquoted trading companies.

In the same budget an Enterprise Investment Scheme was introduced to follow on from the Business Expansion Schemes; it gives 20% tax relief on £100 000 invested in qualifying unquoted companies per year. Income tax and capital gains relief are available on losses. Property-related investments are specifically excluded from the Enterprise Investment Scheme.

REFERENCES

Baring, Houston and Saunders (1991) *Property Report*, Baring, Houston and Saunders, London, November.

Berkley, R (1991) 'Raising Commercial Property Finance in a Difficult Market', *Journal of Property Finance*, vol. 1, no. 4, pp. 523–9.

Beveridge, J A (1991) 'New Methods of Financing', in P Venmore-Rowland, P Brandon and T Mole (eds), *Investment, Procurement and Performance in Construction*, RICS, London.

Catalano, A (1993) 'Paribas Trusts in the Upturn', *Estates Gazette*, 23 October, p. 52.

DTZ Debenham Thorpe (1993) *Money into Property*, DTZ Debenham Thorpe, London, August.

Evans, P H (1993) 'Statistical Review', *Journal of Property Finance*, vol. 4, no. 2, pp. 75–82.

Graham, J (1985) 'New Sources of Finance for the Property Industry', *Estates Gazette*, 6 July.

Jennings, R B (1993) 'The Resurgence of Real Estate Investment Trusts (REITs)', *Journal of Property Finance*, vol. 4, no. 1, pp. 13–19.

Mallinson, M (1988) *Equity Finance*, in S L Barter (ed.) *Real Estate Finance*, Butterworths, London.

Paribas Capital Markets (1993a) *European Equity Research: Rodamco*, Banque Paribas Nederland N.V., October.

Ryland, D (1991) 'Authorised Property Unit Trusts', *Estates Gazette*, London, 9 November, pp. 163–4.

Savills (1989) *Financing Property 1989*, Savills, London.

Savills (1993) *Investment and Economic Outlook*, Savills, London, Issue 3, October.

Sexton, P and Laxton, C (1992) 'Authorised Property Unit Trusts', *Journal of Property Finance*, vol. 2, no. 4, pp. 468–75.

Venmore-Rowland, P (1991) 'Vehicles for Property Investment', in P Venmore-Rowland, P Brandon and T Mole (eds), *Investment, Procurement and Performance in Construction*, RICS, London.

9 Institutional Investment

9.1 INTRODUCTION

The financial institutions consist of the insurance companies and pension funds, the two principal channels for the nation's savings. Because of the nature of the real property market, individual investors generally have withdrawn from the market because the channelling or collectivisation of savings into collective organisations is more tax effective than direct saving.

The institutions dominated the funding of development properties in the early 1980s. The traditional approach to development finance was to obtain short-term finance to complete a development and then arrange a buy-out by an institutional fund. This dominance has since declined. Since 1985, the important new money into commercial property has been from banks, property companies and through overseas investment (Evans 1992, p. 116). Thus, the growth of financial institutions, fuelled by the collectivisation of savings and the decline of personal-sector saving, and evidenced by the expansion of development activity in the post-war period, has now abated and resulted in a significant move away from property investment and funding (Woodroffe and Isaac 1986, p. 12). The decline of the institutions in the commercial property market has been matched by an increase in indirect investment in property companies by way of bank advances. Outstanding bank loans to property companies increased from £5 billion in 1985 to just over £40 billion in the second quarter of 1991 and declined only slightly since to £36.8 billion at the beginning of 1993. Over the period between 1986 and 1992 institutions' purchases have generally exceeded their sales but their net property investment has been a declining share of the total. Institutional net property investment is shown in Table 9.1 and Figure 9.1.

From 1984 there was a noticeable fall in the availability of long-term institutional funding and the reaction of the City to the shortfall was to turn to innovative financing methods. Out of necessity developers turned to alternative finance sources to complement institutional finance (Richard Ellis, 1986). Money flowing into property during the early 1980s increased from £2 billion to £4 billion in the period from 1980 to 1986. Between 1986 and 1989 there was a rapid increase to £14 billion. It then tailed off to £8 billion, £4 billion and finally £0.5 billion in 1992. The pension funds' involvement had been relatively static but has decreased in the late

1980s. The insurance companies have been more stable investors, with an increase in investment in the period 1989–1991. The Stock Exchange has not been a significant contributor except in 1987, 1989 and 1991. Banks rapidly increased their involvement between 1986 and 1991 but this has since decreased quite dramatically (see Figure 9.2 on p. 166).

Table 9.1 *Institutional net property investment 1985–93*

	£ million								
	1985	1986	1987	1988	1989	1990	1991	1992	1993[a]
Insurance companies:									
Life funds	803	789	726	1008	1090	946	1493	668	95
General insurance	12	32	29	94	420	134	−10	−68	−21
	815	821	755	1102	1510	1080	1483	600	74
Pension funds	509	434	240	312	92	−491	467	349	134
Property unit trusts	−5	−101	−516	99	31	−61	19	−12	7
Total	1319	1154	479	1513	1633	528	1969	937	215

[a] First quarter 1993 only.
Source: Evans 1993, p. 79.

Property as a proportion of overall institutional investment has been falling in recent years. The Investment Property Databank *Annual Review* for 1993 suggests that the best end-of-year figures for the proportion of property in institutional portfolios as at December 1992 showed a fall to 7% from the figure in December 1991, which was 9%. The bulk of the drop can be explained, however, in terms of the differential price movements between the different asset classes held in the portfolio. Net property investment by institutions is still positive but at the lowest recorded level since 1980 (Investment Property Databank 1992).

9.2 HISTORY

In the early post-war period the insurance companies in particular played an important role in property financing by lending long-term fixed interest funds. This approach was useful immediately after the war, when inflation was low and thus the returns were not eroded. Financial arrangements between developers and property companies were encouraged because of the shortage of supply of commercial space, the heavy demand and the resultant rental growth and capital value gain. When inflation established itself, the fixed interest approach was no longer attractive to the institutions, and insurance companies which had previously had financial arrangements with major developers broke these and moved into providing funds for sale and leaseback or situations where they could obtain some share in growth. Eventually the institutions carried out direct development, funding the developer on an arrangement whereby the developer received a project management fee with some additional incentives.

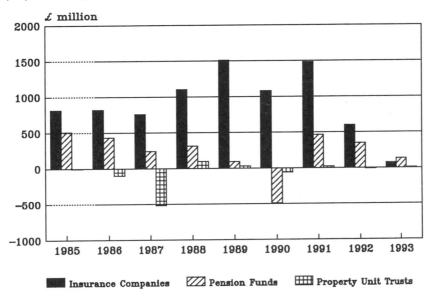

Figure 9.1 *Institutional net investment in property 1985–93. 1993 first quarter only. Source: Evans 1993, p. 79*

The good performance of equities in the 1980s was matched by a poor performance in property. The demand for development sites by the institutional funds increased land values and capital values of completed developments; the level of income arising from the developments in terms of rentals were overexaggerated and thus the yield was poor. The insurance companies had been more firmly established in the development markets and the decline in activity affected them less. The pension funds, except for a few larger ones, cut back their portfolios quite drastically. As has been said, new purchases were still made but marginal or poorly performing properties were removed from portfolios. In 1990 the property holdings of the insurance companies (life and general companies combined) reached £42 billion, with pension funds having holdings of £22 billion (Brett 1990, p.242).

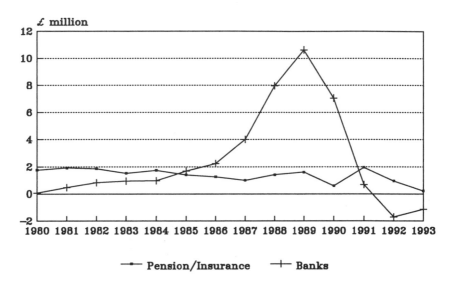

Figure 9.2 *Institutional investment and bank finance into property 1980–93. 1993 first quarter only. Source: Evans 1993, p. 76*

9.3 PARTNERSHIP ARRANGEMENTS

The larger insurance companies and the very large pension funds have extensive property departments, capable in many cases of actually carrying out development as well as advising on the purchase and management of completed investment properties. Smaller funds may choose alternative approaches to investment in property by indirect investment in unauthorised property unit trusts, for instance.

Conventional mortgage finance was replaced by direct development by institutions in the 1980s, as mentioned previously. Alternatively the institution would find a sale and leaseback; this involved the sale of the freehold of the property to the institution and the taking back of a long lease by the developer, who then sublet the development to occupying tenants on conventional 25 year occupational leases. Early deals had no provision for rent reviews but in the late 1960s and early 1970s, as shorter and shorter review periods became the norm, so these interests provided an appropriate inflation-proofed equity investment at the same time minimising any management problems (which were taken on by the developer). Equity-sharing sale and leaseback arrangements are extremely complex and relate to the balance of risk and return of the parties involved. They have been discussed in other chapters, including Chapter 8 on equity.

9.4 DIRECT VERSUS INDIRECT FUNDING

Long-term savings institutions, the pension funds and insurance companies are the main sources of equity finance. The history of the involvement of institutions has been a move towards direct funding of property develop-ment and property investments. Smaller institutions wanting to take a stake in commercial property but lacking the size of resources to invest direct can use indirect routes into property (see Figure 9.3). The main indirect routes are (Brett 1983, p. 107):

(i)   property company shares;
(ii) property bonds – unit-linked life assurance schemes;
(iii) exempt unit trusts and managed funds;
(iv) mortgages and debentures.

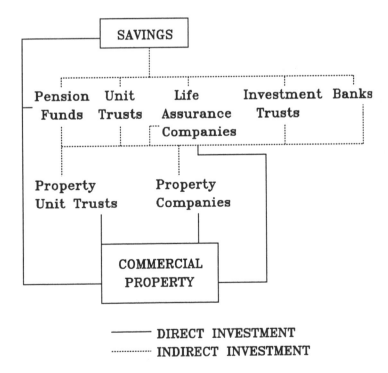

Figure 9.3 *Direct and indirect investment in property. Source: Brett 1983*

The property company differs from the other indirect routes, in that it is a corporate body whose shares can be quoted on the Stock Exchange. The value of its shares will bear some relation to the underlying property assets held in the portfolio of the company but the link is not a direct one. Property bonds and unit trusts work on a different principle. The value of the unit is directly determined by the value of the properties in the fund. Funds which operate on the unit principle are 'open-ended', in the sense that the number of units can increase or decrease with the purchase or sale of assets, whereas the share capital of a company is fixed, apart from new issues of shares or capital reductions requiring legal permission.

9.5   CRITERIA FOR INVESTMENT

Institutions such as pension funds and insurance companies are long-term savings institutions. They invest in equity to support products which have a long duration and could have open liabilities, i.e. products such as pensions or insurance policies for which the payout is not fixed in money terms and so are prone to inflation. Because the liabilities of these institutions extend over long periods, the risks and uncertainties of the returns being affected by inflation are accentuated (Mallinson 1988, p. 38).

The needs of long-term savings institutions in terms of their equity investment relate to the certainty of return. The institution will wish to minimise risk in an investment of course, and associated with this will be the aspects of difficulties of management, which may accentuate problems of the certainty of return. Also, to avoid risk, the institution will require a diversity of interests to avoid putting 'all the eggs in one basket'. Finally, in terms of return, income is required at the present time rather than capital growth.

Recent research by Rydin *et al.* (1990) pointed out that although surveyors and property analysts like to extol the values of property investment and complain that too small a proportion of institutions' portfolios is taken up by property, none the less the proportion of institutional portfolio which is in property assets remains below 20% and fell to 11% in 1987 (Rydin *et al.* 1990, p. 250). This proportion has fallen further, as indicated in the beginning of this chapter.

The results of this survey (Rydin *et al.* 1990) showed that the main reasons for including property in the institutional portfolio and the disadvantages were perceived as follows:

Reasons for including property in portfolio	Disadvantage of property
Long-term return	Poor liquidity
Low level of long-term risk	High unit costs
To achieve a balanced portfolio	
Lack of short-term volatility	

Less important reasons	Less important disadvantages
Low level of short-term risk	Management costs
Inflation hedge	Problems of property as a specialist area (i.e. tax,
Short-term returns	lettings, valuation)

The reasons for including property in the portfolio are consistent with the historic patterns of returns from property investment with a low variability of returns, low correlation between property and equity or gilts returns and relatively low beta coefficients (indicating risk) for property (Rydin *et al*. 1990, p.25; see also Barter 1988, p. 7, for details of the correlation between property, equity and gilt returns.)

Table 9.2 *DTZ Debenham Thorpe survey of institutional investors, August 1993. Source: DTZ Debenham Thorpe 1993, pp. 8–9*

(i) Attractions and disadvantages of property investment in order

Attractions	Disadvantages
Income security	Illiquidity
Performance outlook	Management costs
Spread of risk in portfolio	Indivisibility
Heterogeneity	Research information
Inflation hedge	Performance outlook

(ii) Investment intentions

1993 Activity	% Response for:	
	Purchases	Sales
greater than 1992	75	57
same as 1992	15	23
less than 1992	10	20

1994 Activity	% Response for:	
	Purchases	Sales
greater than 1993	34	32
same as 1993	38	36
less than 1993	28	22

9.6 FUTURE FOR INSTITUTIONAL INVESTMENT

A survey in 1993 of over 50 major insurance companies and pension funds indicated that the planned purchases of property assets for 1993 would be at least 100% over 1992. The institutional investment sector as a whole has a gross investment potential of some £7 billion over the 12–18 months to the end of 1993 and 1994. Disposals by institutions are also likely to rise over this period, as the lack of liquidity since 1990 has prevented the restructuring of investment portfolios. The outlook is for increased expenditure, however, with more new investment funds going to property (DTZ Debenham Thorpe 1993, p. 2). The survey covered what the institutional investors saw as the attractions and disadvantages of property investment as well as their investment intentions into the future; these are set out in Table 9.2 and should be compared with the results of Rydin set out previously. A survey by Chesterton Financial (November 1993) has confirmed the renewed interest of institutions in the property market. The interest in schemes for forward commitment and forward funding was high (94% and 83%, respectively); the sectors of most interest were offices and industrial property, followed by retail warehouses. Retail was the least popular sector (Chesterton Financial 1993).

REFERENCES

Barter (1988) 'Introduction', in S L Barter (ed.), *Real Estate Finance*, Butterworths, London.

Baum, A E and Schofield, A (1991) 'Property as a Global Asset', in P Venmore-Rowland, P Brandon and T Mole (eds), *Investment, Procurement and Performance in Construction*, RICS, London.

Brett, M (1983) 'Indirect Investment in Property', in C Darlow (ed.), *Valuation and Investment Appraisal*, Estates Gazette, London.

Brett, M (1990) *Property and Money*, Estates Gazette, London.

Chesterton Financial (1993) Internal uncirculated reports, Chesterton Financial, London.

DTZ Debenham Thorpe (1993) *Money into Property*, DTZ Debenham Thorpe, London, August.

Evans, P H (1992) 'Statistical Review', *Journal of Property Finance*, vol. 3, no. 1, pp. 115–20.

Evans, P H (1993) 'Statistical Review', *Journal of Property Finance*, vol. 4, no. 2, pp. 75–82.

Investment Property Databank (1993) *Annual Review 1993*, IPD, London, December.

Mallinson, M (1988) 'Equity Finance', in S L Barter (ed.), *Real Estate Finance*, Butterworths, London.

Richard Ellis (1986) 'Development Finance', *Property Investment Quarterly Bulletin*, Richard Ellis, April.

Rydin, Y, Rodney, W and Orr, C (1990) 'Why Do Institutions Invest in Property?', *Journal of Property Finance*, vol.1, no.2.

Woodroffe, N and Isaac, D (1986) 'Corporate Finance and Property Development Funding', Working Paper, Faculty of the Built Environment, Polytechnic of the South Bank.

10 Property Companies

10.1 INTRODUCTION

Property business is defined as extraction of value from land and buildings such that the landlord takes a creditor's view rather than an equity holder's view of the occupiers. In March 1988 the quoted property company sector (this refers to quoted property companies, i.e. ones that are listed on the Stock Exchange), owned property valued at £17 billion, had a market capitalisation of shares worth £13 billion and net assets of £14 billion. This could have been compared at the time with the market capitalisation of BP (£15 billion) and the commercial banking sector (£16 billion)). Seventy per cent of the shares at that time were owned by institutions (Millman 1988, p. 169). The total book assets of the sector increased up to 1990, when they reached a peak of nearly £30 billion but decreased in 1992 to £25 billion (S G Warburg Securities 1993, p. 17). Debt has continued to rise in the balance sheets of the property sector, although less rapidly to 1992. Table 10.1 sets out a summary of asset values and borrowings in the balance sheets of property companies.

Table 10.1 *Quoted property companies: balance sheets, gearing and financing*

Year	Total book assets (£m)	Total borrowings (£m)[a]	Cash (£m)	Debt[b] as a % of book assets	Short-term borrowings (£m)	Short-term borrowings as % total
1986	11 298	3087	437	24.4	1075	34.8
1987	15 172	4254	722	24.4	1506	35.4
1988	19 862	4988	1407	19.4	1748	35.0
1989	27 055	6939	1716	20.6	2648	38.2
1990	30 933	8590	1453	24.2	3642	42.4
1991	27 992	10 132	1223	32.7	4374	43.2
1992	25 462	11 130	1278	38.7	5218	46.9

Notes: [a]Total borrowings include convertible loan stocks and bonds.

[b]Debt is net of cash.

Short-term borrowings are less than 5 years and also include convertible loan stocks and bonds.

Source: S G Warburg Securities 1993, p.17.

In 1993 there was a dramatic rerating of property companies because of a major shift in confidence. In the first half of 1993, equity and convertible issues raised by property companies totalled around £1.3 billion. Capital issues raised subsequently showed a rapid expansion (see Figure 10.1). To the end of 1993, share prices had risen so strongly that they were no longer trading at a discount to net asset value. Property companies were, at the end of 1993, in the rare position of being able to raise money without significant dilution of net asset value or earnings. However, the situation in 1993 was marred by a continued fall-out from the consequences of over-lending, overdevelopment and much-reduced property values (Evans 1993, p. 77). A number of property companies had huge write-offs. For example, London & Edinburgh Trust (LET), the subsidiary of the Swedish Company SPP, had a 1992 pretax loss of £449m against a loss of £138m in the previous year. SPP bought LET in 1990 for £491m. Table 10.2 gives a sample of the main quoted property companies on the Stock Exchange.

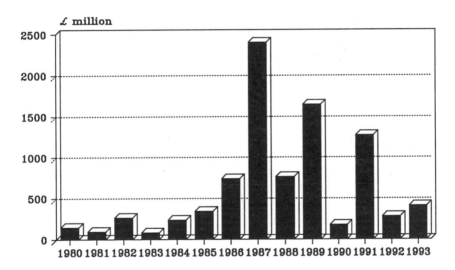

Figure 10.1 *Net capital issues by property companies. The 1993 figure is first two quarters; the second quarter had £445m of issues. Source: Bank of England/Evans 1993, p. 82*

Features of property companies considered by an investor

The property companies listed on the Stock Exchange offer potential investors a range of different opportunities. The main features of a property company to be considered by an investor are:

Table 10.2 Major quoted property companies

Company	Price 29 Oct 1993 (p)	Mkt cap (£m)	Yield (act) (%)	Yield (prosp) (%)	Est'd current nav (p)	Hist-oric book nav (p)	Fore-cast book nav (p)	Dis-count to f'cast book nav (%)
Asda Property	132.00	103.7	2.12	2.08	92	80	95	(38.5)
Bilton	670.00	290.4	3.76	3.64	740	739	740	9.5
Bradford Property	235.00	338.0	3.06	3.19	175	170	185	(27.0)
British Land	401.00	1205.8	2.33	2.40	330	294	365	(9.9)
Brixton	239.00	553.8	4.66	4.11	189	168	195	(22.6)
Burford Holdings	88.00	163.5	1.74	1.99	60	52	63	(39.7)
Capital & Regional	184.00	55.0	0.80	1.02	160	145	165	(11.5)
Cardiff[a]	230.00	5.9	1.39	1.30	215	232	215	(7.0)
Chesterfield[a]	583.00	109.1	2.52	2.57	445	398	475	(22.7)
Compco[a]	300.00	6.2	5.76	5.40	470	461	475	36.8
Derwent Valley	633.00	73.7	1.81	1.78	550	501	565	(12.0)
Frogmore	486.00	243.9	4.39	4.37	417	409	440	(1.05)
Great Portland	228.00	695.5	5.85	4.39	182	170	195	(16.9)
Greycoat[b]	27.00	23.7	0.00	0.00	33	33	n.a.	n.a.
Hammerson 'A'	369.00	905.3	3.61	3.39	393	385	395	6.6
Hemmingway Props.[a]	36.00	34.1	0.00	0.00	27	25	28	(28.6)
Land Securities	737.00	3720.4	4.13	4.07	575	504	620	(18.9)
London & Associated[a]	37.00	25.7	2.09	2.16	41	37	42	11.9
London Merchant Securities	109.00	260.2	4.89	4.82	102	95	110	0.9
MEPC	536.00	2080.3	4.98	4.66	450	445	450	(19.1)
PSIT	168.00	203.9	3.28	3.38	151	142	160	(5.0)
Scottish Met.[c]	107.00	103.9	1.87	1.93	85	82	100	(7.0)
Slough	259.00	995.5	4.17	3.91	260	245	265	2.3
Southend Properties[a]	85.00	78.4	6.67	3.53	100	94	105	19.0
TOPS Estates[a]	223.00	102.8	1.26	1.23	200	189	210	(6.2)
Wates City[c]	91.00	109.2	1.13	0.00	82	73	85	(7.1)

[a]Paribas Ltd is a broker to these companies.

[b]Subject to financial reconstruction proposals.

[c]Adjusted for rights issue.

Source: Paribas Capital Markets 1993b, p. 4

(i) The quality of assets in the portfolio, the age, location and tenure of individual properties and their relative importance in the portfolio. Different types of property and the proportion of overseas investment.

(ii) The perceived quality of management in the company, which is very subjective and is often about single individuals in the company.

(iii) The sources of income of the company. These will vary between well-established property investment companies relying on rents and property development companies whose income arises from selling-on completed developments.

(iv) The capital structure and gearing of the company. A highly geared financial structure is more appropriate for established companies deriving a large proportion of revenue from rental income than for development companies dependent on less secure trading profits. The nature of debt is also important.

The summary for a successful property company from an investor's viewpoint is shown in Box 10.1.

What makes a successful property development company?

1. Ability to understand and forecast external influences.
2. Reputation, track record, style.
3. Links with other developers.
4. Links with financiers.
5. Exploitation of competitive advantages.
6. Efficient use of resources.
7. Management structure.
8. Market leaders rather than followers.

Box 10.1 *Criteria for a successful development company*

Funding of property development by property companies

There are a number of indirect routes into investment in property. The main ones are: property company shares; property unit linked life assurance schemes (so-called 'property bonds'); exempt unit trusts and managed funds; mortgages and debentures. Within this scheme of things, shares are generally available to a wide range of investors, whereas bonds are an investment medium for an individual. Exempt trusts and managed funds, on the other hand, often provide an indirect investment vehicle for pension funds and charities. The property company, unlike the other indirect routes, is a corporate body with its shares quoted on the Stock Exchange. The value of its shares bears some relationship to the value of the property it owns and the income it derives from property operations, but the link is not a direct one. Property company shares will fluctuate on the market, depending on the value of property owned, but the stock market will also tend to discount expected economic and financial events before they happen. An investment trust is a company which holds a portfolio of shares.

Property bonds, exempt property unit trusts and managed funds work on a different principle, the value of the unit in the fund being determined directly by the valuation of the property portfolio of the fund. Thus, the value of the portfolio is divided by the number of units held in the fund and after allowance for the fund's expenses this value becomes the unit price of the fund. The managers of the fund then operate the market at this price by sale of units that owners wish to dispose of and by issue to new investors. There is obviously a margin between offer and bid prices to cover costs of transfer of the units and there is also a need for some liquidity in the system, as sales will not equal purchases in the short term. If demand exceeds supply, then new monies can purchase new investments which are added to the fund. If sales are not matched by new demand for units, then assets have to be disposed of.

Funds operating on the unit principle are 'open-ended' in the sense that the number of units in existence can increase or decrease. Share capital is fixed (the company is 'closed-ended'), apart from new issues authorised by shareholders or capital reductions. Direct and indirect reductions in capital are closely governed by statute and case law and the doctrine of share capital maintenance distinguishes between the income and capital of a company. There are two basic forms of funding for development: corporate finance and direct project funding. In the 1980s, because of the exempt or partially relieved tax status of the principal financial institutions together with the landlord and tenant system established in the UK, which encouraged the investor rather than the owner-occupier, the long-term funding of most commercial developments was usually project-based rather than through the stock market or the company share medium.

An avenue of property development finance was the Business Expansion Scheme. This scheme provided tax concessions involved in development, but as an opportunity for investment with tax relief, this avenue was closed by the 1985 Budget, which excluded certain property development companies from the scheme, and further by the 1986 Budget, which excluded high asset-back activities and effectively closed a loop-hole previously exploited by several property-based activities.

It is difficult to analyse precisely the proportion of new development attributable to property companies, as it is difficult to distinguish between investment funds used for existing and new development. From statistics available it is possible to distinguish broadly the amount of funds available for direct and indirect funding by institutions. Studies in the mid-1980s (Woodroffe and Isaac 1987) show that in 1983 £1498m was invested in property (other than house mortgages) by the institutions; banks advanced £969m to property companies. However, as will be shown in the next section, new development represents a small proportion of the overall investment and the major problem related to funds is how much of the direct and indirect funding relates to new property. At the beginning of 1983 the total market value of the 42 major property companies was in excess of £4274m. Again, it is difficult to analyse the amounts of internal capital available for corporate funding of property but the figures produced by Rowe and Pitman at the beginning of 1983 show a total retained profit of the order of £65m. Looking globally at these figures, it was evident that property companies are playing a significant role in property investment and funding. Using the outline figures mentioned earlier, it may be shown that in 1983 property company investment was running at 70% of institutional funding (there were £969m of bank loans to property companies together with £65m retained profit compared with institutional investment of £1498m).

Investment in existing stock compared with development projects

While the precise percentage of the total investment market effected through corporate funds is unclear, from the previous section, it can be clearly seen as a major contributor. The property companies' funds consist of corporate capital and loans and it should be recalled that the institutions do provide these funds alongside banks, investment trusts, unit trusts, charities, individuals and other corporate investors. Despite the variety of funds, the role of the company in channelling the monies into property developments or investments is a key one.

However, the actual proportion of new to existing development in the market is small. A study of the proportion of new floorspace constructed in 1981–2 showed that it represented less than 2% of the total commercial floorspace in England. New buildings in that period contributed less to the increase in floorspace than extensions and changes of use, but the total gross increase was only 3.5% of the total stock. Thus, the development market relative to existing stock would appear to be small.

Future investment by property companies

The rerating of property companies has meant that in 1993 they have been able to raise new capital and look at investment and development programmes again. The Gallup survey commissioned by *Chartered Surveyor Weekly* in the middle of 1993 indicated that 36% of the major property companies and institutional investors were planning fresh speculative development over the 2 years from August 1993. The investment value of the planned schemes aggregated to £1.94 billion (Kynoch 1993, p. 18). The main results are shown in Figure 10.2. This may indicate a revival of fortunes in the property development market beyond 1995.

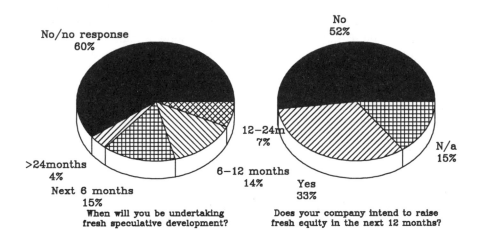

Figure 10.2 *Gallup/CSW survey August 1993. (> 24 months includes those saying yes but not stating a date). Source: Kynoch 1993, p. 19*

10.2 PROPERTY SHARES

Property companies hold all or most of their assets in property; shares are thus a surrogate for property. There should be a close correlation between share prices and property value. Shares are more favoured than direct property because of the general rising share market; because of gearing which can increase returns to equity; because of the benefits of stock selection; and because of the perceived dynamic management of property companies (Barter 1988, p. 70). The drawback of share ownership against direct property investment is the incidence of tax; this affects the returns compared with direct property investment, as the shareholder is in effect double-taxed (as shown later).

Thus, property company shares offer the investor four main features:

Management This takes away the direct problems of management and offers specialist management and entrepreneurial skills.

Gearing Gearing (debt/equity as a percentage is used here, which is common in the market, but, as mentioned earlier, debt/total capital is usually used in economic texts) of the larger quoted companies at January 1993 varied quite dramatically: for instance, Speyhawk (before its demise) had a negative equity of £105m, Stanhope had a gearing of 600%, while Bradford and Warnford had no borrowing. Land Securities had a gearing of 54% (S G Warburg Securities 1993, p. 36). As well as the level of debt, the type of debt is important; whether it is fixed or variable rate, short- or long-term is important. Gearing can increase the equity return, but see Chapter 1 for a more detailed discussion.

Liquidity The market in shares has a central price and there is a speed of entry and exit in and out of the market.

Other participants Liquidity exists because there are other participants in the share market; institutional investors hold a high percentage of shares. Usually the shares are held as part of an equity rather than a property portfolio and thus are managed in the more market-led style of equity shares rather than the more asset-led style of direct property (Mallinson 1988, p. 71).

Tax inefficiency of investing in property shares

There is an innate inefficiency in investing in property shares. This was more marked when there was a wider differential between personal income tax at the basic rate and corporation tax rates. The tax inefficiency can be shown thus (Woodroffe and Isaac 1987 pp. 62–63):

	£
Assume base rate tax is 30% and using corporation tax @ 52%	
Taxable profit	100 000
Less corporation tax @ 52%	52 000
Profit after tax	48 000

Assume all profit is distributed as dividend:

Net dividend is	48 000
ACT paid by company ($^3/_7$ × £48 000)	20 571

Amount received by investors:

Net dividend	48 000
Tax credit (= ACT)	20 571
Profit after tax	68 571

ACT is advance corporation tax and the dividend payment made by the company consists of a net of base rate tax to shareholders. The tax payment is at the rate of 30% on the gross dividend or three-sevenths on the net dividend (i.e. the gross dividend of £68 571 @ 30% tax is £20 571).

If the net dividend is less 30% tax = 0.7 gross dividend, the three-sevenths is a grossing-up factor for the net dividend, as three-sevenths will be 0.3 of the gross. (The formula is $t/(1 - t)$, where t is the tax rate; here 0.3/(1 − 0.3) is 0.3/0.7 or three-sevenths.)

If the shareholder is an individual and is not liable for tax, then he/she can claim back the tax credit. If there is a liability for a higher rate of tax than the 30%, then the taxpayer will receive a further tax bill. The ACT paid by the company is deducted from the total tax liability of the company (£52 000 in the example) and the remainder paid as 'mainstream tax'.

Thus, a gross fund (a pension fund not liable to tax) would receive £100 000 if it invested directly but here it received £68 571 or 68.5%.

If we take a more updated example where the difference between the corporation tax rates and the personal basic rate tax has lessened, then this will look like:

	£
Assume base rate tax is 25% and using corporation tax @ 35%	
Taxable profit	100 000
Less corporation tax @ 35%	35 000
Profit after tax	65 000

Assume all profit is distributed as dividend:

Net dividend is	65 000
ACT paid by company ($^{25}/_{75}$ × £65 000)	21 666

Amount received by investors:

Net dividend	65 000
Tax credit (= ACT)	21 666
	86 606

This is still inefficient, but our gross fund here would have obtained 86.6%, increasing the proportion as the differential between the basic income tax rate and the corporation tax rate lessened from 22% to 10%.

There is also a disadvantage in terms of capital gains taxation. Owning investment properties through UK companies or groups has been systematically disadvantageous since 1972 relative to direct ownership of the same properties by UK taxpayers, gross funds and by non-residents (Millman 1988, p. 174). An example of this is shown in Box 10.2.

A property was purchased in 1965 for £4m, had £6m spent on it and was sold in 1982 for £40m. Consider the different tax position of direct ownership against purchase by a UK holding company, which is sold after sale of the property to put its shareholders in funds:

	£m
Sale proceeds	40
Cost	(10)
Gain	30

	Holding company	*Direct ownership*
Gross gain	30	30
Tax on capital gain	(9)	
Available to shareholders	21	

	Tax on capital gain	*Net proceeds*	*Tax on net capital gain*	*Proceeds*
UK gross funds	–	21	–	30
Non-resident	–	21	–	30
UK taxpayer	6.3	14.7	9	21

Box 10.2 *Capital tax disadvantages of the corporate structure. Source: Millman 1988, p. 174)*

10.3 DISCOUNT ON NET ASSET VALUE

Property investment companies as opposed to trading companies are valued on the basis of their net assets rather than the income produced. A feature of the market in property investment shares was that they traded at a discount to the net assets held. This may not be so in the case of a very bullish market and over longer periods for exceptional performers but generally this discount appeared to be around 20%.

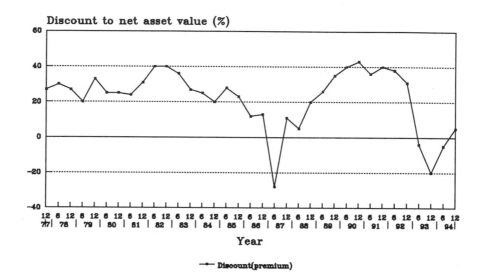

Figure 10.3 *Average discount on net asset value 1977–94. As at December and June. Projected figures for December 1993 and 1994. Source: S G Warburg Research 1993, p. 5*

The discount is measured as:

$$\frac{\text{net asset value per share (NAV / share)} - \text{share price}}{\text{NAV / share}} \times 100\%$$

(see Figure 10.3). This means that the underlying assets were undervalued, and three reasons were commonly given for it:

(i)   problems of possible loss on the forced sale of the company's assets;
(ii) tax liabilities, capital gains tax on disposal of properties and the tax inefficiencies of holding shares as opposed to direct investment;
(iii) disquiet over the valuation by surveyors of the underlying property assets.

Recent research is inconclusive but this situation has effect on financing and activity in the sector. Assets are undervalued and this discourages the growth of property companies through equity expansion and forces them into borrowing to expand. This leads to companies being highly geared (having a high ratio of borrowed capital to total capital). It discourages takeovers within the sector, because takeover situations raise share prices and narrow the discount. Subsequently the share price will tend to fall to a realistic discount as perceived by the stock market. On the other hand, property investment companies could be vulnerable to takeover by firms from other sectors where there are no discounts (Woodroffe and Isaac 1987, p. 1026).

Contingent capital gains tax on a property investment company prior to the 1988 budget (which moved the base date for capital gains tax forward from 1965 to 1982) probably amounted to about 20% of net asset value; subsequently this has fallen to probably 10%. There is an argument for valuing property investment companies by net net asset value (NNAV), which takes into account the contingent liability for capital gains tax. On this basis the discount would be narrowed (Millman 1988, p. 188). Investment trusts are companies which hold investments in shares; they also suffer from discount on net asset value in respect of their ownership of property investment company shares, but are not liable to capital gains tax.

10.4 CORPORATE FINANCE STRUCTURE

Capital structure

The question of an optimal capital structure for a particular company is one which has aroused much debate. The problem is the choice of the best mix of debt (loans, debentures) and equity (ordinary shares, reserves and retained profits). The following factors ought to be considered, but assessing the weight to be given to each one is a matter of judgement.

Cost

The current and future costs of each potential source of capital should be estimated and compared. The costs of each source are not independent of one another. It is generally desirable to minimise the average overall cost of capital to the company.

Risk

It is unwise to place a company in a position where it may be unable, if profits fall, to pay interest as it falls due or to meet redemptions. It is equally undesirable to be forced to cut or omit the ordinary dividend to shareholders.

Control

Except where there is no alternative, a company should not make any issue of shares which would have the effects of removing or diluting control by the existing shareholders.

Acceptability

A company can only borrow if investors are willing to lend to it. Few listed companies can afford the luxury of a capital structure which is unacceptable to the main institutional investors. A company with readily mortgageable assets will find it easier to raise debt.

Transferability

Shares may be listed or unlisted. Many private companies have made issues to the public so as to obtain a listing on the Stock Exchange and improve the transferability of their shares (Isaac and Steley 1991, pp. 154-5).

Cost of capital

A company cannot always choose the cheapest source of capital because of the need to pay attention to the factors indicated in the previous section. The costs of each potential source of capital should be estimated to reduce the average cost of capital. The costs of issuing capital need to take into account any tax benefits: for instance, the interest on loan stock of debentures can be reduced by the tax benefit, as the interest is deductible for tax purposes. This would not be so for preference shares, which would have the same rate before and after tax.

The cost of issue of ordinary shares is more difficult to calculate:

$$\text{gross dividend yield} = \frac{\text{current dividend per ordinary share}}{\text{market price per share}} \times 100\% \times \frac{100}{75}$$

The multiplier 100/75 is to allow for the tax credit. The dividend yield of any company can be compared with dividend yields in general and with those of other companies in the same equity group. The dividend yield prior to the 1960s tended to be higher than the yield obtained on unredeemable Government stocks, because of the greater risk associated with equities. Since that time, the effects of inflation have caused a reverse yield gap in which the yield for equities has fallen below that of gilts as prices are bid higher. This is because equities have an ability to protect the owner against inflation; they tend to be inflation-proof rather than inflation-prone, as gilts are. Redeemable debentures and loans issued by companies would tend to have a higher yield than Government stock because they have a higher risk, but they are also inflation-prone, as the returns are fixed. The dividend yield cannot be regarded as an adequate measure of the cost of equity capital, as it does not take into account future change in the dividend stream and general changes in share price levels (Isaac and Steley 1991, p. 155).

Two possible measures of the cost of equity capital are the earnings yield and the dividend yield plus a growth rate built in. The earnings yield is:

$$\frac{\text{earning per ordinary share after tax}}{\text{market price per ordinary share}} \times 100\%$$

but it is more usual to express this as a price:earnings ratio (*P/E* ratio), i.e.:

$$\frac{\text{market price per ordinary share}}{\text{earnings per ordinary share after tax}}$$

The higher the *P/E* ratio (or alternatively the lower the earnings yield), the more the market thinks of the company and the cheaper the cost of equity capital. Earnings per share are calculated after the deduction of tax and preference dividends.

Dividend cover is also an important tool for analysis. Since the market is interested in future dividends, it prefers to see current dividends reasonably well covered by current earnings; this is a form of guarantee that the dividend will be maintained in the future. The *Financial Times* measure of dividend cover is:

$$\frac{\text{earnings per share on a maximum basis}}{\text{ordinary dividend per share}}$$

Earnings per share on a maximum basis assumes that a company distributes all its profits and is liable to pay advance corporation tax on them.

An alternative approach to the cost of equity capital is to add a growth rate to the dividend yield. If one considers that a company's dividends will grow at the rate of, say, 8%, then this is added to the gross dividend yield to give the total cost of equity capital.

A further approach to calculating the cost of equity capital is that developed by portfolio theory. This cost is estimated as:

$$\overline{R} = R_F + \beta(\overline{R}_M - R_F)$$

where $\overline{R}_M$ is the expected return on the market, $\overline{R}$ is the expected return on the security, R_F is the risk-free rate (from a riskless security such as a Treasury Bill) and β is the measure of risk of the security's sensitivity to movements in an underlying factor. Portfolio theory was discussed in some detail in Chapter 2.

Application of the cost of capital to a project

If a project has a return of 20% to equity capital, it can be refinanced at different levels of debt. The gearing effects are shown by increasing the level of debt, which increases the return to equity capital dramatically.

Example

Assume that the project return = 30% and debt capital costs = 15%. The project is financed by 50% equity and 50% debt. The returns on the project are distributed as returns to the debt holders or to the equity holders on the basis of their holdings:

$$R_p = (0.5)R_e + (0.5)R_d$$

where R_p, R_d and R_e are the returns to the project, debt and equity capital, respectively. Thus:

$$30\% = (0.5)R_e + (0.5)15\%$$

$$R_e = \frac{30\% - 7.5\%}{0.5} = 45\%$$

The value of a project will not alter merely by the way it is financed, but this will affect the way the proceeds are distributed and thus the gearing is affected. If the project is financed 20% equity and 80% debt, then:

$$30\% = (0.2)R_e + (0.8)15\%$$

$$R_e = \frac{30\% - 12\%}{0.2} = 90\%$$

The advantage of using debt is that, besides the gearing effects on the return to equity, the interest on debt is tax deductible and the analysis can be further advanced by using the weighted cost of capital by calculating the returns to equity and debt, and adjusting the debt return for tax relief. Thus, a project may provide a valuable tax shield (Isaac and Steley 1991, p. 157).

10.5 GEARING

The capital structure of a property company is a key factor in how a company is viewed in terms of its attractiveness by an investor or lender. The sector is characterised by a high level of gearing due to the availability of fixed interest finance during the first post-war boom from 1954 to 1964. This availability led to many property companies being highly geared. The term 'gearing' in this context is defined as the proportion of debt to total capital (equity plus debt).

High gearing is of benefit when property values are rising ahead of interest charges but can be dangerous if the real rate of interest is rising at a greater rate than property values. As real interest rates remain higher than growth at the present time, it would appear that property companies should stabilise by de-gearing. However, there are prejudices against such moves: in the 1970s it was argued that the issue of share capital in a well-established company should be restricted only to the acquisition of additional entrepreneurial talent and from takeovers. In the 1960s corporate funding was not popular and leaseback became a major source of funds. This situation was caused in part by the Capital Issues Committee of the Stock Exchange, which for a period of years denied development companies access to the Stock Exchange debenture market. Later, the prejudice against corporate funds was reinforced by the introduction of corporation tax in 1965, which made the institutions less keen to receive their equity interest through shares in development companies, as the corporate structure reduced their gross income.

Thus, the present lack of institutional funding has led to new funds being raised by property companies through loans and debentures, as previously outlined, not by increased equity expansion. It is debenture and loan stock that is being issued rather than ordinary share capital. The risk of even higher gearing has been accepted because of the risks apparent in equity expansion. The use of property company equity for expansion is a difficult process. Firstly, it is not easy for a predator to show shareholders immediate benefits of an acquisition, which are not likely to show through for a number of years. Secondly, there is a fundamental problem that property companies stand at a discount to net asset value and rights issues; convertible rights issues and vendor placings tend to dilute net asset value unless the acquisition is of assets which stand at a greater discount to their net worth.

Capital performance is the most important determinant of share price performance. The discount to net asset value is used in theory, in recognition of the inherent capital gains tax liability within an investment portfolio and other factors discussed in this chapter, but it also acts against the companies having rights issues.

Property companies need to consider the overall level of gearing in respect of both loans which are on the balance sheet and off-balance-sheet loans. This overall level of gearing may depend on a number of factors, including:

(i)   Whether the company involved is an investment company or a trader, i.e. whether the property assets are intended to be held for long-term investment or sold.

(ii) The level of floating debt as against fixed rate debt. This is a measure of the control that the company has over its borrowing costs; fixed rate interest rate can be calculated but floating rates will need to be forecast. This balance of debt has to be viewed in the context of the portfolio held by the company, the certainty of income arising and any risks involved. A portfolio held for trading will differ in terms of the risk profile from a portfolio developed and then held as an investment; this in turn will differ from the risk associated with a portfolio of investment property already let with different risks related to rent voids.

(iii) Whether the company's borrowing is secured or unsecured. If the company is borrowing unsecured, the maximum permitted level of borrowing will be set relative to the amount of the shareholders' funds. However, if the borrowing is secured, then the lender is unlikely to advance more than 70% of the value of the property and thus an input of equity may be required. This input is a major constraint on development activity.

(iv) Any constraints on gearing levels. Some companies will have structured development vehicles which allow off-balance-sheet funding; this will reduce the real gearing ratio. However, any lending on investigation of the accounts will calculate the loan and its price on the basis of the overall risks involved (Beveridge, 1988, p. 166).

10.6 PROPERTY TRADING COMPANIES AND PROPERTY INVESTMENT COMPANIES

A property dealing or trading company is a company primarily concerned with trading or dealing in property. The company buys or constructs with a view to sale and its stock of properties is included in the balance sheet as a current asset and is thus under accounting conventions, shown in terms of value as the lower of cost and market value.

A property investment company retains property and profits from the rental income and capital growth of its assets. A property company can be both an investment and a dealing/trading company.

Profits arising from capital transactions or growth in investment companies are taxed at the capital gains tax rate, whereas dealing/trading companies are taxed at corporation tax rates. The rates are now the same for companies but in the past there was a tax advantage if the profit was deemed to be a capital transaction. This was especially so before March 1983, when the corporation tax was at 52%. All income to both investment and trading companies is taxed at corporation tax rates. If activities are mixed in a company, then all disposals are viewed as trading transactions by the revenue. There is a need to form separate companies for investment and trading. Revenue reserves are called retained earnings in most other industries but in property the distinction is made in investment companies between the capital and revenue reserves. Capital reserves arise in the revaluation of assets, and for property investment companies their articles prevent distribution. If an investment company is being purchased or if it is borrowing funds, it may need to be valued. This can be done internally by a qualified employee. If investment properties form a significant part of the resources of an enterprise, such valuations should be made annually and supplemented by an independent valuation every 5 years. If the valuation exceeds the book value, this is termed a revaluation surplus and is subject to the rules of distribution outlined above.

The boundary between investment and trading companies was fairly clear until the tax year 1987–8. Before this there were lower tax rates on capital gains than on income from profits; therefore companies were careful to preserve the distinction between the two activities. Large groups therefore have separate investment and trading companies. Investment companies still formed 85% of the market capitalisation of the quoted property sector in 1988; the remaining 15% were trading companies or service companies, including chartered surveying practices (Millman 1988, p. 178). However, because of acquisitions and mergers, property investment companies are shrinking in number. Before the downturn in the market in 1990, the trading companies had increased dramatically in number. Whereas the stock market values property investment companies and investment trusts on a discount to net asset value, other companies such as traders or service companies are valued on a multiple of their earnings. Hybrids do exist where development is combined with investment portfolios. Trafalgar House and Taylor Woodrow are examples where civil engineering and contracting are combined with a property portfolio. An example of a hybrid is Sterling Guarantee Trust (SGT). Sir Jeffrey Sterling, the founder, was a shrewd proponent of aligning cash-flow businesses with a property portfolio. The development of SGT is shown in Figure 10.4.

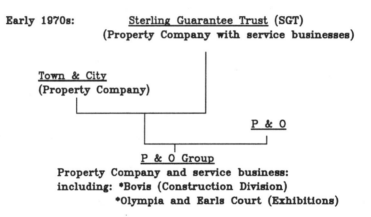

Figure 10.4 *Sterling Guarantee Trust. Development of hybrid business. Source: Millman 1988, p. 180*

10.7 TAKEOVERS

Introduction

Acquisitions of other companies are investment decisions and should be examined by the same criteria as other investments. However, there appear to be two main differences. Firstly, because takeovers are often contested, there may be little information beyond published data on which the investment decision can be made. Secondly, many takeovers are for longer-term strategic reasons, which may be difficult to quantify now and may be even more difficult to quantify in the future when a company's 'goalposts' may have changed along with those of competitors and those of the market. Many of the large takeovers of companies generally in the market in the 1980s failed because of the lack of information and lack of a clear strategy. Experience has shown that any problems arising will be accentuated if the size of company acquired is large, especially relative to the bidder. Risk analysis confirms that, when acquisitions have highly uncertain outcomes, the larger they are, the more catastrophic the impact of any adverse outcomes (Pike and Neale 1993, p. 515).

Motives for takeover

The motives for takeover often concern a feeling that the assets of the company to be acquired are valued at less than market value or there is some synergy in operating the organisations together. Thus, the motives concern the assets, which may be undervalued, or the marriage value in purchasing a management team, using your own or merging the skills. The choice between assets and management team in a takeover may also be linked to whether a bidder is looking to invest or trade in the property portfolio. In the latter case, management and entrepreneurial skills may be critical. Motivation for takeover is summarised in Box 10.3.

- The acquisition of skilled/technical management.
- The obtaining of a supply of sites and projects.
- The obtaining of potential benefits from the merging of property interests.
- The ability to restructure funding facilities.
- Diversification (geographical or sectoral).
- If the acquired assets are at a discount to the share price, then they are cheap
- Tax advantages.
- Access to cash or advantageous loan facilities.

Box 10.3 *Motivation for takeovers*

Discount to net asset value

The traditional discount on net asset value experienced in the share price of an investment property company may lead to a discouragement of take-overs and rationalisation in the property investment sector. Takeover situations raise the share prices of the company being taken over and thus narrow the discount. Subsequently, the share price will tend to fall towards the previous discount level, the extent of the fall depending on the view the market takes. Thus, the takeover will generally mean a dilution of net asset value per share and a greater discount unless the company being taken over is standing at a greater discount to the bidder (Isaac and Woodroffe 1987, p. 1024).

Takeovers: procedure

A takeover could proceed by an offer of shares in the predator company, a cash offer or offer of other securities, e.g. convertible loan stock issued by the predator. These offers would have to be at a higher level than the market price of the company being acquired, to induce sale or swaps by the investors. Any tax liabilities in the portfolio of the company being acquired would need to be considered (Brett 1990, p. 131).

Hostile takeovers had their origins in the post-war property sector. There have been recent suggestions by stockbrokers that many of the quoted property companies could disappear over the next few years as a result of liquidation, receiverships or takeovers. In the past, takeovers were more prominent in the early stages of an upswing in the property cycle as predators sought to take advantages of discounted net asset value or exploit marriage values (Temple 1992, p. 476).

The takeover code and statutory background

Takeovers are regulated by:

(i) *The Takeover Panel*   The rules are set out in the City Code on takeovers and mergers.
(ii) *The Office of Fair Trading*, which considers investigation of take-overs if competition, consumer choice or the public interest is threatened.
(iii) *The Companies Acts*   There has been a progressive reduction in the level at which substantial share investment must be disclosed and this is now at 3%. The use of nominees to build up share ownership is now more difficult; a Section 212 notice under the Companies Act 1983 can be served requiring disclosure of the bidder. Other aspects also serve to deter a potential bidder, e.g.:

   (a) If the bidder buys 10% of the shares prior to an offer being made, the subsequent offer must include a cash alternative equivalent to the highest price paid for the shares.
   (b) If the bidder buys more than 30% of the shares, an offer is usually mandatory at the highest price previously paid with a fully underwritten cash alternative (Temple 1992, p. 477).

Hostile takeovers are best avoided by ensuring a good track record, low overheads and enhancement of shareholder value. It is important as well that others know how well you are doing to discourage bidders and encourage a good press and investor/institutional loyalty.

Analysis for takeovers

The stock market can be an efficient medium for raising capital finance but it also enables control of existing companies to be effected. The ability to identify and evaluate suitable takeovers in the property sector will depend on the investigation of a number of factors, including:

(i)   the company's property assets, existing and potential income, value and trading potential;
(ii) the overall state of the company's financial position, its borrowings, liabilities and earnings;
(iii) the price and performance of the issued shares, dividend history and market capitalisation.

Techniques of analysis for takeover and other purposes include:

Assessment of the Price/Earnings ratio (P/E)

$$P/E = \frac{\text{market price per share}}{\text{earnings per share}} = \frac{1}{\text{earnings yield}}$$

A high *P/E* ratio indicates a strong expectation of growth and confidence in the share (comparable to a high year's purchase or YP in property valuation). Property companies tend to have higher *P/E* ratios but this income approach to valuation of the companies is used only for trading companies and not investment companies.

Net asset value per share

The property assets may be shown in the accounts at valuation, cost or net realisable value, if different.

Share price discount

In the past there have been substantial discounts on the net asset value as expressed by the share price. This makes the undervalued assets vulnerable to predators.

Share dividend

The dividend provided over a period of time.

Dividend cover

The number of times current dividends are covered by the profits available for distribution = earnings/dividends.

10.8 SUMMARY

To summarise, the criteria for the successful financing of property companies can be considered as:

(i)   The ability to raise equity if and when required.
(ii) The flexibility to use fixed or floating rate finance and to have access to a wide range of secured and unsecured finance.
(iii) The ability to achieve financing with long maturity money. This is especially important to property investment companies, where the length of maturity of the loan is more important than interest margins. If interest can be fixed, then future income can be more confidently forecast.
(iv) The importance of flexibility in the financial structure, because each individual property company and project is unique and thus each company must be in the position to achieve the appropriate mix of financing required.

Above all, a wide variety of financial sources and instruments should be available so that the directors of the company can make decisions as to the appropriate mix, given the prevailing market conditions (Beveridge 1988, p. 167).

REFERENCES

Beveridge, J (1988) 'The Needs of the Property Company', in S L Barter (ed.), *Real Estate Finance*, Butterworths, London.
Brett, M (1990) *Property and Money*, Estates Gazette, London.
Evans, P H (1993) 'Statistical Review', *Journal of Property Finance*, vol. 4, no. 2, pp. 75–82.
Fraser, W D (1993) *Principles of Property Investment and Pricing*, Macmillan Press, London.

Isaac, D (1986) 'Corporate Finance and Property Development Funding: An Analysis of Property Companies' Capital Structures with Special Reference to the Relationship between Asset Value and Share Price', Unpublished thesis, Faculty of the Built Environment, South Bank Polytechnic, London.

Isaac, D and Steley, T (1991) *Property Valuation Techniques*, Macmillan Press, London.

Isaac, D and Woodroffe N (1987) 'Are Property Company Assets Undervalued?', *Estates Gazette*, London, 5 September, pp. 1024–6.

Kynoch, R (1993) 'Firms Predict £2bn Spending Surge', *Chartered Surveyor Weekly*, 26 August, pp. 18–21

Mallinson, M (1988) 'Equity Finance', in S L Barter (ed.), *Real Estate Finance*, Butterworths, London.

Millman, S (1988) 'Property, Property Companies and Public Securities', in S L Barter (ed.), *Real Estate Finance*, Butterworths, London.

Paribas Capital Markets (1993b) *Monthly Property Share Statistics*, Banque Paribas, November.

Pike, R and Neale, B (1993) *Corporate Finance and Investment*, Prentice Hall, London.

S G Warburg Research (1993) *U.K. Property: Monthly Review*, S G Warburg, London, November.

S G Warburg Securities (1993) *U.K. Property: Review of 1992 and Prospects for 1993*, S G Warburg, London.

Savills (1989) *Financing Property 1989*, Savills, London.

Savills (1993b) *Investment and Economic Outlook*, Savills, London, Issue 3, October.

Temple, P (1992) 'How to Beat a Hostile Takeover', *Journal of Property Finance*, vol. 2, no. 4, pp. 476–83.

Woodroffe, N and Isaac, D (1987) 'Corporate Finance and Property Development Funding', Working Paper of the School of Applied Economics and Social Studies, Faculty of the Built Environment, South Bank Polytechnic, London.

11 Joint Ventures

11.1 INTRODUCTION

There are a number of different types of joint venture arrangements but basically they involve the joining together of two or more parties to undertake a transaction. These parties may include institutions, banks, contractors, overseas investors, local authorities and public sector bodies.

The reasons for forming a joint venture may be numerous but essentially are about two areas – finance and expertise. A property company may not have sufficient finances to enable it to complete a transaction and find the development costs; in this case financial advisers may market the scheme to attract a third party investor. Developers may also form joint ventures and other forms of partnership with owners of land or a development where the latter do not have the expertise to develop; this may be the case where the landowner may be unused to the process of development and engaged essentially in non-property-oriented activities. In recent years other factors have influenced the formation of joint ventures and these basically relate to the reduction of debt in the arrangements for development and, related to this, the reduction in risk.

Thus, additional reasons for forming joint ventures could be listed as:

(i) the increased risk in property development;
(ii) the lack of equity in the property market and property companies unable to raise new funds of their own accord in the market;
(iii) pressure to reduce debt in the property sector, by the Bank of England and lenders;
(iv) demands of overseas investors who have a preference for joint venture arrangements in their dealings.

11.2 CRITERIA FOR CHOICE OF JOINT VENTURE STRUCTURE

The main types of joint venture structure are the partnership and the joint venture company (JVC), which are now explained. The decision to choose between the two will rest on a number of criteria, including:

(i) favourable tax treatment;
(ii) tax benefits;

(iii) limitations of liability;
(iv) control mechanisms;
(v) the number of participants;
(vi) the timescale for the development, its disposal and whether this is a one-off or one of a number of schemes;
(vii) proposed methods of financing the development.

In the analysis it is generally assumed that the joint venture has been formed for trading purposes, i.e. to develop a property, let it and sell on the investment created to a third party. An example of the factors to be considered in negotiating a joint venture agreement to develop a business park are set out in Box 11.1.

(i)   Level of funding to be provided.
(ii)   Infrastructure, amount and timing.
(iii) Who is in control of the decision-making process?
(iv)   How is the scheme to be phased and what types of buildings are going to be developed in terms of investment or owner-occupied property?
(v)   On completion of the first phase, how are subsequent phases going to be financed?
(vi)   How is the profit to be divided following a substantial increase in the land value due to the success of the first phase?
(vii) How is the profit going to be distributed?
(viii) What are the dissolution provisions in the event of failure?
(ix)   How are disputes to be settled?

Box 11.1 *Factors to be considered when negotiating a joint venture agreement*

11.3 TYPES OF JOINT VENTURE

The main types of joint venture structure considered here are the limited company and the partnership. As well as these common forms, a limited partnership and management agreement are also considered. Joint ventures will also differ on the funding arrangements. Examples of these types of partnership, including profit sharing and forward funding, which relate to the division of profit rather than the structure of the joint venture vehicle, will also be discussed.

11.4 JOINT VENTURE COMPANY (LIMITED LIABILITY COMPANY)

Trading companies will often form a separate company for carrying out a particular project; it may be that the company will only have one site and finance is obtained on a project by project basis relating to each company formed. The advantage of the use of a limited company is that the structure is well known and can be utilised to provide a range of debt and equity interests, which, as with any other corporate financial structure, can reflect the risk and rewards of the shareholders and creditors. The limited company is a separate legal entity and shareholders are limited, in terms of losses, to the extent of capital provided.

There are tax benefits and disbenefits. Group relief will be available to the parent companies who have shareholdings but this advantage may be offset by the disadvantage that liabilities from subsidiary companies will need to be consolidated in group accounts. Previously 50:50 joint companies were established to keep the borrowings of the JVC out of the consolidated accounts. Traditionally the definition of a subsidiary company is one where the parent has a shareholding and controls the composition of the Board of Directors or where it has more that 50% of nominal equity capital. To avoid consolidation of accounts a different type of company was established termed a 'controlled non-subsidiary'. This in effect meant that although the subsidiary was controlled, its accounts were not consolidated into the group accounts of the parent. The Companies Act 1989 has changed this and the accounts of a joint venture will now have to be consolidated into one or more of the parent companies. A number of tests will determine whether consolidation of the accounts takes place, including a revised definition of a subsidiary based on the board of directors and voting control. The most significant test in the context of a 50:50 joint venture is whether a parent has the right to or can exercise a dominant influence (Albert and Watson 1990, p. 190). Thus, a controlled non-subsidiary will be treated as a real subsidiary in the company accounts. A controlled non-subsidiary is regarded as a company, trust or other vehicle, directly or indirectly controlled and a source of benefits or risks that are, in substance, no different from those that would arise were the vehicle a subsidiary (Bramson 1988, p. 141). The joint venture company is thus distinguished, if it is a subsidiary as defined above, from an associated company, in which a parent has a significant stake but may not have technical control. In the case of an associated company, the debts are regarded as off-balance-sheet and not consolidated. This may thus give a false accounting picture, because although profits may be apportioned from the associate company and consolidated in the accounts, interest charges may not. At all events, a company owned 50:50 with another party, where each party has the same number of directors and votes, will probably not constitute a subsidiary of either (Brett 1990, p. 96).

Although the joint venture company, because of the Companies Acts, may provide a lack of flexibility and secrecy of operation, the corporate structure could be used as a vehicle which could be expanded in the future. This could be done by increasing the portfolio being developed and attracting more funds by the issue of new shares, and the vehicle could then be floated on the Stock Exchange.

11.5 PARTNERSHIPS

Partnerships are governed by the Partnership Act 1890. Partnership is a form of joint venture where each partner has a direct interest in the property and will with its fellow-partners be a co-owner of the whole of the property. If companies want to set up a joint venture, they could acquire the property jointly, but usually wholly owned subsidiaries are used which may have been established particularly for this transaction. A co-ownership structure may be difficult for those dealing with the partnership property. The property itself may be held by a nominee company whose shares in turn are held by the partners. A partnership is easy to form and has a flexible structure. The disadvantage is that each partner has unlimited liability; however, this can be avoided by the use of limited liability companies. Minority interests are protected, as they have the ability to dissolve the partnership at any time and ask for assets to be sold. Partnerships are taxed as if they are a company by assessing the trading profit; once this has been done, the profit or loss is allocated to the partners. The partners then pay tax on the allocated amount.

11.6 OTHER TYPES OF JOINT VENTURE

Limited partnerships may be feasible as another form of joint venture and the regulations for these are laid down under the Limited Partnership Act 1907. The limited partnership has two kinds of partner, general partners and limited partners. The obligations of a limited partner will be limited by the amount of capital originally invested, provided that the limited partner does not take part in the management of the partnership (Albert and Watson 1990, p. 194). General partners have full liability and are thus liable for losses beyond the original capital subscribed. Limited liability partners are able to make some strategic decisions without losing their limited liability; these could include decisions to end the partnership. Also it would be possible for the general partner to be a limited company, thus effectively limiting the liabilities of both parties (Bramson 1988, p. 144).

Management agreements are also possible where one party will hold on to the property on completion. These agreements could be on a project management basis with a developer assisting a landowner/investor for a project management fee or else sharing in the profits of the scheme.

Possible arrangements for profit sharing in partnership arrangements are discussed later.

11.7   PARTNERSHIP ARRANGEMENTS

These relate more to a method of funding a development than to a true joint venture and are explored more fully elsewhere. They may include arrangements such as participation lending and forward funding. In participation lending, the lender will take a share of the proceeds of a scheme and this may occur where a lender is taking a higher risk, by lending more or at more advantageous rates of interest.

Forward funding is where the purchaser of a development assists the funding of the development. This provides security for the purchaser by having some control as the development proceeds. It may be that the forward funder will fund the development at a lower rate of interest. The subsidy of the interest rate and the reduction of risk to the developer will thus lead to a reduced developer's profit payable and a higher yield on purchase of the completed development (because of reduced risk and reduced cost to the developer). Thus, the purchaser purchases at a reduced price.

The problem with joint ventures and more general partnership arrangements is that the interests held by the parties are going to be difficult to resell until the development is complete, so the partners involved have no security to offer to tenders.

11.8   THE FORMAL AGREEMENT

The participants in a joint venture need to ensure that there is proper documentation between them. The nature of the agreement needs to look at the overall control of the projects, the day-to-day operation and the exit of the parties. In detail the agreement governing the activities of a joint company will be embodied in its Articles of Association. In the joint venture arrangement it is important to distinguish between the overall control and day-to-day management. The important point is to avoid destructive deadlocks.

The formal agreement should clearly indicate elements such as:

  (i)   the level of funding proposed;
  (ii) the development period;
  (iii) the control mechanism for decision making;
  (iv) provision for dissolution;
  (v)   arrangements for settlement of disputes.

If things go wrong in a joint venture, then dissolution of the joint venture may be the only option. This could be done by one party buying out the other parties at an agreed valuation. The formula for the valuation could be previously agreed; it may well be that the triggering of such dissolution may be at an inappropriate time for one or other of the joint venture partners, especially in respect of the valuation of any work in progress. One approach suggested is that, if there is a deadlock, either party may offer to purchase the other's interest within a given timescale and at a figure quoted by the offeror. The offeree then has the option of either accepting the offer or buying the offeror's interest at the same price. If interests are not equal, then this will need to be done on a pro rata basis. This approach is known as the 'Texas Option', among other things (Bramson 1988, p. 148).

Forms of Joint Venture

Limited liability companies
Partnership
Partnership arrangements for profit division

Purposes of Joint Venture

One-off, or for a number of projects
Tax advantages
Attract financial investment
Attract development expertise
Reduce debt/risk
Buy into an existing development programme

Joint Venture Agreements

Should contain details of:
    funding level
    development period
    control
    profit distribution
    dissolution
    disputes

Clients for Joint Ventures

Landowners without development expertise or finance
Developers without finance or land
Owner-occupiers with land banks
Banks and other lending institutions

Box 11.2 *Summary of joint ventures*

11.9   EXAMPLE OF A JOINT VENTURE: Rosehaugh Stanhope Developments

In 1987 Rosehaugh and Stanhope Properties set up a joint venture, Rosehaugh Stanhope Developments (Holdings) PLC (RSD). RSD developed the Broadgate Complex in the City of London. The accounts of the joint venture partners were prepared prior to the changes which tightened up on off-balance-sheet finance for joint venture companies. The separate accounts for Rosehaugh and Stanhope were prepared separately to 30 June 1987. These disclosed RSD's affairs. Rosehaugh's debt relating to RSD included in the consolidated balance sheet was £71m and that of Stanhope was £8.5m. The debt of RSD was £183m; thus, the borrowing included in the consolidated balance sheets of Rosehaugh and Stanhope understated the true level of the group's indebtedness. However, both partners followed existing accounting conventions and made detailed disclaimers – the issue here is whether the conventions allow the balance sheet to show the proper financial position (Peat 1988, p. 123).

11.10 SUMMARY

A summary of the points discussed in this chapter are shown in Box 11.2. If a property development is undertaken through a joint venture, it has the advantage of bringing together the resources and expertise of the parties. It also spreads the risk of the project between the parties. Before the 1989 Companies Act, neither the borrowings of a joint venture company nor its related property interests needed to appear in the balance sheets of the parent companies. Because joint venturers tend to set up a separate joint venture company for each project, finance can be applied to the project as a non-recourse or limited-recourse loan. The changes in the Companies Acts suggest that the accounts of a company should reflect the commercial effect of a transaction rather than the form. The practice of not showing the borrowings of 'off-balance-sheet' companies is likely to continue in the case of genuine 50:50 joint ventures, even though the definitions of what constitutes a subsidiary company are being tightened.

REFERENCES

Albert, D and Watson, J (1990) 'An Approach to Property Joint Ventures', *Journal of Property Finance*, vol. 1, no. 2, pp. 189–95.

Bramson, D (1988) *The Mechanics of Joint Ventures*, in S L Barter (ed.), *Real Estate Finance*, Butterworths, London.

Brett, M (1990) *Property and Money*, Estates Gazette, London.
Chesterton Financial, Internal uncirculated reports.
Peat, M (1988) *The Accounting Issues*, in S L Barter (ed.), *Real Estate Finance*, Butterworths, London.

12 Unitisation and Securitisation

12.1 DEFINITIONS

Securitisation is the creating of tradeable securities from a property asset. *Unitisation* is also the creation of a tradeable security but the aim in this case is to parallel a return comparable to that from direct ownership.

This distinction may sound confusing but going back to the original analysis relating to debt and equity as outlined in earlier chapters should clarify matters. To begin with, one must consider a single property rather than a portfolio. For a single property, if we divide the interest into a number of holdings, then we divide the equity and this is unitisation. If we divide the interest and add debt securities, in the way a company may have shares and loan stock, this is securitisation. In fact, securitisation is rather like imposing a corporate finance structure on a property, i.e. a single-asset property company, but this approach simplifies matters because it is important to understand the objectives of securitisation and unitisation, which will differ from the operation of a property company. From the above, securitisation thus includes unitisation and can be used as a general term incorporating unitisation, and this will be done here except when discussing securitisation historically or when the securitisation of the equity alone is considered. The distinction between securitisation and unitisation is shown in Figure 12.1.

Figure 12.1 *Securitisation and unitisation*

The distinction of a single property is important to this analysis; if a portfolio of properties is considered, then unitisation is basically akin to property units, as in an authorised property unit trust, while securitisation of a portfolio would be a property company's shares and loanstock/debentures. A matrix of options will clarify this as shown in Figure 12.2.

Securitisation

	Equity	Debt
One Property Asset	Unitisation Securitisation	Securitisation
Portfolio of Assets	Unit Trusts Shares in a Property Company	Mortgage Backed Securities Loan Stock/Debentures in a Property Company

Figure 12.2 *Securitisation matrix*

A further analysis used in the past by the Barkshire Committee (Barkshire 1986) related to the distinction between the unitised property market, in which the investor gets a percentage interest in the ownership of the property investment and property income certificates, where an investor gets a percentage income that the investment produces. This distinction of structure is not very useful and confuses the elements of debt and equity. Nevertheless, so that the clarification can be exaggerated, the framework is outlined in Table 12.1.

The vehicles for unitisation and/or securitisation are:

- single-property ownership trusts (SPOTs),
- single-asset property companies (SAPCOs),
- property income certificates (PINCs).

Thus, SPOTs, because they only deal with equity are vehicles for unitisation, whereas SAPCOs and PINCs can be securitised. To summarise, securitisation in general is the conversion of an asset into tradeable securities (these are certificates of ownership or rights to income). In the property context used here, securitisation is the conversion of a single property and the tradeable securities may be debt- or equity-based.

Unitisation is included in securitisation but specifically refers to the securitisation of the equity interest. In its simplest form this unitisation will provide a share of the rental and capital growth with no obligation of management. This approach contrasts to property share ownership in the sense that, with unitisation, the investor selects specific property assets in which ownership is held rather than having to accept an existing managed portfolio. In this respect Barter, writing in 1988, suggested the income yield which could arise from unitisation (which, because of its tax transparency, will be the equivalent of investing directly in property) may be twice the dividend yield from property company shares (Barter and Sinclair 1988, p. 213). Aspects of tax transparency are discussed later in this chapter.

Table 12.1 *Unitisation and securitisation vehicles*

Vehicle	Ownership			Securitisation of equity (unitisation)	Securitisation of debt (total securitisation)
SPOTs	Direct	}	Unitised property market	Yes	No
SAPCOs	Direct			Yes	Yes
PINCs	Income owned			Yes (Initially unitised but debt securities could be added.)	Possible

12.2 HISTORY

The pattern of investment in commercial property has changed substantially over the post-war period. There has been a collectivisation of savings and the property investment market has become dominated by the major institutions, the insurance companies and the larger pension funds. This has been less so in recent years, where property investment and development has been funded by banks and by raising equity in property companies.

Problems with the ownership of property investment have arisen because of the lack of liquidity in the market. There are difficulties in transferability, and extended negotiations are necessary to achieve matched deals. Other investment media such as quoted shares have a centralised market and do not experience these problems. Further problems with illiquidity have been experienced in terms of the increasing investments available. A number of recent property developments are too large to fit neatly within the portfolio of existing institutions. Institutions would not commit a large proportion of their available funds to a single-property investment where this may be contrary to existing policy or where overcommitment to one project may increase risk within the portfolio related to the balance of the investments.

The number of potential purchasers for a larger investment (say more than £20m) is thus limited and this will affect the price of the asset. The problem of illiquidity will affect the demand, supply and value of large projects because of the way the asset is traded.

Other problems with large investments may relate to situations where a partial disposal is required or where developers may wish to retain the investment but recoup some of the project cost. There is also a lack of opportunity to spread investment portfolios by incorporating larger buildings which because of location and prestige may be attractive assets. Finally, there will be problems associated with the valuation of such properties by traditional methods, where comparable evidence is lacking and a bulk discount relating to size or a discount reflecting the lack of ease of transferability, especially important in the event of a forced sale, will need to be incorporated.

Indirect investment in property shares and unit trusts has been readily available to investors and to some extent has addressed the problems of illiquidity. For a long period until recently, property unit trusts (PUTs), where they were unauthorised, had not been able to invest in real property. Exempt unauthorised unit trusts could not under previous law (the Prevention of Fraud (Investment) Act 1958) be openly offered for sale to the public. The result is that only the main institutions have been involved in this form of investment. Property bonds exist but also suffer from illiquidity problems and some contain provisions which may delay repayment of investments for up to 6 months. Property share investment has been popular since the Second World War and the growth of property investment companies over this period has been a major factor in the property market. Company share ownership suffers from three major difficulties. Firstly, there is a tax problem relating to double taxation of income (the shares are not tax-transparent). Secondly, there is not purity of investment in that the portfolios of properties can be large, varied and changing, and it is therefore difficult to identify the asset ownership related to the share ownership. Finally, the net asset values are discounted on the stock market in respect of property investment companies, while property trading companies are valued on the assessment of future probability, which may not readily be related to existing asset values.

Three major vehicles had originally been suggested to deal with the problems. For simplicity these structures have been considered as single-asset property companies (SAPCOs), single-property ownership trusts (SPOTs) and property income certificates (PINCs). In the first two cases, the single-property vehicles are divided up on the basis of ownership of the asset. In the case of SPOTs, the interest is divided up into equity units which are identical; in the case of SAPCOs, the division is by securitisation, the layering of negotiable interests in the investment on a risk/reward basis and including debt as well as equity interests. Different interests are thus created in relation to the assets in much the same way as companies are financed through a variety of corporate funding techniques. Finally, PINCs differ from the previous two vehicles in that they provide ownership rights to the income arising from the investment rather than direct investment in the asset. Other vehicles which have been considered are property unit trusts (PUTs) (already discussed) and mortgage-backed securities (MBSs), which are common in the USA.

Mortgage-backed securities originally developed in the residential market. They enable a building society or specialist mortgage lender to raise funds using a pool of mortgages as collateral, the strength of which means that the issue receives a high credit rating. MBSs allow the issuer to repackage their mortgage assets for sale in capital markets freeing capital for additional loans. Subsequent to the Building Societies Act 1986 the building societies have been committing funds to the commercial property sector, although, as has been mentioned elsewhere, there have been some bad experiences. Despite this, the presence of building societies in the market may accelerate the take-up of MBS issues (Savills 1989, p. 10).

Objectives of securitisation: a summary

(i) Provides for liquidity in the market and, associated with this, the need to keep values up, increase the size of the market and speed up time taken for transactions.

(ii) Assists in the diversification of risk. Securitisation provides a range of opportunities to have a mixed portfolio and to invest in different development proposals more precisely. Securitisation offers the ability also to invest in debt and equity security in themselves having different risk profiles.

(iii) Provides the opportunity to avoid management of property, as occurs with direct ownership and hopefully to leave the task to the more skilled and experienced.

(iv) Provides tax transparency and avoids the double taxation which exists with property company shares.

(v) Provides a more flexible financial structure to encourage debt instruments and thus gearing situations, making the funding market more flexible for the sale of the developer's interest or part interest, and provides a better opportunity for refinancing development funds with long-term investment.

12.3 PROBLEMS IN THE DEVELOPMENT OF SECURITISATION

A number of statutory and legal constraints have stalled the development of securitisation in the property field. These basically relate to legal ownership, financial disclosure, tax and share listings.

Legal ownership

The Law of Property Act 1925 basically reduces the number of legal owners to four; where there are more than four, separation must be made between legal owners and those receiving the beneficial interests. If those joining together form a trust for sale or a partnership, then both of these structures have important limitations and, in respect of the latter, the risk of unlimited liability. Really, only a company or a unit trust, where the asset is held by trustees on trust for members holding units, are suitable vehicles for securitisation of a single property (RICS 1985, Appendix II).

Financial disclosure

Before 1986 the Prevention of Fraud (Investments) Act 1958 prevented dealings of the public in unauthorised unit trusts. The Department of Trade and Industry would not authorise trusts made up of property assets because of the perceived illiquidity and lack of diversification of interests. The Financial Services Act 1986 introduced 'collective investment schemes' for property, and authorised property unit trusts (APUTs) have now been established. APUTs have been previously discussed. Single-property schemes could now be promoted under this legislation.

Taxation

Tax transparency is defined as the ability through securitisation to achieve the same level of net after tax return as would be achieved through direct ownership. The primary objective of securitisation was to avoid the double taxation that shareholders in property companies suffer. This relates to both capital gains tax and income tax and was discussed in Chapter 10 on property companies.

Share listing

The Stock Exchange would not originally permit the listing of single property vehicles and thus there was no ready market for the shares. In May 1987 the International Stock Exchange permitted listing of single property schemes.

12.4   THE VEHICLES

Single-property unit trust

This is envisaged as vehicle rather like an existing property unit trust but will involve investment in a single-property asset. The trust would be authorised and would enable multiple direct ownership in a property or financial terms no less favourable than those available for single direct ownership in property (RICS 1985, p. 11). SPOTs involve a trustee holding the legal title to the property with the trust deed providing details of the operating framework for the scheme. Income accruing to the trust as a result of rents received passes straight to the investor (unit holder). Rental income is secured by the covenant of the tenant and by the form of lease agreement.

Thus the vehicle is a trust which could be floated on the Stock Exchange, management is through trustees who retain the ownership, there are no debt interests. SPOTS require the law to be changed to achieve tax transparency; the Inland Revenue classed them as unauthorised unit trusts and thus liable to corporation tax (Savills 1989, p 10). In 1988 the Treasury confirmed it would not grant SPOTS tax transparency and thus the vehicle is in abeyance (Barter and Sinclair 1988, p. 229).

Single-asset property companies (SAPCOs)

A SAPCO is a company structure rather like a property company only in this case the company hold a single property rather than a portfolio. SAPCOs can be listed on the Stock Exchange but suffer from the same problems as property companies, in that they are not tax-transparent. SAPCOs are the best examples of complete securitisation and an example is given later. SAPCOs fulfil the opportunities of securitisation by providing various financial instruments such as debt, preferred equity and equity secured on a single asset in order to access the widest possible pool of investment capital and thereby enhance liquidity through tradeability. Layers of securities of different characteristics are created to appear to different classes of investor who will be looking for different returns and risks (Gibbs 1987, p. 350).

Property income certificates (PINCs)

A PINC is a tradeable share. The share represents a right to the income arising from rent and capital appreciation of the single-property asset. It has the benefit of tax transparency and the ability to be listed. Debt instruments can be issued to create gearing. A PINC is a composite security encompassing two elements:

(i)   the right to receive a share of the property's income;
(ii) an ordinary share in a company which exercises control and management.

A PINC is a limited liability equity share in a tax-transparent single-asset property company. A suggested structure for a 80% flotation, where the developer or vendor retains 20%, is shown in Figure 12.3.

12.5   ISSUES IN SECURITISATION

Problems of valuation of the units

The units may change hands at a discount to the asset value as perceived by the valuer and will thus mirror the market movement of shares in property investment companies. The possibility of discount runs counter to the views of the organisers of the market, who suggest that there should be a premium on the price of units because of liquidity. By taking the whole and dividing it into smaller units, the increased liquidity should avoid any bulk discount on the whole and thus trade at a premium to the value. The initial value may vary: the issue price will reflect the market conditions. There will be problems of revaluation in the sense of when these should take place and who should carry them out. The significance is that, like company accounts, there needs to be an adjustment of market value. The valuation here will be the assessment of profit and net asset value (NAV) through the company accounts. Periods for revaluation could be 1 year or 5 years. There may be problems for the valuation profession, in the sense that there may be less need for valuations generally but still the need for revaluation. The basis of valuation may be different here to reflect the discount and the increased liquidity.

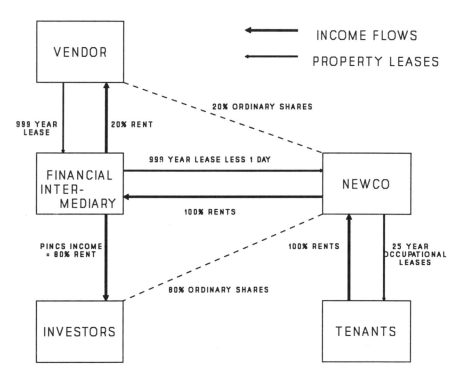

Figure 12.3 *PINCs structure. Source: Orchard-Lisle 1987, p. 365*

Problems of management of the units

The managers of the units will need to make decisions relating to the sale of the asset, refurbishment and financial management. For instance:

(i)   They will need to provide maintenance and sinking funds.
(ii) They will need to decide on any programme for refurbishment.
(iii) They will have to provide guarantees to perform and to protect the investor's interests.

Problems of marketability

The problems of marketability will depend on demand, premiums and discount trading, the size of the market and alternative investments, including property shares.

Size and membership of the market

There needs to be a critical mass for the market to operate properly. The net worth of the members of the market will need to be decided for both market makers and others. The initial fee and subsequent membership fee will need to be decided.

There needs to be a diversity of investors, as otherwise the market can be manipulated by one party. The surveyor will have a role here in the provision of financial services. The initial number of properties will have to be agreed. There is a debate as to whether freehold or long-leasehold properties should be unitised.

Conflicts of interests and insider trading

Rent review considerations of tenant versus landlord surveyors: the unit holders may be tenants as well of the buildings which are securitised or of comparable buildings. 'Chinese Walls' (which establish clear divisions of information so that inside information obtained in one area of the firm cannot be used elsewhere) will need to be established within firms to prevent transactions on the basis of insider information; what constitutes insider information may be difficult, given the nature of the property market. Disclosure of property information, including structural defects and dangerous materials, will be necessary.

12.6   EXAMPLE OF SECURITISATION (from Gibbs 1987, pp. 350–2)

Case Study: Billingsgate, Lower Thames Street, EC2

Joint developers: London & Edinburgh Trust
S & W Berisford

£20m raised internally   (30% construction cost)
£44m raised on market   (70% construction cost)

The money raised on the market was non-recourse borrowing from a syndicate of banks. Finance for the construction and letting was to be repaid on resale or refinancing.

Valuation:

Let to Samuel Montagu on a 35 year lease with 5 year upward only reviews.

Rental	£5 000 000
Yield	6.2%
Capital value	£79 000 000

London & Edinburgh Trust sold out interest to S & W Berisford, who in turn did not wish to hold a £79m investment.

Securitisation solution:

3 layers of security:

(i) *Debt security*

£52.5m of 6⅝% deep-discounted first mortgage bonds expiring 2006 offered at 32.5% discount. (Gross redemption yield 10.6%, which was 1.15% over the yield provided by Treasury 13.5% 2004–2008, the equivalent gilt.) This raised £35.5m.

(ii) *Preferred equity security*

£25.8m cumulative preferred equity shares of 1p each at a price of 100p per share. Shareholders guaranteed 30.2% of the rental income to be paid as dividends (on basis that the current rent shows a 5.9% return). Gross dividend rises to 20% p.a. by year 20 from the initial 5.9%.

(iii) *Ordinary equity security*

The rest was kept as ordinary shares. These are highly geared. There was no dividend entitlement till the next review. The shareholders get 69.56% increase in rental and capital growth. Value of the share is £79m, less debt and preferred equity = £17m.

There was little investor interest in the shares despite the booming market at the time in City offices and the massive leap in rents expected at the next rent review. In September 1988, Berisford made a bid for the outstanding preference shares and now controls more than 50%. The Billingsgate experience may have damaged prospects for further SAPCOs (Savills 1989, p. 10).

12.7 CONCLUSION

The vehicles discussed above have floundered for a number of reasons, the inability to be listed and problems of developing a market that is rapidly changing. Securitisation does offer an approach to counter the illiquidity of the market and will return once the market generally has picked up. Securitisation and liquidity will provide certainty about market price but will mean that investors will no longer have direct control.

The RICS in their research have provided the following advantages (Maxted 1988, p. 137) for holding a single property in multiple ownership:

(i) to stimulate investment in large urban renewal projects;
(ii) to enable small investors to enter the market;
(iii) to create a vehicle which would supplement the involvement of the major institutions in the market;
(iv) to introduce liquidity to the benefit of all classes of investor;
(v) to open a wider range of property investment opportunities and enable an investor to spread risk through a tax neutral vehicle.

A survey by Rydin *et al.* (1990) asked a number of financial institutions about the prospects for a unitised property market. The respondents considered unitised property as a substitute for direct property holding and not as a substitute for equities or gilts. The need for an active market was stressed before they would become involved. The main criteria stated for the emergence of an active unitised market were:

(i) choose quality properties;
(ii) install active management to ensure capital growth.

In the analysis 43% considered the opportunities for gearing unimportant, thus were satisfied with a unitised rather than a completely securitised market (Rydin 1992, p. 256). The response of those surveyed as to what they believed unitisation acted as a substitute for in alternative investments is shown in Figure 12.4.

Direct Property
72%

Gilts
3%

Equities
8%

Property Co Shares
17%

Figure 12.4 *Unitisation: substitution of other investments (%). Source: Rydin et al. 1990, p. 256*

REFERENCES

Barkshire, R (1986) *The Unitised Property Market*, Working Party of the Unitised Property Market, London, February.

Barter, S and Sinclair, N (1988) 'Securitisation', in S L Barter (ed.), *Real Estate Finance*, Butterworths, London.

Gibbs, R (1987) 'Raising Finance for New Development', *Journal of Valuation*, vol. 5, no. 4, pp. 343–53.

Maxted, B (1988) *Unitisation of Property*, College of Estate Management, Reading

Orchard-Lisle, P (1987) 'Financing Property Development', *Journal of Valuation*, vol. 5, no. 4, pp. 343–53.

Royal Institution of Chartered Surveyors (1985) *The Unitisation of Real Property*, RICS, London.

Rydin, Y, Rodney, W and Orr, C (1990) 'Why Do Institutions Invest in Property?', *Journal of Property Finance*, vol.1, no. 2.

Savills (1989) *Financing Property 1989*, Savills, London.

13 Financial Accounts

13.1 PROPERTY ACCOUNTS

Company financial statements

A company's financial statements are contained in the report sent to their shareholders. The report provides details of the operations of the company. It contains a Chairman's review which looks at the preceding year and prospects for the future. There is also a Director's Report, which comments on such matters as profits, dividends, fixed assets and finance, and includes the report of the auditors and a summary of the accounting policies of the company, which can be useful in the analysis of the position of the firm. Accounting policies are important in the property sector in respect of asset valuation and there will be different bases according to whether a property company is an investment or a trading company. Attached to the report are the financial statements. These financial statements would be:

- the profit and loss account;
- the balance sheet;
- notes to the accounts;
- current cost accounts;
- a statement of source and applications of funds;
- a statement of value added.

The balance sheet and the profit and loss account are the main statements of the financial situation of the company. The balance sheet would be for an individual or group of companies, but if there were a parent company, then this might be included in addition. The main accounts would be in accordance with historic cost conventions but current cost accounts would attempt to take into account inflation of asset values. It is useful to remind ourselves, at this stage, of those particular groups who need to use published accounts, because it is their needs for information which will have to be satisfied. These are set out in Box 13.1.

The balance sheet

The balance sheet lists the balances of assets and liabilities as at the accounting date. As a result of the EC's fourth directive on company accounts, balance sheets must now be in a standardised form. The balance sheets are built up from three categories of entry: assets, liabilities and shareholders' funds. Thus, total assets are equal to the sum of shareholders' funds plus liabilities if one looks at the balance sheet from the point of view of the company; alternatively, from a shareholder's view one can see that the difference between assets and liabilities is the shareholders' funds:

> *Business view*:   assets = shareholders' funds + liabilities
> *Shareholder's view*:   assets − liabilities = shareholders' funds

Fixed assets + net current assets (current assets less current liabilities) = capital employed (shareholders' funds + long-term liabilities). This is a modification of the business view, taking current liabilities to the asset side of the equation.

The balance sheet model of the firm, first introduced in Chapter 1, is set out in Figure 13.1 to clarify these concepts.

Who are the users of published accounts?

- *The equity investor group*, including existing and potential shareholders and holders of convertible securities, options or warrants.
- *The loan creditor group*, including existing and potential holders of debentures and loan stock, and providers of short-term secured and unsecured loans and finance.
- *The employee group*, including existing, potential and past employees.
- *The analyst-adviser group*, including financial analysts and journalists, economists, statisticians, researchers, trade unions, stockbrokers and other providers of advisory services such as credit rating agencies.
- *The business contact group*, including customers, trade creditors and suppliers and, in a different sense, competitors, business rivals, and those interested in mergers, amalgamations and takeovers.
- *The Government*, including tax authorities, departments and agencies concerned with the supervision of commerce and industry, and local authorities.
- *The public*, including taxpayers, ratepayers, consumers, and other community and special interest groups such as political parties, consumer and environmental protection societies and regional pressure groups

---

Box 13.1 *The users of published accounts (Westwick 1980, p. 4)*

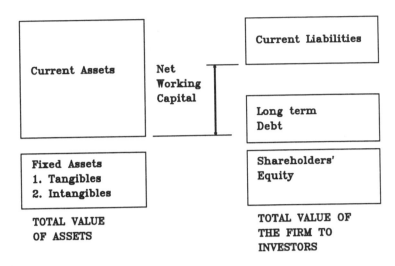

Figure 13.1 *Balance sheet model of the firm. Source: Ross* et al. *1993, p. 5*

Profit and loss account

While the balance sheet is for a particular moment, a profit and loss account is for a year ending on the accounting date; it is the result of the year's activities. The profit is shown before and after tax; profit attributable to minority interests arises from investment in other companies amounting to 50% or less of ownership and these profits are now allowed to be consolidated in the sheet. The accounts also show the proportion of profit distributed and retained. To grow, a company will need to increase its assets. The balance sheet shows that assets = liabilities plus shareholders' funds, so that the ways to grow would be to increase liabilities (borrow more) or increase shareholders' funds. There are two ways of increasing the shareholders' funds: by issuing more shares or ploughing back profits. Ploughing back profits is not necessarily the cheapest source of long-term funds for the company and it also restricts the payment of dividends.

Examples of a balance sheet and a profit and loss account

Balance sheet as at 31 March 1993		
	£000	£000
Fixed assets		
(Investment properties for property companies)		3000
Land and buildings for occupation		400
Plant and machinery		200
Fixtures and fittings		200
		3800
Current assets		
Stocks (trading properties for property companies)	3000	
Debtors	100	
Cash	100	
	3200	
Current liabilities		
Bank overdraft	400	
Trade creditors	600	
	1000	
Net current assets		2200
Total assets less current liabilities		6000
Capital and reserves		
Issued share capital		2000
Revenue reserves		1000
Capital reserves		1000
Shareholders' interest		4000
Long-term liabilities (over 1 year)		
Loans		2000
Total long-term capital		6000
(Adapted from Asch and Kaye 1989, p. 25)		

The following notes to these accounts refer to an ordinary trading company. Notes relating to the peculiarities of property companies are in parentheses.

Fixed assets
Assets were normally valued at historic cost for an ordinary company. Land and buildings were shown at original cost less depreciation in normal accounts, but because this does not reflect worth, companies now revalue to market value. Depreciation is an annual allowance for wear and tear and reduces the balance sheet valuation; it is deducted from profit as a cost. (For a property company the valuation should be market value for an investment property or the lower of cost and realisable value for a property in the course of development, but intended as an investment property – that is, intended as a fixed asset.) Fixed assets are intended to be permanent features of the company's assets; current assets are turned into cash, usually within 1 year. Plant and machinery and fixtures and fittings are shown at cost less depreciation.

Current assets
Stocks are valued at cost. (For a property company, properties to be traded are stocks and are valued at the lower of realisable value or cost.) Cost includes the expenses paid out on a property since purchase and interest.

Current liabilities
These are the amounts due to creditors within 1 year. The balance of current assets less current liabilities is called the net working capital.

Capital and reserves
Issued share capital is the amount paid in by the shareholders when they originally bought the shares in the company. Reserves arise because profits are not distributed to shareholders but ploughed back in the company; these are called revenue reserves. Revenue reserves have to be distinguished from capital reserves, which arise on the revaluation of assets and which then may give rise to a surplus. (Capital reserves are especially important in property companies arising from revaluation of the assets rather than profits from rents or trading.)

Long-term liabilities
These are amounts owed by the company at a future date, longer than 1 year.

Profit and loss account for the year ended 31 March 1993		
	£000	£000
Turnover		10 000
less cost of sales (direct costs)		6500
Gross profit		3500
less (indirect costs):		
Administration expenses	1000	
Selling and distribution costs	200	
Interest on loans	150	
		1350
Net profit before tax		2150
Corporation tax		750
Profit on ordinary activities after tax		1400
Extraordinary item after taxation		200
Profit for the year		1200
Dividends		600
Transfer to reserves		600

(Asch and Kaye 1989, p. 28)

Whereas the balance sheet reveals the state of affairs of the company at one point in time, the profit and loss account shows how much net cash has been generated by activities over the accounting period by matching the expenditure of the year against the revenues. The cost of sales is the cost of raw materials, production or direct labour, power and other factory costs. An extraordinary item is unusual in terms of size and frequency. They are infrequent and thus need to be omitted when considering profit trends over a period of years – for instance, a large profit may have been made from disposal of part of the business, an event which is unlikely to occur again and which distorts the profit figure for that year.

Basic accounting concepts

The financial statements are produced and based on accounting concepts. Four rules or concepts are observed in all published accounts unless it is otherwise stated. These rules are:

- the going concern concept;
- the accruals concept;
- the consistency concept;
- the prudence concept.

The going concern concept assumes that the business will be continuing its activities for the foreseeable future on a similar scale. Thus, the values attaching to assets and liabilities in the balance sheet reflect going concern values. This concept is important in property asset valuation for accounts purposes. The accruals concept says that it is vital for an accurate assessment of profit and loss for the accounting period to compare costs and benefits accurately. It is important to assign costs and financial returns to the period incurred, which may not be the same time period when money costs are incurred or financial returns received. For instance, if a sale has legally taken place, whether or not cash has been received from the customer for the goods delivered, the transaction will be taken as a sale and included as part of the sales revenue appearing in the profit and loss account. The consistency concept is necessary so that approaches to the formulation of the accounts remain the same and so valid comparisons and analysis can be made against previous results and with other companies. The prudence concept covers the attitudes of dealing with costs and revenues; it is the cautious way an accountant approaches the problem of accounting for these items unless the outcome is certain. Based on the above concepts, the Companies Acts makes it a legal requirement that a company's balance sheet should show a true and fair view.

Techniques for analysis

The analysis of company accounts involve the initial consideration of three problems:

(i) Is the company making a satisfactory profit?
(ii) Is the company short of cash or cash-rich?
(iii) What should be the source of long-term funds?

These problems relate to profitability, liquidity and capital structure, and are as applicable to individual property projects as they are to property companies or any firm. The techniques applied are based on relationships between the elements in the financial statements (financial ratios) and rates of return (yields). The area of capital structure is of major interest to financing arrangements and also has parallels in the financial construction of property projects.

Profitability measures

The key ratios used to analyse the profitability of an enterprise are:

(i) Trading profit as a percentage of turnover.

(ii) Profit before interest and tax as a percentage of average capital employed.

(iii) Earnings per share, either basic (based on issued share capital) or fully diluted (based on authorised share capital, which is the total share capital that can be issued).

(iv) Dividend per share.

(v) Number of times covered – that is, the number of times a dividend is covered by earnings. This is also a measure used by property managers to access the security of a tenant by testing the number of times the rent is covered by the net profit of the tenant company.

(vi) Assets per share – the asset backing of shares based on the value of the net assets divided by the number of shares. There has been much discussion in this area in relation to the share price of property investment companies, as one would expect the asset value per share to relate to the market price of the share. However, traditionally the market has discounted the net asset values of property investment companies historically by an average of approximately 20%. The discount is measured by (Isaac and Woodroffe 1987, p. 1024):

$$\frac{\text{net asset value per share - share price}}{\text{net asset value per share}} \times 100\%$$

Return on investment

This is defined as

$$\frac{\text{profit}}{\text{assets}} \times 100\%$$

Thus, profit is looked at as a percentage of capital and this is further influenced by two further ratios comprising the profit margin (profit as a percentage of sales) and the rate of asset turnover (sales dividend by assets):

$$\frac{\text{profit}}{\text{assets}} = \frac{\text{profit}}{\text{sales}} \times \frac{\text{sales}}{\text{assets}}$$

or

$$\text{return on capital} = \text{profit margin} \times \text{turnover}$$

The return on capital may vary from one industry to another but wider variations may be found in the profit margin and rates of turnover. For instance, a return of 20% could be achieved by a high profit margin and a low turnover (the corner shop) or a low profit margin and a high turnover (the supermarket piling the goods high and selling cheap).

A sector comparison should show that the capital-intensive industries with long production cycles would have a low rate of turnover but a high profit margin. From the key ratios above, a number of subsidiary ratios relating costs or assets to sales can be formulated. Depending on the use to which the ratio is put, the definition of profit and assets will differ. Generally a wider view of company performance is taken:

$$\text{return on capital} = \frac{\text{profit before tax, interest and dividends}}{\text{total capital employed}}$$

The comparison of profitable ratios enables firms within a sector to be compared against one another and for the various sectors to be compared.

Liquidity and cash flows

As well as being profitable, it is also important that a company should be liquid. A profitable and fast-expanding company may find that it has tied up its profits in fixed assets, stocks and debtors, and that it has difficulty paying its debts as they fall due. There are two main ratios to examine the liquidity of a company: the liquidity ratio and the current ratio.

The liquidity ratio is also called the acid test ratio because it is a most important test. It is the ratio of liquid assets to current liabilities and a 1:1 ratio means that a company has sufficient cash to pay its immediate debts. Liquid assets are defined as current assets excluding stocks of goods which cannot be quickly turned into cash. In effect liquid assets are debtors, cash and any short-term investments like bank deposits or Government securities. A company can survive with a liquid ratio of less than 1:1 if it has an unused bank overdraft facility.

The other test of a company's liquidity is the current ratio, which includes stocks and work in progress on the grounds that stocks eventually turn into debtors and then into cash itself. It is calculated by relating all current assets to current liabilities. A norm of 2:1 is generally regarded as being satisfactory but this will depend on the norm for a particular industry.

Thus:

$$\text{liquidity ratio} = \text{liquid assets : current liabilities}$$

$$\text{current ratio} = \text{current assets : current liabilities}$$

Gearing ratio and interest cover

Two important measures of financial analysis are the gearing ratio and interest cover.

The gearing (or leverage) ratio is the ratio of debt to shareholders' funds. This could be expressed as the ratio of debt to net operating assets, and this is the approach used in most economics texts, but normally in the market it is stated as:

$$\text{gearing ratio} = \frac{\text{debt (borrowings)}}{\text{shareholders' funds}}$$

This is also known as the debt-to-equity ratio.

Interest cover is the profit available to pay interest charges:

$$\text{interest cover} = \frac{\text{profit before interst and tax}}{\text{net interest}}$$

An example is given in Box 13.2.

The gearing ratio is used to compare levels of debt between companies. Interest cover indicates the safety margin before profits become inadequate to cover the interest charge. Gearing and interest cover are used by lenders to determine whether a company's borrowings are at a reasonable level and whether it is prudent to lend more.

Investors are concerned with the company's capacity to absorb a down in profit without having to sell assets in possibly unfavourable market conditions. Also, gearing is a measure of the potential to finance expansion without recourse to the shareholders, which would depress share price. If a company requires additional debt to fund a new project, the resultant gearing effect may depress share price and restrict flexibility to respond to future opportunities. There is thus pressure to record the project, the asset and debt off-balance-sheet.

	Co. A	Co. B
Balance Sheet	£m	£m
Net operating assets	100	100
Financed by: Debt	20	80
Shareholders	80	20
	100	100
Profit and Loss Account		
Operating profit	15.0	15.0
Less interest payable @10%	(2.0)	(8.0)
Profit before tax	13.0	7.0
Tax @ 35%	(4.55)	(2.5)
Net Profit	8.45	4.5
Gearing ratio	20 ÷ 80 = 25%	80 ÷ 20 = 400%
Interest cover	15 ÷ 2 = 7.5 times	15 ÷ 8 = 1.88 times

Box 13.2 *Gearing ratio and interest cover*

Financial gearing and operational gearing

This section is based on the analysis of Asch and Kaye (1989, pp. 83–4). Many organisations have some control over production methods – that is, they can use either a highly automated process with its associated high fixed costs, but low variable costs, or alternatively a less-automated process with lower fixed costs but higher variable costs. If the enterprise chooses to use a high level of automation, its break-even point is at a relatively high sales level, and changes in the level of sales will have a magnified effect on profits. In other words, the degree of operating gearing is high. This is the same effect as that produced with financial gearing, in that the higher the gearing factor, the higher the break-even sales volume and the greater the impact on profits.

The degree of operating gearing can be defined as the percentage change in operating profits associated with a given percentage change in sales volume. Operating gearing can be calculated using the following formula:

$$\text{degree of operating gearing} = (S - VC)/(S - VC - FC)$$

where *S* represents the level of sales (quantity × value), *VC* is total variable cost and *FC* is total fixed cost (Asch and Kaye, 1989, p. 83).

For example, let us suppose that a firm has a level of sales of £100 000 total variable costs of £50 000 and total fixed costs of £20 000. Its degree of operating gearing would be:

$$(100\,000 - 50\,000)/(100\,000 - 50\,000 - 20\,000) = 1.67 \text{ or } 167\%$$

Therefore, if sales increase by 100%, profit increases by 167%. Operating gearing affects earnings before interest and taxes (EBIT), whereas financial gearing affects earnings after interest and taxes, i.e. the amount available to equity holders in the company. Financial gearing will intensify the effects on earnings available to equity after the effect of operating gearing has been taken into account.

The degree of financial gearing can be defined here as: the percentage change in earnings available to equity that is associated with a given percentage change in earnings before interest and taxes (EBIT). That is, the change in equity return relative to overall return before tax. An equation has been developed for calculating the degree of financial gearing:

$$\text{degree of financial gearing} = EBIT/(EBIT - I)$$

where *EBIT* is earnings before interest and taxation and *I* is interest paid (which is the return to debt capital, so *EBIT* − *I* is the return to equity capital).

Thus, in the earlier example, we can compute the degree of financial gearing if we now assume that further debt is required involving interest payments (*I*) of 5000. The degree of financial gearing would be:

$$30\,000/(30\,000 - 5000) = 1.2 \text{ or } 120\%$$

If *EBIT* were to increase by 100% this would result in an increase of 120% in the amount available to equity. We can combine operating and financial gearing to reveal the overall effect of a given change in sales on earnings available to the owners as follows (which in effect merely reflects the addition to the interest cost to fixed costs):

$$\text{combined gearing effect} = (S - VC)/(S - VC - FC - I)$$

which for our example would be:

$$(100\,000 - 50\,000)/(100\,000 - 50\,000 - 20\,000 - 5\,000) = 2 \text{ or } 200\%$$

Therefore, if sales change by 100% this would cause the earnings available to equity investors to change by 200%. In this example, the combined gearing effect of 2 was obtained from a degree of operating gearing of 1.67 and financial gearing of 1.2, but clearly other combinations would have produced the same effect. It is possible to make trade-offs between financial and operating gearing. The concept of the degree of gearing allows an organisation to predict the effect of change in sales on the earnings available to ordinary shareholders, in addition to revealing the interrelationship between financial and operating gearing. The concept can be used to predict, for example, that a decision to finance new plant and equipment with debt may result in a situation where a small change in sales volume will produce a large variation in earnings, whereas a different operating and financial gearing combination may reduce the effect on earnings (Asch and Kaye 1989, pp. 83–4).

Analysing a property company: a summary

In order to analyse a property company, its accounts and finances, the following criteria (from Brett 1990, pp. 87–92) will be important:

(i) *Net asset value per share* If the net assets are £10m and the issued share capital is 5m share at £1, then the net asset value per share is £10m/5m, i.e. £2 or 200p per share.

(ii) *Gearing* If the shareholders' funds are £5m and the debt capital is £3m, then the gearing is £3m/£8m, i.e. 0.375 or 37.5%.

(iii) *Composition of interest rates in the debt* What is the percentage of variable rate loans to total loans? A company with a lot of debt with floating rates may find its share price suffering, especially in a period of volatile interest rates.

(iv) *Valuation of assets* When were they last valued? Property companies are meant to value their properties internally annually and have an external independent valuation every 5 years.

(v) *Comparison of the amount of properties shown at cost* (development properties in the process of being developed) *with the amount shown at value* (investment property) This analysis gives an indication of the level of development activity.

(vi) *The legal interests in properties held* The breakdown of properties into freeholds, long leaseholds and short leaseholds can give an indication of the type and amount of income arising and the nature of the reviews.

(vii) *Comparison of profit* A year-on-year comparison excluding extraordinary items is a valuable analysis.

(viii) *Capital*   How is it financed, what capital commitments are there?
(ix)   *Contingent liabilities*   Has the company guaranteed the borrowing of associate companies which increases its liabilities? Are there any off-balance-sheet transactions?

13.2   PROPERTY ACCOUNTS: ISSUES

Capitalisation of interest for property companies

One aspect of financial reporting attracts more adverse comment than others; this is the process of capitalising interest into the cost of property developments rather than treating it as an expense. Thus, the cost increases the asset value in the balance sheet rather than reducing the profit in the profit and loss account. The difference between capitalising and expensing interest can have a high impact on the reported results and net assets of business during the development period. It is somewhat surprising that generally accepted accounting practice in the UK permits both policies (Smee 1992, p. 15). The capitalisation of borrowing costs into most types of property development appears a logical and appropriate policy. Interest is a development cost and is no different from construction and land costs in this respect. The policy of capitalising interest is mandatory in the USA and looks set to become so elsewhere in the world.

The arguments against capitalisation are set out in Exposure Draft (ED) 51 (Accounting Standards Committee 1990) and are briefly:

(i)   It is illogical to treat finance costs as a period expense normally and then treat them as a cost during the period of construction and revert to treating them as a period expense once the asset is complete, as finance costs are probably continuing to be incurred.
(ii) Borrowing costs are often for the whole enterprise and allocation of cost to a particular fixed asset will be arbitrary.
(iii) Capitalisation of borrowing costs results in similar fixed assets carrying different levels of interest. A highly geared company will carry its fixed assets at a higher amount than one which is not.

Smee (1992, p. 22) stated that capitalisation results in a proper matching of income and capital return with the development expenditure and best reflects, from an accounting view, the management's judgement of a project's viability rather than being creative accounting.

Treatment of interest on debt instruments is dealt with in Section 13.5.

Goodwill

When a company acquires a business, it often seeks to write off the goodwill against capital reserves to avoid having to amortise the goodwill in its profit and loss account. The company can thus increase net profit and earnings per share. On resale of the business, the company can record a greater gain, as the original price will not reflect the additional sum paid for goodwill. After 23 January 1992 the profit and loss account on the date of disposal should be determined by reference to the attributable amount of purchase goodwill, where this has not previously been charged to the profit and loss account. This ruling was made by the Urgent Issues Task Force set up by the Accounting Standards Committee and the Accounting Standards Board (see Ryland 1992, p. 36).

Structure of financial statements: reporting in financial statements

The Accounting Standards Board (ASB) has issued an exposure draft on financial statements – this requires additional matters to be included in the statements to make it more difficult for companies to inflate net profits and earnings per share. The ASB requires each company to prepare a cash flow statement as part of their financial statements for accounting periods ending after 23 March 1992 (Ryland 1992, p. 37).

Valuation of assets

Through time, the value of investment property will increase and the upward revaluation will create a surplus, being the difference between the open market value and its historic cost. This gain (loss) can be dealt with in three ways:

(i)   It can be passed through the profit and loss account as ordinary, exceptional or extraordinary item.
(ii) If the company's articles prevent option (i), then the gain can be transferred to the capital reserve.
(iii) It can be shown in a separate capital profit and loss account. This is best practice, to place gains or losses in a proper reserve and show it in the accounts as a capital profit and loss account which thus makes a distinction between realised and unrealised surpluses (Purdy 1992, p. 343).

Information in property company accounts

In May 1990 chartered accountants Stoy Hayward and researchers from the University of Reading set up a panel of experts to look at the provision of information in property company accounts and the main areas of problems relating to loans and interest, the nature of the assets and joint ventures. The recommendations of the panel are listed below (Purdy 1992):

(i)   Property company accounts should be placed in context, in terms of: what has happened over the year; how the company has been performing over the last 5 years; a view of the future and what accounting policies are used.

(ii) More details should be included about loan arrangements, the payment of interest and the capitalisation of interest.

(iii) An analysis of properties should be included showing their use as either trading stock, investment properties or development properties.

(iv) A list of properties with a worth greater than 5% of the total property portfolio should be included.

(v)   An external revaluation, on an open market basis, should be carried out in accordance with the guidelines of the Royal Institution of Chartered Surveyors.

(vi) All revaluation gains or losses should be passed into a property revaluation reserve, shown in the accounts as a capital profit and loss account which distinguishes between realised and unrealised amounts.

(vii) Details of costs and revenues from all developments relating to, and details of, all joint ventures should be included.

13.3   THE REGULATION OF ACCOUNTS

There are several sources of regulation with which statutory accounts have to comply. These are:

(i)   The Companies Acts, which describe the principles which should be followed in preparing statutory accounts. They indicate that accounts should show a true and fair view. The Companies Acts also set out the detailed disclosure requirements.

(ii) The accounting profession publishes SSAPs (Statements of Standard Accounting Practice) and these cover accounting and disclosure.

(iii) If the company is listed, the Stock Exchange specifies mandatory disclosure requirements.

The company accounts are independently examined by the auditor, who has to report to the shareholders that the accounts show a true and fair view and are properly prepared in accordance with the Companies Act. Auditors are under a professional obligation to ensure the accounts comply with SSAPs. If the accounts do not accord with the regulations, the auditor must state this in his report unless, in exceptional circumstances, he concurs with a departure from an SSAP. This seldom happens. If the auditor is going to qualify the accounts, he will discuss this with the directors and often they will amend the accounts to avoid qualification. The auditor will also advise of any failure to observe the relevant requirements of the Stock Exchange.

13.4 OFF-BALANCE-SHEET FUNDING

Off-balance-sheet funding has become common in the last few years because there is less equity and more debt in the balance sheets, small developers have limited equity resources, and banks have become more competitive, flexible and innovative in their lending. In the 1980s banks contrived with the lenders to encourage off-balance-sheet funding for their own marketing (Peat 1988, p. 117). Also in the UK, the SSAPs have never been intended to be applied mechanistically but intended to set out the broad principles which are to be applied in drawing up accounts; there is thus a tendency for the broad approach of the SSAPs to be ignored and for some property lenders to pursue accounting treatments which, while consistent with the letter of accounting standards, may be at variance with their spirit.

Examples of off-balance-financing are provided by Peat (1988, pp. 118–23) and these are set out and discussed in the following paragraphs.

Controlled non-subsidiary

If a developer sets up a debt-financed subsidiary to undertake a project, the consolidated balance sheet of the parent company would have to show the debt of the subsidiary. An alternative is to form a company which is not technically a subsidiary within S.736 of the Companies Act 1985. A company is a subsidiary of another if the latter is a member of the company and controls the board. If the parent company has only the right to appoint half the board but its directors each have two votes while the others have one, it will not control the composition of the board, although it will effect almost total control. Similarly, a company is a subsidiary of another if the latter holds more than half its equity share capital in terms of nominal value. The technique in this respect is for a company to own shares which represent no more than half of the nominal value of the share capital but give a right to, say, 99% of the company's profits. The company would not technically be a subsidiary, even though its 'parent' enjoyed 99% of its profits, as referred to previously, and effectively controlled the Board. This kind of structure is called a diamond structure.

Example of a 'diamond structure'

The definition of a subsidiary set out in S.736 of the Companies Act 1985 provides that a company is a subsidiary of a parent company only:

  (i) If the parent is a member of the board and controls the board of directors of the subsidiary.
  (ii) If the parent company holds more than half the nominal value of the equity share capital of the subsidiary.
  (iii) The subsidiary will be regarded as a subsidiary of the parent, if it is itself a subsidiary of a subsidiary of the parent.

The diamond structure set out in Figure 13.2 avoids the definition of subsidiaries indicated in the previous paragraphs.

Diamond Structure

Figure 13.2 *Off-balance-sheet funding: diamond structure*

A and B shares have the same number of votes except on a vote to appoint directors. The holders of the A shares have the right to appoint three directors without reference to the holders of the B shares; similarly, the B shareholders have the right to appoint three directors without reference to the holders of the A shares. However, at Board meetings of the off-balance-sheet vehicle (the quorum for which requires an A director) the A directors each have six votes, while the B directors have one each. Rights to dividends and returning capital on a winding up may be split so that the A shareholders received 99% and the B shareholders 1%.

Although the parent receives nearly all the profit and can control decisions, because the membership of the Board is 50:50 it was not considered under the Companies Act 1983 to be a subsidiary; the fact that the directors appointed by the parent carry a majority of the votes which may be cast at Board meetings is not addressed in this legislation.

This diamond structure also means that the parent does not hold more than half of the nominal value of the equity share capital. A and B shares are equity share capital within the meaning of the Act. Equity share capital is defined as the issued share capital excluding capital which carries rights to participate beyond a specified amount in the distribution. In this example there is no specified amount as a ceiling. Although the dividend right of the A shares is far greater than that of the B shares, the definition of a subsidiary requires that the measure of the relative weight of the shares is to be their nominal value.

A similar result to above could be arranged by having the B shares of the off-balance-sheet vehicle held by the bank, but the structure above exists for tax reasons. For example, it may be necessary to ensure that the off-balance-sheet vehicle and its parent would be treated as falling within the same group for group relief purposes or for corporation tax on capital gains, or it may be necessary to minimise the stamp duty payable on transfers of property between the parent and the off-balance-sheet vehicle.

Prior to the publication of the draft SSAP on Accounting for Special Purpose Transactions (Exposure Draft 42), most accountants held that it was not permissible to consolidate a company which was not a legal subsidiary; thus, a note to the accounts would disclose these interests. This approach is not appropriate if the notes present a view contradictory to the main accounts rather than supplementing them.

Other examples of off-balance-sheet funding will now be considered:

Sale and leaseback

If sale and leaseback are at fair market values, the accounting transaction is that as summarised as follows:

- the property is taken off balance sheet;

- the net sale proceeds are included as cash or debtors in the balance sheet;
- the profit or loss is recognised (difference between net sale proceeds and value in accounts);
- the rent payable is charged to profit over term of the lease.

Variations in this may include put and call options where the seller has a right to buy back the property at a predetermined price (preserving an interest in the capital growth of the asset) and the lender has a put option to require the seller to repurchase at the same price (protecting the lender from capital losses). Accounting for leases is dealt with in SSAP 21. This distinguishes between a finance lease and a standard lease. A finance lease is defined as 'a lease that transfers substantially all the risks and rewards of ownership of an asset to the lessee'. Any other lease is an operating lease. In property a lease is likely to be an operating lease where:

(i)   There are regular rent reviews to a market rent.
(ii) There is a reversion of the asset to the landlord on the expiry of the lease. Thus, the landlord takes the risk/rewards of the rental income and the capital appreciation.

The categorisation of the leaseback as a finance or operating lease determines whether the asset and the related financing can be taken off balance sheet. This can only really be done if the lease is an operational lease; the presumption with other leases is that they are finance leases on the basis that the lessee has uninterrupted use of the property. If the lease is a finance lease, then under the provisions of SSAP 21 it will need to be capitalised by the lessee. The property asset is included in the balance sheet at its fair value and the obligation to pay rentals included as a liability of a similar amount; alternatively the sale proceeds can be included on the balance sheet as a liability.

Sale and repurchase

This comprises two agreements, one for sale and one for the repurchase, entered into simultaneously. The price payable to repurchase will be the sale price plus interest. The intended effect is that the seller's balance sheet after sale and before repurchase includes the sales proceeds but neither the property nor the obligation to repay (the debt is taken off balance sheet). It is not likely that the auditors would accept that the property and obligation to repay should be off-balance-sheet, because the seller (repurchaser) retains substantially all the beneficial interest in the property. A more sophisticated approach has been used by house builders to finance showhouses and can take the finance off balance sheet.

Example of sale and repurchase:

(i) The builder sells the completed showhouses to the financier.
(ii) The financier grants the builder a right to use houses for a fee which equals the interest on funds advanced by the financier.
(iii) The builder undertakes to sell the showhouses as an agent for the financier.
(iv) The builder retains from sale proceeds an agency fee equal to the excess sale proceeds over the amount due to the financier.

The critical difference here is that the sold houses are unlikely to revert to the housebuilder, nor will he probably have to make good any shortfall in sale proceeds. The builder will guarantee that the houses will be sold in a certain period of time and he will make good the shortfall, but the time period and the values included in the agreement would be such that he would be unlikely to have to do so. The builder may also report a profit in the period he enters into the sale agreement rather than waiting for the actual sale.

Options

Property transactions frequently involve the grant of options to purchase a property. The accounting profession has no prescribed rules for options. Options are often used as an alternative to secured borrowings and to create off-balance-sheet structures, as with buy-back options in sale and finance leaseback.

Example of an option arrangement

The direct purchase of a property may look like:

Equity	£1m
Debt	£9m
Value	£10m

These elements could be shown on a balance sheet. As an alternative a bank could purchase the property on the investor's behalf for £10m and the investor could pay £1m for an option to purchase the property at some future time for a predetermined price. The predetermined price equals the purchase price plus the bank's interest and other costs less rent received.

The bank will have a put option, if the value declines, to force the investor to acquire the property for the same amount as the purchase price. The idea is to take the asset and debt off the balance sheet because here it appears that the beneficial ownership has been acquired by the financier. However, as before, because the investor has the cost/benefits of the option, the option will be shown in the accounts with disclosure of the contingent obligation under the put option. More strictly, it would be viewed that the effect of the option, because of the likelihood of repurchase, is, in effect, to purchase the property.

Lease and finance leaseback

This is a variant of the sale and leaseback and is a useful means of structuring the finance of a property which is going to be developed by a developer.

A manufacturer acquires a site on which to build a building for his own use; the finance agreement with the bank might be:

- Manufacturer grants the bank a lease for 25 years, no premium and peppercorn rent.
- Bank enters into contract with a builder to build the warehouse.
- Bank leases back building to manufacturer for 25 years. No premium is paid; rents reimburse the bank for development costs and interest.

This approach is a finance one rather than an attempt to obtain an accounting advantage. Thus, the property and the obligation to pay would be on the balance sheet. This approach is motivated by tax considerations, the desire for the bank to obtain the benefit of capital allowances. This benefit (reducing the bank's tax) will be shared with the manufacturer, as it will be reflected in the lower rentals payable under the leaseback.

Joint ventures

Joint ventures are covered in Chapter 11. Joint ventures are reflected in the accounts of the parent companies (the joint venturers) as an investment asset, at the cost of the investment plus investor's share of profits; the borrowings of the joint venture company, however, may not appear.

Non-recourse debt

Lenders' rights are restricted to a charge over a particular asset which is pledged as security. Some suggestions, especially by bankers, are that non-recourse debt in the balance sheet be netted against the asset it is financing. These suggestions reflect the bankers' and lenders' primary interest in the balance sheet, which in their case is used to determine whether there are sufficient assets available to repay future and existing debt. Netting off of non-recourse debt is not generally an acceptable approach, as accounts extend beyond just credit and liquidity assessment.

Recent moves to account for off-balance-sheet transactions

Exposure Draft (ED) 42 says that transactions should be accounted for in accordance with their economic substance, having regard to their effect on the enterprise's assets and liabilities. ED42 as incorporated in the Companies Act 1989 affects the off-balance-sheet vehicles described above dramatically. For instance:

Controlled non-subsidiary   Should be accounted for as a subsidiary.

Sale and leaseback   Would be treated as a borrowing transaction and the terms of arrangement need to be reworded.

Lease and finance leaseback   Is unaffected.

Sale and repurchase   Need to clearly account for the transaction as borrowing.

Options   Transaction or arrangement should be accounted for on the basis of the likelihood that the option will be exercised, if it is probable that it would be exercised. This would be the case where two options, one to sell and one to buy, exist.

Joint ventures   If a joint venture is a genuine sharing of risk and reward, a participant who has an interest of 50% or less will not need to disclose the separate joint venture asset and borrowing on the parents companies' balance sheets.

Non-recourse debt   It is not appropriate to offset the asset against its liability. If the accounts are used solely for lending decisions, there may be a basis for netting off. Assets and liability should be separate categories in the balance sheet (Peat 1988, pp. 125–6).

Implementation of the EEC Directive on Company Law

This deals with group accounts, voting rights and problems discussed with the diamond structure. There is a new definition of subsidiary. It is a subsidiary if the parent holds a participating interest in the subsidiary and either:

(i)   it exercises a clear influence over the subsidiary or
(ii) the subsidiary and parent are managed on a unified basis.

Overall there is still the requirement that the accounts present a true and fair view.

13.5   OFF-PROFIT-AND-LOSS-ACCOUNT FUNDING

This approach basically charges operating costs directly to shareholders rather than to the profit and loss account. Share options renumeration, for instance, where directors and employees receive share options rather than income, is a dilution of share capital not charged to the profit and loss account. Another example is convertible loan stock, which has a lower interest rate but gives the holder rights to convert to equity at a fixed price (Peat 1988, pp. 127–31). Other structures which provide off-profit-and-loss-account financing are as follows.

Deep-discount debentures

These bonds are issued at a lower rate of interest, which may remain at this level or be stepped up. The accruals concept of accounting (see earlier in the chapter) should mean that revenues and expenses should be matched for the appropriate time period. The real rate of interest should be thus accounted for over the life of the bond, which reflects the use of the loan over the period, and this should be taken out of profit.

Share premium accounts

There is a need to credit the share premium account when the proceeds of an issue of shares exceeds the nominal value. At the same time one is able to write off costs of the issue of shares and debentures, including commission and discounts against the account. It is possible therefore to write off the deep discount of a bond against the share premium account.

The appropriate method should be to amortise the discount through the profit and loss account (as notional interest), then transfer (by way of a movement of reserves) an amount from the share premium account to retained profits.

Redeemable convertibles

These are redeemable, convertible loan stock. The interest coupon is lower than on the conventional convertible and this is compensated for by the inclusion of a redemption option. If the share price does not increase sufficiently to make conversion worth while, the holder may opt for redemption at a premium over issue price, and this has an appropriate return to compensate. The issue is: should the potential redemption premium be accrued and charged to the profit and loss account as interest to the date when it may be exercised? The approach should be that the potential premium should be accrued and charged to the profit and loss account rather than held as a contingency for a possible claim.

Convertible preference shares

This has the same problems and issues as redeemable loan stock. Convertible issues are usually bonds, but convertible preference shares with a redemption premium option have been issued. The preference shares thus convert to ordinary shares under this procedure, but if the price is low, they can be redeemed with a premium to make up for the low yield. Systematic accrual should be made through the profit and loss account for the potential redemption premium, however remote its potential redemption appears to be.

Debt with equity warrants

This is an issue of debt with equity warrants which are rights to subscribe for shares at fixed price. These warrants are redeemable, i.e. the amount paid for the warrant is repayable if the warrant is not exercised. The debt instruments and the warrants are traded separately. The objective is (as for convertible debt) to secure lower interest rates for the debt issued. Thus, to account properly for this the proceeds from the issue should be allocated between debt and the warrants and accounted for separately. If the warrant is redeemable, accrual should be made through the profit and loss account for potential redemption.

REFERENCES

Accounting Standards Committee (1990) *Exposure Draft 51, Accounting for Fixed Assets and Revaluations,* ASC, May.

Asch, D and Kaye, G R (1989) *Financial Planning: Modelling Methods and Techniques,* Kogan Paul, London.

Barkham, R J and Purdy, D E (1992) 'Financial Company Reporting: Potential Weaknesses', *Journal of Property Valuation and Investment,* vol. 11, no. 2, pp. 133–44.

Brett, M (1990) *Property and Money,* Estates Gazette, London.

Calachi, R and Rosenburg, S (eds) (1992) *Property Finance, An International Perspective,* Euromoney Books, London.

Isaac, D and Woodroffe N (1987) 'Are Property Company Assets Undervalued?', *Estates Gazette,* London, 5 September, pp. 1024–6.

Peat, M (1988) 'The Accounting Issues', in S L Barter (ed.) *Real Estate Finance,* Butterworths, London.

Pike, R and Neale, B (1993) *Corporate Finance and Investment,* Prentice Hall, London.

Purdy, D E (1992) 'Provoking Awareness through the Provision of Relevant Information in Property Company Accounts', *Journal of Property Finance,* vol. 3, no. 3, pp. 337–46.

Ross, S A, Westerfield, R W and Jaffe, J F (1993) *Property Finance,* Irwin, Boston.

Ryland, D S (1992) 'Changes in Accounting Rules', *Journal of Property Finance,* vol. 3, no. 1, pp. 28–37.

Smee, R (1992) 'Capitalisation of Interest for Property Companies', *Journal of Property Finance,* vol. 3, no. 1, pp. 13–22.

Westwick, C A (1980) *Property Valuation and Accounts,* Institute of Chartered Accountants in England and Wales, London.

14 Financial Services

14.1 INTRODUCTION

The provision of financial services by property consultants will obviously vary according to the expertise of the firm, its clients and any niche market in which the firm is operating. This section relies heavily on the study of the operation of Chesterton Financial, the financial services company of Chesterton International, international property consultants. Chesterton Financial deal mainly with:

- debt finance;
- joint ventures;
- equity participation;
- professional advice;
- tax-based leasing.

Most activity is in the area of debt finance.

The role of financial services is to make contact with a number of funders; these will include banks, building societies, insurance companies and finance houses operating in the UK market. Chesterton Financial in 1992 were in contact with 170 such lenders. The role of financial services is to be an intermediary and to know the lending criteria of the various institutions, their likes, dislikes, procedures, and also to know the staff and personnel who may be doing the lending. When a client approaches a financial services company, the company will ascertain the requirement and then refine it to convert the enquiry into an application to a lender. In addition, the terms are agreed on which the financial services company will act for the client. Typical fees for acting are set out in the following section. In the early stages of discussion with the client, a general idea of the terms of the loan can be guessed but it is necessary to research the market, to phone lenders who may be interested, outline the deal to them and establish whether they would wish to look at it in more detail.

The research should provide three or more options for the transaction. An information memorandum is then prepared for those lenders who have expressed an interest in the deal, which, in most instances, covers the following basic headings:

- Introduction to the transaction.

- Background to the transaction.
- Description and history of the borrower.
- Amount and purpose of the loan.
- Description and location of the property for which the loan is sought.
- Costs and valuations related to the property.
- Financial analysis of cash flows and analysis of return.
- The equity investment proposed and the proposals for securing the loan.
- The terms of the loan and its proposed interest rate margin.
- The security being provided for the loan, the status of the borrower.
- A summary of the proposal with recommendations.
- Appendices, which may include detailed and financial analysis, structural surveys, formal valuations and legal report on the property, planning permissions, etc. Also, accounts and site plans/maps. While most of the material will be readily available from the client, detailed cash flows are usually prepared by the financial services company.

The proposal is then sent to the lender, who may reject the application outright once the full proposal is known or else put the application to the Credit Committee. Usually, however, the lender will ask for more information. This process will continue with one or more lenders until an acceptable deal is structured.

The financial services company will follow the process, giving legal and commercial advice through to the drawdown of the loan. This process may mean providing relevant information to the solicitors involved and ensuring all the information needed is available. Any fresh valuations will need to be provided and any conditions set by the lender will need to be fulfilled.

14.2 PROVIDERS OF FINANCIAL SERVICES

Besides the special departments and companies working with surveying firms and property consultants, there are financial services ranging from the large insurance groups to small specialist property finance intermediaries. Lenders thus have thousands of sources of potential new business.

Lenders will tend to differentiate between the intermediaries on two counts:

(i) quality clients (borrowers);
(ii) quality transactions (quality of security, property transaction, cash flow, etc.).

Chartered surveyors who have some activity in the financial services area include Chesterton, Jones Lang Wootton, Healey & Baker, Savills, Richard Ellis and Drivas Jonas. Savills (1989) carried out research on the average size of debt issued in 1989 and on the types of financial structures used; this information is given, respectively, in Figures 14.1 and 14.2. More recent analysis of the types of financial instrument used in 1992, for instance, shows a much more restricted range based on term loans, revolving credit and bonds with a very small rights issue usage (see Figure 14.3).

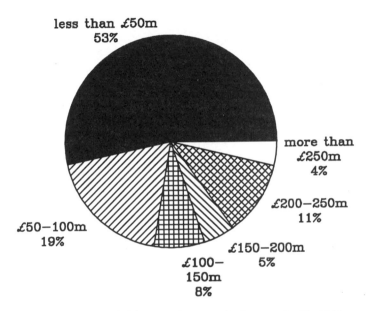

Figure 14.1 *Average size of debt issued 1989 (%). Source: Savills 1989*

New forms of finance have brought increased competition in the markets for the property professionals, the chartered surveyors. As debt finance and the capital markets have become more important, investment banks have attempted to compete more openly with surveyors providing specialist property financing services. Competition has also come from the accountants, particularly in the area of project management and corporate advice. The key argument is whether to act as principal or advisor; in certain corporate transactions it is necessary to take a principal role but historically professional partnerships have given advice. To the more financial services orientated firms there is a need for capital if they are to take principal positions – for instance, the ability to underwrite a debt – financing facility or an equity placing for a development or property company. In the context of securitisation, there is the need to underwrite a flotation or make markets (Barter 1988, p. 31). The ability to structure or arrange deals may not be sufficient to ensure the appropriate instructions. Clients want to see the arranger of the finance taking the lead with its own funds while accepting that the majority of the funding will be syndicated elsewhere.

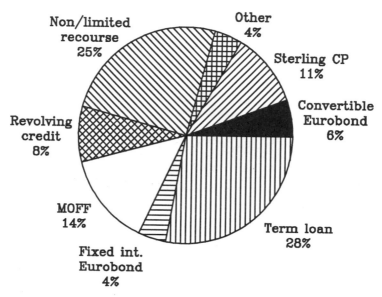

Figure 14.2 *Types of debt issued 1989 (%). Source: Savills 1989*

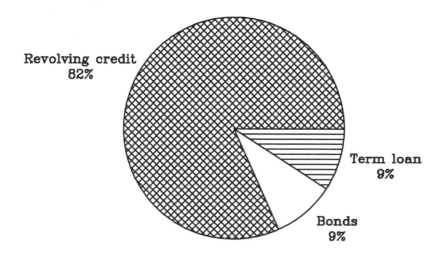

Figure 14.3 *Types of debt issued 1992 (%). Source: Savills 1993a*

The training for people in financial services is very important; it is a key opportunity for developing property professionals in the finance field. The weak players in this market at the moment are the medium-sized firms, which do not have the niche markets of the small firms and lack the international perspective, specialised departments and research backing of the larger diversified practices.

The funding of property

The decision as to which funding strategy to pursue depends on the financial policy of the client. Major perspectives may include:

Private versus public client Clients in the private sector may have firm views on the use of public sector money, especially where management control or equity share may be dissipated. Funding may be available from the public sector in terms of grants or loan facilities from European, national and local government bodies. Public sector clients, because of preference policy or legislation, may be limited in their use of different sources of funds.

Debt versus equity alternatives The extent to which a developer is willing to share the risks and rewards of a project will determine the more likely source of funds and the terms that might apply.

Tax considerations Fiscal measures impinge on the process of property development and are crucial in assessing the viability of a given project and on deciding the best way of organising a programme of acquisition, construction and disposal.

Current arrangements Many client developers will have access to existing sources of finance; large organisations will often have multiple funding arrangements with funds and banks. A general funding facility could be provided giving wider flexibility to project finance.

14.3 FEES FOR PROVIDING FINANCIAL SERVICES

The fees charged by financial services companies may be options of:

(i) An abortive fee plus a success-related fee on the facility. This could be, say, a £10 000 fee (payable even if the project is abortive) plus a success related fee of, say, ½% of the facility.

(ii) A speculative fee, say 1% of the facility; this is the traditional approach.

(iii) A partnership approach, perhaps 1% if the agent brings in the funding partner, ⅔% if the client brings in partner (if they have contacts).

If the fees are based exclusively on transaction costs, fees for acting will be greater, perhaps on the following scale:

Transaction size	Fee
£250,000 plus	2%
£500,000 plus	1.5%
£1m plus	1%

14.4   THE DEBT FINANCE MARKET

In the 1990s the debt market is tough going. The banks are highly exposed in property, the highest since the collapse of 1973–4. If the problems of the banks were confined to property, then the debt finance market would not be too badly affected. Bank lending problems are not confined to property and there are problems in other sectors, including retailing, housing construction and manufacturing. Banks themselves have operational problems. Bad debt problems are thus making banks reluctant to lend unless an improvement in the economic situation is seen. This makes the work of financial services and the placing of the loans more difficult.

The financial services intermediaries do have two positive aspects to look to, though.

(i)   Banks need to lend money to make money. They need to lend it more so now. A bank which loses £1000 may need to lend £50 000 for a year to make up that loss. The clearing banks have written off billions of pounds in the last few years and this must act as an incentive to lend.

(ii) As finance becomes more difficult to obtain, so the intermediaries with wider contacts become more important, as do their skills in negotiating and presenting the deals. Thus, the paradox is of greater importance for financial services in a more discerning lending market.

14.5 PRESENTATION OF LOAN PROPOSALS

Proper presentation of loan proposals is essential, especially for those developers and investors whose credibility and track record is unknown. Leading institutions put great store by the proper presentation of material backed up by appropriate research, comparable evidence, valuations and cash flow projections. Obviously in a situation like this it is also important for the lender to be aware of the business strategy of the borrowers, their background and experience. The CVs of the key people involved in the project will be required. For small developers this is especially important; recent research by O'Grady and Isaac (1993) indicates that there are four main reasons why lenders turn down applications for funding from small developers. These are in order:

(i) Lenders are not convinced of the overall viability of the development.
(ii) Lack of adequate equity provided by the developers.
(iii) Poor presentation of the documents applying for finance.
(iv) Unfavourable results arising from investigations into the developers past record.

This presentation approach is best seen as an example of how an agreed facility is presented as shown in Box 14.1.

14.6 CRITERIA OF ACCEPTANCE

For the acceptance of a loan arrangement, both sides are looking at basic investment criteria of risk and return:

Lender looks at:

- Risk of borrower defaulting
- Risk of property not achieving a sale price to cover debt
- Return on capital relative to cost of capital

Borrower looks at:

- Risk of falling values
- Risk of higher interest rates
- Risk of unemployment or inability to pay
- Return on equity in property

Consists of:

- Principal terms and conditions
- Description of premises
- Details of the group of companies

Enclosures:

- Property particulars
- Valuation report
- Certificate of title
- General brochures of borrowing company
- Annual company report of borrower
- Financial accounts of borrower

Principal terms and conditions:

- Description: e.g. Medium-term loan facility
- Borrower:
- Guarantor:
- Underwriters:
- Lender:
- Arranger: lead manager and agent
- Amount:
- Purpose: say, to assist the finance of the purchase
- Term: e.g. 5 years from the signing of the facility document
- Drawdown: e.g. in one amount.
- Repayment: Minimum instalment amounts, e.g.

Months from signing	Instalment amounts (£m)
12	7
24	4
36	4
48	2.5

- Interest: e.g. the aggregate of:

  margin of $\frac{7}{8}$ (year 1) or if later, till all monies guarantee is released (guarantee to repay all monies) a margin of $\frac{3}{4}$%

  LIBOR (1, 3 or 6 months, borrower's option or 12 months subject to availability from bank)

  associated costs rounded up to the nearest $\frac{1}{16}$%

Box 14.1 *Example of a presentation of an offer of a facility*

A simple comparison of what is required in terms of information by a lender can be made in an area with which we are all generally familiar, the mortgage application to purchase a house. The principal area of interest to the lender and the fundamental criteria are the same (see Box 14.2). Wyles (1990) suggests a number of criteria which would be used in underwriting commercial mortgage indemnities (CMIs – see Chapter 4 for a discussion of these). These criteria are useful as lending criteria on which a proper presentation of a loan proposal should be based. These criteria are presented as two lists, one for investment property and one for speculative development (Wyles 1990, p. 384):

Investment property	*Speculative development (see comments in left column)*
Financier – nature of/requirements	Financier
Borrower – details/requirement	Development – proposals
Asset – details, value	Site
Cash-flow projections, assumptions	Appraisal
Estimated rental value (ERV) – comparables	Voids – repercussions
Site – details/constraints	Profit on cost
Loan duration	Cost overrun risk
Structure of finance	Completion risk
Costs and values	Basis of feasibility
Loan-to-value ratio	

14.7 COMPARISON OF FINANCE TERMS

There are four main areas to be considered prior to entering into a facility to ensure that a suitable structure can be arranged. These are cost, flexibility, risk and accounting presentation.

Cost Best rates are available for the best-quality covenants. Where the lending institution takes more risk, a higher return is required. For non-recourse transactions an interest rate between 1% and 2% over LIBOR is currently required.

Flexibility The greater the level of security and recourse, the less likely there is to be any restriction on management control. Flexibility depends on the interest rate structure.

Risk The greater the lender's risk, the greater the cost to the borrower.

Accounting A number of creative packages are available which can remove debt from the balance sheet.

1. Information required by lender	2. Information required by borrower
(a) Details of borrower: status date of birth nature of employment length of service financial commitments evidence of bankruptcy	(a) Maximum loan: multiplier of income % property value

(b) Details of property to be mortgaged
 	
age
location
type
use, may need to be wholly
   residential
	(b) Interest rate and repayment
	   period

(c) Details of occupants	(c) Fixed/variable rate
(d) Details of previous applications	(d) Arrangement costs/ redemption costs
(e) Details of loan requirements payment details	

Box 14.2 *Information required for loan proposal (house mortgage)*

14.8 FINANCIAL REGULATIONS

The rules on financial advisers have changed radically over the last 5 years or so. There is now a clear line between independent advice and straight salesmanship. All independent advisers are regulated by the Financial Intermediaries, Managers and Brokers Regulatory Association (FIMBRA). The idea of the regulation was to encourage protection for the investor; however, the amount of paperwork and accounting procedure has made the process difficult for the individual operator and thus many FIMBRA members have now linked themselves to a single insurance company.

The Financial Services Act has introduced new administrative and disclosure obligations. Authorisation to advise under the Act may include other departments of professional practices, including investment agents and property management. The Act has brought new regulations and issues of compliance and conflicts of interest. While there will have to be formal compliance requirements within the authorised part of a surveyor's business, the inevitable consequence of the more diversified firm may be a need for compliance policy and a compliance officer for the whole firm. The compliance officer would have knowledge of all transactions being undertaken within the firm as a whole and would have the power to enforce disclosure of conflicts of interest, establish 'Chinese Walls' and discipline staff (Barter 1988, p. 31).

Financial Services Act 1986

The Financial Services Act 1986 is an act to regulate investment business. The main principle of the Act is the requirement that a person be authorised or exempted in order to carry out an investment business. Sections 3 and 4 of the Act provide that it is a criminal offence to carry on investment business without authorisation. Section 5 provides that contracts, generally, entered into by an unauthorised person are unenforceable against the client dealing with that unauthorised person.

Part 1 of the Act regulates investment business and investment protection has been delegated to the Securities and Investments Board (SIB). It is financed by a levy on self-regulating organisations (SROs) and recognised professional bodies. The SROs are listed in Box 14.3. The rulebooks used by these regulators encompass principles of fairness, skill and diligence, and stipulate the minimum required financial resources required to operate a business.

To be within the scope of the Act, the business activity must be concerned with an investment. Business is defined as dealing in investments, arranging deals in investments, managing investments, giving investment advice and establishing collective investment schemes. Investments are defined as (Estates Gazette 1991, p.193):

- stocks and shares;
- debentures, loan stock, bonds and certificates;
- loan stock, bonds and other documents of indebtedness to Government or to local authorities or to public authorities;
- warrants or other instruments entitling the holder to subscribe for any of the above;

- certificates respecting any of the above;
- unit trusts;
- options to acquire (among other things) investments, currency, gold or silver;
- futures;
- contracts for differences;
- long-term insurance contracts;
- rights and interests in investments.

Self-regulating organisations (SROs) are:

SFA (the Securities and Futures Authority), which is made up of members of the Stock Exchange market makers, brokers and those working in the futures and options markets

IMRO (the Investment Managers' Regulatory Organisation), which is made up of managers of large investment portfolios

LAUTRO (the Life Assurance and Unit Trust Regulatory Organisation), which is concerned with the marketing of life assurance and unit trusts

FIMBRA (the Financial Intermediaries, Managers and Brokers Regulatory Association), which concerns itself with the selling of investment services

Recognised professional bodies (RPBs) are:

The Institutes of Chartered Accountants of England and Wales, Scotland and Ireland

The Association of Certified Accountants

The Law Society

The Institute of Actuaries

The Insurance Brokers Registration Council

Box 14.3 *Self-regulating organisations and recognised professional bodies under the Financial Services Act*

REFERENCES

Barter, S L (1988) 'Introduction', in S L Barter (ed.) *Real Estate Finance*, Butterworths, London.

Estates Gazette (1991) 'Mainly for Students: The Law of Financial Services', *Estates Gazette*, London, November 16, pp. 193–4.

O'Grady M and Isaac D (1993) *Funding for the Small Developer, the Importance of Research and Presentation*, University of Greenwich, School of Land and Construction Management.

Savills (1989) *Financing Property 1989*, Savills, London.

Savills (1993a) *Financing Property 1993*, Savills, London.

Wyles, M (1990) 'Mortgage Indemnity – A Risk/Reward Arbitrage', *Journal of Property Finance*, vol. 1, no. 3, pp. 378–86.

Bibliography

Accounting Standards Committee (1990) Exposure Draft 51, Accounting for Fixed Assets and Revaluations, ASC, May.

Albert, D and Watson, J (1990). 'An Approach to Property Joint Ventures', *Journal of Property Finance*, vol. 1, no. 2, pp. 189–95.

Armon-Jones, C H (1992) 'Underwriting Property Sales', *Journal of Property Finance*, vol. 2, no. 4, pp. 497–500.

Asch, D and Kaye, G R (1989) *Financial Planning: Modelling Methods and Techniques*, Kogan Paul, London.

Bank of England (1993) Quarterly Bulletin, vol. 33, no. 3, August.

Baring, Houston and Saunders (1991) Property Report, Baring, Houston and Saunders, London, November.

Barkham, R J and Purdy, D E (1992) 'Financial Company Reporting: Potential Weaknesses', *Journal of Property Valuation and Investment*, vol. 11, no. 2, pp. 133–44.

Barkshire, R (1986) *The Unitised Property Market*, Working Party of the Unitised Property Market, London, February.

Barter, S L (1988) 'Introduction', in S L Barter (ed.), *Real Estate Finance*, Butterworths, London.

Barter, S and Sinclair, N (1988) 'Securitisation', in S L Barter (ed.), *Real Estate Finance*, Butterworths, London.

Baum, A E and Schofield, A (1991) 'Property as a Global Asset', in P Venmore-Rowland, P Brandon and T Mole (eds), *Investment, Procurement and Performance in Construction*, RICS, London.

Berkley, R (1991) 'Raising Commercial Property Finance in a Difficult Market', *Journal of Property Finance*, vol. 1, no. 4, pp. 523–9.

Beveridge, J (1988) 'The Needs of the Property Company', in S L Barter (ed.) *Real Estate Finance*, Butterworths, London.

Beveridge, J A (1991) 'New Methods of Financing', in P Venmore-Rowland, P Brandon and T Mole (eds), *Investment, Procurement and Performance in Construction*, RICS, London.

Bramson, D (1988) 'The Mechanics of Joint Ventures', in S L Barter (ed.), *Real Estate Finance*, Butterworths, London

Brett, M (1983) 'Growth of Financial Institutions', in C. Darlow (ed.), *Valuation and Investment Appraisal*, Estates Gazette, London.

Brett, M (1983) 'Indirect Investment in Property', in C. Darlow (ed.), *Valuation and Investment Appraisal*, Estates Gazette, London.

Brett, M (1990) *Property and Money*, Estates Gazette, London.

Brett, M (1991) 'How Property Futures Work', *Estates Gazette*, 18 May, p. 71.

Briscoe, G (1988) *The Economics of the Construction Industry*, Mitchell, London.

Brown, G R (1991) *Property Investment and the Capital Markets*, E & F Spon, London.

Cadman, D and Catalano, A (1983) *Property Development in the UK – Evolution and Change*, College of Estate Management, Reading.

Calachi, R and Rosenburg, S (eds) (1992) *Property Finance, An International Perspective*, Euromoney Books, London.

Catalano, A (1993) 'Paribas Trusts in the Upturn', *Estates Gazette*, 23 October, p. 52.

Central Statistical Office (1992) *Financial Statistics: Explanatory Handbook*, CSO, December.

Central Statistical Office (1993) *Financial Statistics*, CSO, September.

Chartered Surveyor Weekly (1991) 'Editorial: Crisis at London Fox Leaves Futures Uncertain' *Chartered Surveyor Weekly*, 10 October, p 5.

Chartered Surveyor Weekly (1991) 'Editorial: UPS Offers New Option to Property Strugglers' *Chartered Surveyor Weekly*, 17 October.

Chesterton Financial (1991) *Property Lending Survey*, Chesterton Financial, London, February.

Chesterton Financial (1992) *Property Lending Survey*, Chesterton Financial, London, February.

Chesterton Financial (1993) *Property Lending Survey*, Chesterton Financial, London, February.

Chesterton Financial/CSW Property Confidence Barometer, Bi-annual Survey 1991–1993, Chesterton Financial, London.

Chesterton Financial Internal uncirculated reports, Chesterton Financial, London.

Clarke, R J (1990) 'Refinancing', *Journal of Property Finance*, vol. 1, no. 3, pp. 435–9.

Cohen, P (1992) 'Non-recourse Property Funding', *Journal of Property Finance*, vol. 3, no. 3, pp. 319–24.

Copeland, T E and Weston, J F (1988) *Financial Theory and Corporate Policy*, Addison-Wesley, Wokingham.

Darlow, C (1988) 'Direct Project Funding', in C Darlow (ed.), *Valuation and Development Appraisal*, Estates Gazette, London.

Darlow, C (ed.) (1983) *Valuation and Investment Appraisal*, Estates Gazette, London.

Debenham, Tewson and Chinnocks (1984) *Property Investment in Britain*, Debenham,Tewson & Chinnocks, London.

Dent, P and Weeks, C (1993) 'Is there LIFFE after FOX?', *Estates Gazette*, 9 October, pp. 132–6.

DTZ Debenham Thorpe (1993) *Money into Property*, DTZ Debenham Thorpe, London, August.

Dubben, N and Sayce, S (1991) *Property Portfolio Management*, Routledge, London.

Estates Times (1993) 'Swaps Not Cash', *Estates Times*, 19 November, p 24.

Estates Gazette (1991) Mainly for Students: The Law of Financial Services, *Estates Gazette*, London, November 16, pp. 193–4.

Evans, P H (1992) 'Statistical Review', *Journal of Property Finance*, vol. 3, no. 1, pp. 115–20.

Evans, P H (1993) 'Statistical Review', *Journal of Property Finance*, vol. 4, no. 2, pp. 75–82.

Fielding, M and Besser, A (1991) 'Syndicated Loans – Caveat Borrower', *Estates Gazette*, 15 June, pp. 78 and 103.

Fox, J W W (1993) 'Sale and Leasebacks: A Case Study', *Journal of Property Finance*, vol. 4, no. 1, pp. 9–12.

Fraser, W D (1993) *Principles of Property Investment and Pricing*, Macmillan Press, London.

Freed, N (1992) 'Bridging Finance', *Journal of Property Finance*, vol. 3, no. 2, pp. 187–90.

Gallinger, G W and Healey P B (1991) *Liquidity Analysis and Management*, Addison-Wesley, Wokingham.

Gemill, G (1990) 'Futures Trading and Finance in Housing Market', *Journal of Property Finance*, vol. 1, no. 2, pp. 196–207.

Gibbs, R (1987) 'Raising Finance for New Development', *Journal of Valuation*, vol. 5, no. 4, pp. 343–53.

Goldsmith, G C (1992) 'Sterling Interest Swaptions', *Journal of Property Finance*, vol. 3, no. 3, pp. 315–8.

Goodman, T (1991) 'Property Futures Idea is Still Alive – Just', *Chartered Surveyor Weekly*, 10 October, p 11.

Graham, J (1985) 'New Sources of Finance for the Property Industry', Estates Gazette, 6 July.

Hargitay, S E and Sui-Ming, Y (1993) *Property Investment Decisions*, E & F Spon, London.

Investment Property Databank (1992) *Annual Review 1993*, IPD, London, December.

Isaac, D (1986) 'Corporate Finance and Property Development Funding: An Analysis of Property Companies' Capital Structures with Special Reference to the Relationship Between Asset Value and Share Price', unpublished thesis, Faculty of the Built Environment, South Bank Polytechnic, London.

Isaac, D and Steley, T (1991) *Property Valuation Techniques*, Macmillan Press, London.

Isaac, D and Woodroffe N (1987) 'Are Property Company Assets Undervalued?', *Estates Gazette*, London, 5 September, pp. 1024–6.

Jennings, R B (1993) 'The Resurgence of Real Estate Investment Trusts (REITs)', *Journal of Property Finance*, vol. 4, no. 1, pp. 13–9.

Jones Lang Wootton (1989) *The Glossary of Property Terms*, Estates Gazette, London.

Journal of Valuation (1989) 'Market Data', *Journal of Valuation*, vol. 8, no. 1, pp. 87–9.

Kynoch, R (1993) 'Firms Predict £2bn Spending Surge', *Chartered Surveyor Weekly*, 26 August, pp. 18–21

Lee, C F (1985) *Financial Analysis and Planning*, Addison-Wesley, Wokingham.

Mallinson, M (1988) 'Equity Finance', in S L Barter (ed.), *Real Estate Finance*, Butterworths, London.

Marriott, O (1962) *The Property Boom*, Hamish Hamilton, London.

Marshall, P and Kennedy, C (1992) 'Development Valuation Techniques', *Journal of Property Valuation and Investment*, vol. 11, no. 1, pp. 57–66.

Maxted, B (1988) *Unitisation of Property*, College of Estate Management, Reading.

McIntosh A and Sykes S (1985) *A Guide to Institutional Property Investment*, *Macmillan Press*, London.

Millman, S (1988) 'Property, Property Companies and Public Securities', in S L Barter (ed.), *Real Estate Finance*, Butterworths, London.

Mitchell, C and Peake, J H (1991) 'The Management of Interest Rate Exposure', *Journal of Property Finance*, vol. 1, no. 4, pp. 530–38.

O'Grady M and Isaac D (1993) *Funding for the Small Developer, the Importance of Research and Presentation*, University of Greenwich, School of Land and Construction Management.

Orchard-Lisle, P (1987) 'Financing Property Development', *Journal of Valuation*, vol. 5, no. 4, pp. 343–53.

Paribas Capital Markets (1993a) *European Equity Research: Rodamco*, Banque Paribas Nederland N.V., October.

Paribas Capital Markets (1993b) *Monthly Property Share Statistics*, Banque Paribas, November.

Parker, R H (1983) *Understanding Company Financial Statements*, Penguin, London.

Peat, M (1988) 'The Accounting Issues', in S L Barter (ed.), *Real Estate Finance*, Butterworths, London.

Pike, R and Neale, B (1993) *Corporate Finance and Investment*, Prentice Hall, London.

Pugh, C (1991) 'The Globalisation of Finance Capital and the Changing Relationships Between Property and Finance', *Journal of Property Finance*, vol. 2, nos 2 and 3.

Purdy, D E (1992) 'Provoking Awareness through the Provision of Relevant Information in Property Company Accounts', *Journal of Property Finance*, vol. 3, no. 3, pp. 337–46.

Ratcliffe, J (1978) *An Introduction to Urban Land Administration*, Estates Gazette, London.

Ratcliffe, J (1984) 'Development Financing: Drawing up the Agreement', *Architects Journal*, 22 and 29 August, p. 63.

Richard Ellis (1986) 'Development Finance', *Property Investment Quarterly Bulletin*, Richard Ellis, London, April.

Richard Ellis (1991) 'A look at Commercial Property Futures', *Investment Research Review*, no. 2, Richard Ellis, London.

Riley, M and Isaac, D (1991) 'Property Lending Survey 1991', *Journal of Property Finance*, vol. 2, no. 1, pp. 74–7.

Riley, M and Isaac, D (1992) 'Property Lending Survey 1992', *Journal of Property Finance*, vol. 2, no. 4, pp. 38–41.

Riley, M and Isaac, D (1993) 'Property Lending Survey 1993', *Journal of Property Finance*, vol. 4, no. 1, pp. 43–8.

Riley, M and Isaac, D (1993) 'Commercial Property Lending: Confidence Survey', *Journal of Property Finance*, vol. 4, no. 3.

Ross, S A, Westerfield, R W and Jaffe, J F (1993) *Corporate Finance*, Irwin, Boston.

Royal Institution of Chartered Surveyors (RICS) (1985) *The Unitisation of Real Property*, RICS, London.

Rydin, Y, Rodney, W and Orr, C (1990) 'Why Do Institutions Invest in Property?', *Journal of Property Finance*, vol. 1, no. 2, pp. 250–58.

Ryland, D (1991) 'Authorised Property Unit Trusts', *Estates Gazette*, London, 9 November, pp. 163–4.

Ryland, D S (1992) 'Changes in Accounting Rules', *Journal of Property Finance*, vol. 3, no. 1, pp. 28–37.

S G Warburg Securities (1993) *U.K. Property: Review of 1992 and Prospects for 1993*, S G Warburg, London.

S G Warburg Research (1993) U.K. *Property: Monthly Review*, S G Warburg, London, November.

Samuel, J M and Wilkes F M (1987) *Management of Company Finance*, Van Nostrand Reinhold, Wokingham.

Savills (1989) *Financing Property 1989*, Savills, London.

Savills (1991) *Financing Property 1991*, Savills, London.

Savills (1993a) *Financing Property 1993*, Savills, London.

Savills (1993b) *Investment and Economic Outlook*, Savills, London, Issue 3, October.

Scott, I P (1992) 'Debt, Liquidity and Secondary Trading in Property Debt', *Journal of Property Finance*, vol. 3, no. 3, pp. 347–55.

Scrimgeour Vickers & Co (1986) *United Kingdom Research, Annual Property Report*, Scrimgeour Vickers & Co, London.

Sexton, P and Laxton, C (1992) 'Authorised Property Unit Trusts', *Journal of Property Finance*, vol. 2, no. 4, pp. 468–75.

Shayle, A (1991) 'The Use of Deep Discount and Zero Coupon Bonds in the UK Property Market', *Journal of Property Finance*, vol. 2, no. 1, pp. 11–7.

Sieracki, K (1993) 'U.K. Institutional Requirements for European Property', *Estates Gazette*, July 17, p. 116.

Smee, R (1992) 'Capitalisation of Interest for Property Companies', *Journal of Property Finance*, vol. 3, no. 1, pp. 13–22.

Temple, P (1992) 'How to Beat a Hostile Takeover', *Journal of Property Finance*, vol. 2, no. 4, pp. 476–83.

UBS Global Research (1993) *UK Equities: Property Perspective*, UBS Ltd, London, No 3, April.

UBS Phillips & Drew (1993) *Global Research Group: UK Property Service*, UBS Ltd, London.

Van Horne, J C (1989) *Financial Management and Policy*, Prentice Hall, London.

Venmore-Rowland, P (1991) 'Vehicles for Property Investment', in P Venmore-Rowland, P Brandon and T Mole (eds), *Investment, Procurement and Performance in Construction*, RICS, London.

Westwick, C A (1980) *Property Valuation and Accounts*, Institute of Chartered Accountants in England and Wales, London.

Wolfe, R (1988) 'Debt Finance', in S L Barter (ed.), *Real Estate Finance*, Butterworths, London.

Woodroffe, N and Isaac, D (1987) 'Corporate Finance and Property Development Funding', Working Paper of the School of Applied Economics and Social Studies, Faculty of the Built Environment, South Bank Polytechnic, London.

Wyles, M (1990) 'Mortgage Indemnity – A Risk/Reward Arbitrage', *Journal of Property Finance*, vol. 1, no. 3, pp. 378–86.

Index